Modernizing Insurance Regulation

Founded in 1807, John Wiley & Sons is the oldest independent publishing company in the United States. With offices in North America, Europe, Australia, and Asia, Wiley is globally committed to developing and marketing print and electronic products and services for our customers' professional and personal knowledge and understanding.

The Wiley Finance series contains books written specifically for finance and investment professionals as well as sophisticated individual investors and their financial advisors. Book topics range from portfolio management to e-commerce, risk management, financial engineering, valuation, and financial instrument analysis, as well as much more.

For a list of available titles, visit our Web site at www.WileyFinance.com.

Modernizing Insurance Regulation

JOHN H. BIGGS
MATTHEW P. RICHARDSON

EDITORS

WILEY

Cover Design: Wiley
Cover Image: © iStockphoto/skegbydave

Published by John Wiley & Sons, Inc., Hoboken, New Jersey.
Published simultaneously in Canada.

For general information on our other products and services or for technical support, please contact our Customer Care Department within the United States at (800) 762-2974, outside the United States at (317) 572-3993 or fax (317) 572-4002.

Wiley publishes in a variety of print and electronic formats and by print-on-demand. Some material included with standard print versions of this book may not be included in e-books or in print-on-demand. If this book refers to media such as a CD or DVD that is not included in the version you purchased, you may download this material at http://booksupport.wiley.com. For more information about Wiley products, visit www.wiley.com.

ISBN 978-1-118-75871-7 (Hardcover)
ISBN 978-1-118-75875-5 (ePDF)
ISBN 978-1-118-75884-7 (ePub)

Printed in the United States of America
10 9 8 7 6 5 4 3 2 1

To my wife Penelope,
for 55 years of companionship
—J.B.

To my wife Julie,
for 27 wonderful years,
hoping for at least another 28
—M.R.

Contents

Preface

With the onset of the financial crisis in the summer of 2007 and the emergence of systemic risk with the fall of Lehman Brothers in September 2008, the faculty at the New York University (NYU) Stern School of Business embarked on an ambitious project of trying to understand the root causes of the crisis and make suggestions for fixing the financial system. This project involved at different stages 35 or so faculty aligned with NYU. The result was three books—*Restoring Financial Stability: How to Repair a Failed System* (John Wiley & Sons, 2009), *Regulating Wall Street: The Dodd-Frank Act and the New Architecture of Global Finance* (John Wiley & Sons, 2010), and *Guaranteed to Fail: Fannie Mae, Freddie Mac and the Debacle of Mortgage Finance* (Princeton University Press, 2011). As part of our analysis, it became clear to us that a much-understudied area of the financial system was the insurance sector.

To address this, we, along with our colleagues Viral Acharya and Stephen Ryan, and PhD student Hanh Le, wrote a 62-page article entitled "Systemic Risk and the Regulation of Insurance Companies" (Chapter 9 of *Regulating Wall Street: The Dodd-Frank Act and the New Architecture of Global Finance*). The paper had some traction within regulatory circles. However, there was sufficient disagreement with our views in the paper by practitioners in the industry that we decided to put on a conference on September 21, 2009, at the Salomon Center for the Study of Financial Institutions at the NYU Stern School of Business, titled "Regulation of the Insurance Industry: Current Issues." The conference featured leading practitioners, regulators, and academics. The purpose of the conference was to debate important issues surrounding regulation of insurance companies. A follow-up conference took place on March 2, 2012, titled "Conference on Alternative Designs for a Modern Insurance Regulatory Structure."

Three important points emerged. First, there was general agreement that the insurance sector is a key part of the financial system and needed to be regulated as such. Second, there was sharp disagreement on the form the regulation should take and which type of companies would fall under a given regulation. Third, the arguments on both sides were well constructed and therefore worthy of future discussion. Therefore, we thought it worthwhile that the participants of the conferences lay out the arguments of these various sides in a written form to help academics, regulators, and practitioners alike see these arguments up against each other.

This book is very much organized around this principle. All the chapters have as an author at least one of the participants—whether a regulator, practitioner, or academic—of the conference. The chapters focus on three key areas: (1) whether state regulation of insurance companies is sufficient in today's world of modern finance, (2) whether insurance companies are systemically risky and need to be regulated as such, and (3) whether the guaranty associations are sufficiently structured given the risks of insurance companies. The chapters are organized so that the reader can read the arguments side by side and decide on their own the merits of all the arguments. We therefore hope that this book serves as a useful tool to navigate the world of insurance regulation.

Acknowledgments

First and foremost, we would like to thank all the academics, regulators, and practitioners who wrote chapters for this book. Their contributions have made this book a unique compilation of arguments from leading thinkers in the field. The disagreements and various views offered for and against particular forms of insurance regulation provide the reader with an interesting perspective from all sides.

Second, and equally important, we would like to thank other participants and attendees of the two conferences on insurance regulation at the Salomon Center at the NYU Stern School of Business, "Regulation of the Insurance Industry: Current Issues" (September 21, 2009) and "Conference on Alternative Designs for a Modern Insurance Regulatory Structure" (March 2, 2012). We are sure that all the contributors to this book, but the editors especially, benefited and were influenced by discussions that arose during these two days. In particular, we would like to thank those participants who did not write in this volume but presented at these conferences, including William Berkley (CEO, W.R. Berkley Corporation); Scott Campion (Oliver Wyman); Douglas Elliott (Brookings Institution); Frank Keating (former CEO of the American Council of Life Insurers); Howard Mills (Deloitte & Touche, former Superintendent of the New York State Insurance Department); Mark Parkin (Deloitte & Touche); Stephen Ryan (NYU Stern School of Business); Ingo Walter (NYU Stern School of Business); and Roy Woodall (independent member of the Financial Stability Oversight Council).

Third, a very special thanks needs to be given to our finance colleague, Viral Acharya (coauthor of Chapter 9 of this book), and our accounting colleague, Stephen Ryan. Their input was invaluable towards NYU Stern's undertaking of studying insurance regulation. The conferences and books would not have happened without them. We would also like to thank Hanh Le, our PhD student, who not only was involved in the original chapter on insurance regulation but has been involved in many of the school's initiatives on systemic risk. We also want to acknowledge the Salomon Center staff for the smooth running of the conferences, especially Mary Jaffier and Robyn Vanterpool. Finally, we need to acknowledge practitioners who were instrumental in putting together the conferences, including

Gary Hughes (General Counsel, American Council of Life Insurers), Jack Egan (American Council of Life Insurers), Elizabeth Palmer (TIAA-CREF), and Tom Workman (President, Life Insurance Council of New York). These individuals in particular put large amounts of time into organizing the conferences. Even though some of our work was at odds with their views, their willingness to hold an open academic forum made the conferences successful and has led to what (we hope everyone agrees) is a unique book in the insurance area.

CHAPTER 1

Modernizing Insurance Regulation: An Overview

John H. Biggs and Matthew Richardson

Stern School of Business, New York University

INTRODUCTION

The insurance sector is an important part of the U.S. economy. For example, premiums collected by life and health (L/H) and property-casualty (P-C) insurers totaled $1.28 trillion in the United States in 2008, according to the National Association of Insurance Commissioners (NAIC).[1] Insurance allows individuals and businesses to protect themselves against potentially catastrophic financial risks. The traditional model of insurance is one in which insurers pool and diversify these idiosyncratic risks. In competitive markets, insurers price diversifiable risks on an actuarial basis, yielding tremendous utility gains to the previously exposed individuals and businesses.

Within this traditional model of insurance, it is reasonable to argue that systemwide defaults across insurance companies are unlikely because much of the risk is diversified away. If this type of risk is therefore not the primary concern, then it should not be surprising that the focus of regulation of insurance companies has been consumer protection in terms of individual firm solvency and the types of products offered. This partially explains why a regulatory system, dating back some 150 years, has revolved around state, not federal, regulations.

That said, why precisely insurance companies are regulated at the state rather than the federal level can be explained through two Supreme Court decisions, one in 1868 and the other in 1944. (See, for example, Harrington [2000], Webel and Cobb [2005], and Tyler and Hornig [2009], among others.)[2] In the earlier decision, in the *Paul v. Virginia* opinion, the Court determined that insurance was not interstate commerce and so for all practical purposes insurance companies were not subject to federal regulation. Seventy-six years later, the court reversed that decision in the *United States v. Southeastern Underwriters Association* case, which ruled that insurance is interstate commerce and subject to federal antitrust laws.

However, in response to the 1944 ruling, Congress elected not to take on insurance regulation and quickly passed into law in 1945 the McCarran-Ferguson Act, which permitted states to continue the regulation of insurance companies, as long as state regulation was not deficient (albeit subjecting the insurers to the antitrust laws). The latter provision affected mostly property-casualty (P-C) companies because of their use of state rating bureaus and their standardized pricing of personal insurance.

Since the passage of the McCarran-Ferguson Act, a tug-of-war between federal and state regulation has been a regular source of conflict. As the equilibrium between state and federal regulation has been disturbed by exogenous shocks in insurance products and markets, the regulatory process has been for the states and its regulatory body, the NAIC, to respond by adapting the state system to these shocks or criticisms. The NAIC is a de facto national organization, albeit made up of the chief insurance officials of the 50 states.

But there is growing evidence that the insurance industry has moved away from the traditional model, exposing itself to fragility similar to other parts of the financial sector. While this process started some 50 years ago as banks and asset management firms began to compete for similar customers, it likely escalated with the passage of the Gramm-Leach-Bliley Act in 1999. This Act effectively repealed the Glass-Steagall Act, further blurring the lines between financial services companies by allowing affiliation among banks, securities firms, and insurance companies. Insurance companies, whether through their asset holdings, their product offerings like variable annuities (VAs) and guaranteed investment contracts (GICs), or their funding, look less like the insurance companies of a few decades ago. It should not be a controversial statement that financial markets of the twenty-first century are substantially different from those of the nineteenth and twentieth centuries, suggesting possible revisions in how insurance companies are regulated.

Many large, complex financial institutions effectively failed during the most recent financial crisis. While one can argue that the insurance industry was less impacted (for the reasons given in paragraph 2), it is clear that the industry was not entirely spared—for example, from the failure of American International Group (AIG) to severe financial distress at some monoline insurers to large increases in default risk at some of the largest life insurers.

The most recent financial crisis has exposed serious holes in the architecture of the U.S. financial system. As a result, the Congress passed the Dodd-Frank Wall Street Reform and Consumer Protection Act, and it was signed into law by President Barack Obama on July 21, 2010. The Dodd-Frank Act did not create a new direct regulator of insurance but did impose on nonbank holding companies, possibly insurance entities, a major new and unknown form of regulation for those deemed "systemically important financial institutions" (SIFIs)—sometimes denoted "too big to fail" (TBTF)—or presumably any entity that regulators believe represents a "contingent liability" for the federal government in the event of severe stress or failure.[3]

Such a holding company would be subject to regulation by the Federal Reserve, where the list of companies subject to that regulation and its form is still being worked out, but now features AIG and Prudential Financial as two insurers in the SIFI list.[4] This initiative arose due to the concern of massive support for AIG with direct funding from the Federal Reserve or the more limited bailouts of $950 million for Lincoln National and $3.4 billion for the Hartford Group under the federal Troubled Asset Relief Program (TARP). Other insurers, faced with large losses, made corporate moves so as to qualify for support from federal resources but were able to survive without actual drawdowns.

Because of the lack of any significant insurance expertise in Washington, the Dodd-Frank Act did create a Federal Insurance Office (FIO) in the Treasury Department, with a broad mandate to make recommendations and gather information but no broad regulatory responsibility. Significantly, it required that the director of the FIO submit a report to Congress with recommendations to modernize and improve insurance regulation within 15 months of the passage of the Dodd-Frank Act.

The law also provides that a person with "insurance expertise" should be nominated by the President and approved by the Senate as one of the 10 voting members of the very powerful Financial Stability Oversight Council (FSOC). It further provided that at least one other individual with "insurance expertise," to be nominated by the NAIC, should be one of the five nonvoting members of the FSOC. In fact, three of the appointments have been made and all three are former state commissioners.

In light of the financial crisis and the somewhat benign changes to insurance regulation contained in the Dodd-Frank Act (regulation of SIFIs aside), how should a modern insurance regulatory structure be designed to deal with twenty-first-century insurance companies?

The purpose of this book is to lay out the arguments for and against various types of regulation. The book focuses in particular on three key areas of insurance regulation: (1) state versus federal, (2) systemic risk, and (3) guaranty associations. The book purposefully provides opposing arguments by leading academics, regulators, and practitioners.

This chapter summarizes the arguments laid out in the book and is separated into the following three sections, covering each of the three key areas.

STATE VERSUS FEDERAL REGULATION

As described in the introduction, the regulatory framework for insurance companies revolves around state, not federal, regulation. Aside from the advisory role of the new FIO housed in the Treasury Department, the only significant change is federal oversight of insurance companies deemed to be SIFIs. The question is whether this is sufficient for a modern insurance sector that includes companies operating across state and national lines and engaging in nontraditional insurance activities.

While not the primary focus of all the chapters of this book, almost all of the chapters touch on the issue of state versus federal regulation. The book starts with Chapter 2, by Dirk Kempthorne, CEO of the American Council of Life Insurers (ACLI) and former U.S. senator and governor of Idaho and U.S. Secretary of Commerce. While not calling for federal regulation per se, he argues that insurance regulation should be (1) uniform across different jurisdictions, (2) consistent with the business model of insurance companies (and not banks), and (3) efficient and, in particular, not duplicative. One could view points 1 and 3 as being more consistent with federal than multistate regulation. At the very least, Governor Kempthorne suggests that the new FIO will have to play a role in modernizing the system, especially with respect to coordination with international regulatory standards.

In Chapter 3, Roger Ferguson, CEO of TIAA-CREF and former vice chairman of the Federal Reserve Board of Governors, goes one step further and argues for the need for a federal regulator option for insurance companies. He argues that there has been a blurring of lines of business among financial companies, and that existing state regulation of insurance companies has led to a competitive disadvantage for those companies with a national footprint. Many of his concerns mirror those of Governor Kempthorne's in Chapter 2. Vice Chairman Ferguson admits that the NAIC has tried to fix some of these problems for multistate insurers. Nevertheless, he argues that, because the NAIC has no jurisdictional power across the states, national insurance companies cannot achieve speed to market for products and must satisfy a complex web of regulations for managing insurance sales. In addition to these issues, Vice Chairman Ferguson explains that a federal regulator for nationwide insurance companies would be better able to handle rules within an international setting and industry-wide threats or crises. He surmises that the majority of insurance companies would remain state regulated but, for the select few national companies, a federal insurer would serve them better.

In Chapter 4, Therese Vaughan, former CEO of the NAIC, sees the state versus federal regulation issue quite differently. Vaughan views the state system for insurance companies as a much more effective way to regulate the insurance sector. She describes historical evidence of the success of the state system and cites other international agencies' praise of its hands-on approach to regulation. Vaughan describes her experience at the NAIC and how the organization led to improvements in many of the state system's design faults described in Chapters 2 and 3. In contrast to those chapters, Vaughan questions the benefits of uniform regulation and cites examples of how federal regulation failed with respect to banks during the most recent financial crisis. She also sees a benefit of collaboration among state regulators. That said, there is recognition that inefficiencies remain, especially with respect to life insurers focused on asset management.

Chapter 5, by Eric Dinallo, partner at the law firm Debevoise & Plimpton and former insurance superintendent for the State of New York, concurs with Vaughan's Chapter 4. Commissioner Dinallo describes his experience in particular at regulating certain insurance subsidiaries of AIG before and during the financial crisis. He points out lapses in federal regulation and the danger of regulatory arbitrage, especially with respect to AIG's holding company and its use of credit derivatives. In his view, the strong protections of the operating companies at the state level through ring-fencing and tight capital regulation provide a robust solvency regime in times of financial distress. Commissioner Dinallo very much questions the need to federalize existing state regulation. Interestingly, however, the chapter places the business of insurance in a historical context and questions whether some of the activities performed by modern-day insurance companies are insurance per se and not some form of other financial activity.

With respect to solvency of insurers, in Chapter 11, Peter Gallanis, who leads the National Organization of Life and Health Insurance Guaranty Associations (NOLHGA), provides theoretical arguments and evidence in favor of the existing state-based system. In particular, Gallanis describes the success of the current state guaranty associations system in protecting policyholders over the years, with respect to both the size of the safety net and the resolution of failed insurance companies prior to 2008. In contrast, in Chapter 10, John Biggs, who is the former CEO of TIAA-CREF and an executive-in-residence at the NYU Stern School of Business, takes an opposite view. Biggs sees the system as particularly weak with a lack of uniformity and risk-based pricing across state guaranty associations. In pointing out well-known problems with systems based on post hoc assessments, Biggs is especially concerned that a number of guaranty associations did not or could not effectively participate in resolving the stress of large insurance companies in 2008 (such as AIG, Hartford Financial, and Lincoln Financial). Because there is a presumed reliance on the federal taxpayers in the event of widespread distress of large companies, and putting aside the Dodd-Frank Act's designation and resolution of SIFIs, Biggs calls for a risk-based, prefunded, federal insurer guaranty system.

With respect to state versus federal regulation, Chapters 6 through 9 of the book discuss this issue peripherally and for the most part argue either for or against federal regulation, depending on a given chapter's case for whether the insurance sector is systemically risky. For example, in Chapter 9, Viral Acharya and Matthew Richardson of the NYU Stern School of Business call for federal regulation. The argument is twofold: (1) It is simply inconceivable that federal regulation would not be required for a systemically risky sector since different state jurisdictions would not be able to manage the risk of such a sector, and (2) the Dodd-Frank Act's reliance on FSOC to look at a limited number of insurance SIFIs is not sufficient to pick up potential emerging systemic risks within the sector. While the chapter recognizes the advantage of state regulators' proximity to the ground and the relatively dismal performance of federal regulators, Acharya and Richardson also point out that a multistate system is prone to regulatory arbitrage, citing a recent paper by Koijen and Yogo (2013) as one such instance.[5]

In contrast, consistent with arguments made in some of the aforementioned chapters, in Chapter 7, David Cummins and Mary Weiss of Temple University and, in Chapter 8, Scott Harrington of the University of Pennsylvania's Wharton School point out that insurers have generally fared well through this and other crises. They argue that this is partly due to the success of the state regulatory framework and are concerned with any radical change to the current system. While Cummins and Weiss find some evidence for systemic risk for certain nontraditional insurance activities, their view is that federal regulation should focus in this area and not more broadly. Similarly, while Harrington is less convinced about systemic risk, to the extent that some new federal regulation will inevitably take hold for SIFIs, this regulation should be tailored specifically to insurance companies and focus on the nontraditional activities of these firms.

Of course, at the end of the day, the question of state versus federal regulation, particularly as it relates to systemic risk, is very much about the degree to which the insurance sector is systemically risky. The book devotes four chapters to this issue, and we briefly summarize the relevant arguments in the following section.

SYSTEMIC RISK

In the book *Regulating Wall Street: The Dodd-Frank Act and the New Architecture of Global Finance* (edited by Acharya, Cooley, Richardson, and Walter [2010]), seven chapters are devoted to systemic risk regulation with a special emphasis on analyzing the economic implications of the Dodd-Frank Act's approach to systemic risk regulation. One of those chapters in particular focuses on insurance companies.[6] As such, the four chapters devoted to systemic risk of insurance companies in this book take a step back and ask the essential question: Are insurance companies systemically risky? Chapters 6 through 9 provide a broad range of views on this question.

On the one hand, as described earlier, insurance companies are not banking institutions and should be regulated differently than banks. All four chapters agree that the traditional insurance model is unlikely to produce much systemic risk. In fact, in Chapter 2 Governor Kempthorne argues that life insurance companies are not systemically risky. His chapter describes life insurance companies very much in the traditional sense.

On the other hand, as also described in the introduction and in some of the aforementioned four chapters, insurance companies have moved away from the traditional model of insurance. For example, the argument is given that the insurance industry is no longer traditional and instead (1) offers products with nondiversifiable risk, (2) is more prone to a "run," (3) insures against macroeconomy-wide events, and (4) has expanded its role in financial markets. If the insurance sector performs poorly in systemic states, that is, when other parts of the financial sector are struggling, then as an important source for products to the economy (i.e., insurance) and a source for financing (i.e., corporate bonds and commercial mortgages), disintermediation of the insurance sector can have severe consequences for the real economy.

Before summarizing Chapters 6 to 9's debate about whether insurance firms are systemically risky, it is first worthwhile to describe the exact procedure for determining whether an insurance company is systemically risky using the Dodd-Frank Act and subsequent rulings. Chapter 8, by Scott Harrington, provides an excellent discussion of the procedure involved in designating nonbank financial institutions SIFIs, including insurance companies.

The Dodd-Frank Act created the Financial Stability Oversight Council (FSOC) with the primary purpose of identifying and monitoring risks to the U.S. financial system arising from the distress or failure of large, interconnected bank holding companies or nonbank financial companies. FSOC is made up of 10 voting members from the major regulatory agencies such as the Federal Reserve, Securities and Exchange Commission (SEC), Commodity Futures Trading Commission (CFTC), Federal Deposit

Insurance Corporation (FDIC), Office of the Comptroller of the Currency (OCC), Consumer Financial Protection Bureau (CFPB), Federal Housing Finance Agency (FHFA), National Credit Union Administration (NCUA), Treasury, and, most important for our purposes, a presidential appointee with expertise in insurance. With respect to nonbank financial companies, the Dodd-Frank Act gives the FSOC (by a two-thirds vote) the authority to designate any nonbank financial company a SIFI subject to enhanced regulation by the Federal Reserve.

If a nonbank financial company is deemed to be a SIFI, then the Federal Reserve must determine a set of enhanced regulatory rules for the SIFI, including additional risk-based capital requirements, leverage and liquidity restrictions, resolution standards (especially with respect to capital structure rules), and short-term funding limits. The FSOC lays out six risk categories from which the SIFI designation will be determined. In particular, FSOC will consider (1) size, (2) leverage, (3) liquidity risk, (4) interconnectedness, (5) lack of substitutes for the firm's services and products, and (6) existing regulatory scrutiny.

The process involves three stages. The first stage will look at the six factors using publicly available data and information from regulatory agencies. The second stage involves a more detailed analysis of the company, involving additional information from the company, if certain quantitative thresholds are reached with respect to the six categories or if the global consolidated assets are over $50 billion. If FSOC deems that a company needs additional evaluation after the second stage, then a third stage is triggered. This final stage involves information collected directly from the company. After this stage is the required two-thirds vote of the FSOC to determine whether a company is a SIFI. If requested, a company can ask for a hearing, after which there is a new vote. Currently, AIG and Prudential have been designated as SIFIs and MetLife is in the third stage of review.

Governor Kempthorne's Chapter 2 and Scott Harrington's Chapter 8 both argue that insurance companies are not banks and that they are therefore not systemically risky, and focus their arguments on the fact that traditional insurance does not have systemic consequences. While the analysis in Chapter 8 allows for the fact that some noninsurance activities may pose additional risks, Harrington suggests that the regulation should be differentially focused on these risks and should not place the rest of the insurance company under the same regulatory regime. Harrington in particular is concerned with the potential consequences of FSOC's recent determinations on AIG, but especially Prudential Financial and MetLife.

Chapter 7, by David Cummins and Mary Weiss, provides a more detailed analysis of the FSOC risk factors in the context of the insurance industry. Their general conclusion is that most of the core activities of insurance companies are not systemically risky with respect to the six risk factors. Some exceptions they cite are for the large life insurers and possible interconnectedness in the property-casualty area. That said, Chapter 7 points out that noncore activities of the type mentioned earlier may be more problematic, such as investing in privately placed bonds and asset-backed securities, offering guaranteed investment contracts for annuities, writing financial guarantee insurance, and so on.

In Chapter 6, Anna Paulson, Thanases Plestis, Richard Rosen, Robert McMenamin, and Zain Mohey-Deen of the Federal Reserve Bank of Chicago provide some evidence that the U.S. life insurance industry is less traditional than commonly assumed. Specifically, they provide a detailed analysis of the liquidity of the life insurance industry's asset holdings and liabilities. They provide evidence that approximately 50 percent of liabilities are in a moderately to highly liquid category, allowing for some type of withdrawal. In light of the possibility that life insurance premiums are no longer as sticky, they also describe the liquidity of the insurance industry's asset holdings. In particular, they analyze stress scenarios in which the insurance industry would have to liquidate some of its assets. They find that, relative to runnable liabilities, these firms would have to dip fairly deeply into their holdings of corporate bonds and other less liquid securities (i.e., nonagency and nongovernment securities).

In Chapter 9, Viral Acharya and Matthew Richardson describe systemic risk in a different way than FSOC's risk factors. Using theoretical arguments in Acharya, Pedersen, Philippon, and Richardson (2010), they estimate a firm's systemic risk as its expected shortfall in a financial crisis, denoted systemic expected shortfall (SES, or SRISK on NYU Stern's systemic risk website at http://vlab.stern.nyu.edu/welcome/risk).[7] In particular, systemic risk of a financial firm is its relative contribution to the aggregate capital shortfall of the financial sector. Chapter 9 then provides a detailed descriptive analysis of how insurance companies contribute to this shortfall and therefore to systemic risk.

Like Cummins and Weiss's Chapter 7, Chapter 9 also stresses the nontraditional nature of current insurance companies, yet argues that the insurance sector is more systemically risky than implied by Chapter 7. One of the main differences between these chapters is the different interpretation of systemic risk. Using the SRISK definition, it is likely that the impact of noncore activities will be greater because these activities expose insurance companies to aggregate shocks. Moreover, while there is some disagreement among Chapters 6, 7, 8, and 9 on how to measure systemic risk and with respect to the degree to which insurance firms are no longer in traditional lines of business, there is also a different interpretation about how to view systemic risk. Chapter 9 argues that systemic risk arises when there is an aggregate capital shortfall in the financial sector and the sector as a whole begins to disintermediate. For insurance companies, this disintermediation might involve insurance companies no longer supplying the full slate of insurance products, or no longer being a primary financier of many of the credit-linked activities in the economy, such as corporate bonds or commercial mortgages.

Acharya and Richardson's Chapter 9 analyzes SRISK before, during, and after the financial crisis. They use publicly available pricing data from equities and credit default swaps of insurance firms. Their basic conclusion is that the pricing data shows that insurance companies contribute to the expected aggregate capital shortfall of the financial sector in a crisis. Interestingly, since the financial crisis ended, insurance companies have become systemically more important as a fraction of their assets. This is in contrast to the banking sector, which appears to have reduced its systemic risk. Cummins and Weiss, in Chapter 7, also employ the SRISK measure, albeit in a different way. Their focus is on trying to understand what characteristics of insurance companies are statistically related to SRISK. Consistent with much of the intuition across all of the systemic risk chapters, they document that firms engaged in noncore insurance activities or certain core activities, like separate accounts and group annuities, tend to be more systemically risky.

Harrington's Chapter 8 questions some of the assumptions underlying these systemic risk measurements; in particular, what constitutes a capital shortfall in banking may be different for insurance companies. Moreover, equally of issue, the assumption that an additional dollar of capital shortfall in the insurance sector has the same systemic consequences as that in the banking sector may be problematic. That said, Paulson et al.'s Chapter 6 suggests insurance companies are more banklike in their liquidity mismatch than implied by the common view of insurance. The assumption of equal consequences of capital shortfall may therefore be reasonable.

GUARANTY ASSOCIATIONS

In Chapters 10 and 11, respectively, John Biggs and Peter Gallanis consider the modernizing of the safety net for insurance company policyholders in the event of an insolvency of an insurance company. These authors represent extreme opposites in opinion. Peter Gallanis highlights the success of the existing state-based guarantee system based on an after-the-failure assessment of surviving companies to cover losses. His chapter provides assurance to policyholders that the system would protect them in the future. In contrast, John Biggs critiques the state system from a variety of points of view. He suggests in Chapter 10 that a federal prefunded system would be more consistent, transparent, and more capable of coping with major industry-wide failures (as in 2008) without federal government intervention.

Gallanis contrasts the success of state regulation and resolution, with only 15 life insurance companies liquidated compared to the failure of over 400 banks and other financial institutions. He focuses on the regulation and resolution of life and health insurers, but his presentation also covers similar matters for property and casualty companies (although their liability structure is markedly different from life companies and more similar to health insurance companies).

Gallanis outlines the macro prudential aspects of state insurer regulation in describing the basic financial model of insurers, and the resulting regulatory system. He highlights the important role of the NAIC and NOLHGA in standardizing regulation across the states. He reviews the way the "receivership" and "guaranties" operate. Those interventions over the years have resulted in relatively small assessments against the industry. He shows graphically how little the past decade's assessments to the life companies have been compared to the end of the last century, when several very large companies became insolvent. He also points out that a large percentage of those small assessments were recovered through credits against state-imposed premium taxes.

It is surprising how little the insurers themselves had to pay out in net assessments during the most drastic failure of the financial sector since the Great Depression. Yet this contrasts sharply with the enormous sums provided and guaranteed by the federal sector in its intervention to protect the insurance sector. Gallanis also provides data showing the capacity of the state assessment to be roughly $10 billion a year or at least $100 billion over 10 years. He points out at some length the long payout structure of a life insurance company's obligations and the matching of that with the annual assessments. Gallanis concludes that the insurance industry weathered the storm of the 2008 crisis rather well and met its commitments to consumers when a few relatively small companies did fail.

Related to the Gallanis chapter is Dinallo's Chapter 5, which defends state insurance regulation in spite of the federal intervention in AIG, which largely held insurance company assets. Dinallo, Gallanis, and others see the AIG crisis as due to poor regulation of insurance holding companies, and especially the lack of regulating the enormous guarantees through credit default swaps.

In Chapter 10, Biggs does not question the success of NOLHGA and the state commissioners in dealing with insolvencies under the existing state guaranty structure. He sees the structure itself as weak and not providing a stronger safety net for insurers. In his view, little of the 2008 burden was shouldered by the industry itself.

In his critique of the system, Biggs points out the opaqueness of having 50 different benefit patterns depending on the insured person's residence, further aggravated by a provision in most state laws preventing any communication of the existence of the system. Also, the usual state provisions are inconsistent with the other widely publicized safety nets, like the Federal Deposit Insurance Corporation (FDIC) and particularly the Pension Benefit Guaranty Corporation (PBGC).

He criticizes the post hoc assessment system as (1) creating uncertainty in the speed of resolution, (2) preventing any form of risk-based charges, and (3) being "procyclical" (i.e., in making assessments against the industry when a broad-scale crisis creates stress on the entire industry). Biggs cites the economic literature that favors risk-based premiums for two reasons. The first is simply fairness since cautious underwriters and well-capitalized insurers would pay in less than more risky companies. The second is for reduction of moral hazard since risk takers relying on the government "put" would see their premiums rise.

Biggs also points out that the liability structure for many of our largest life insurers has moved to a large provision for immediately withdrawable preretirement annuities that are rarely annuitized into traditional long payment streams. These liabilities are more like bank deposits, and therefore more subject to risks of a run than are traditional life insurance obligations.

To counter these limitations of the varying laws of the 50 states, he proposes a uniform prefunded federal system that would strengthen the financial backing and make transparent to prospective policyholders the guarantees. Furthermore, he sees several additional advantages. A prefunded federal system could have responded to the 2008 crisis in some form, particularly in providing temporary TARP-type funding for prudently financed companies that could pay back at a penalty rate. Such an existing fund would accordingly provide a "last window of opportunity" to insurers comparable to what the Federal Reserve provides U.S. banks.

Additionally, Biggs sees the existence of a federal insurer guaranty system as providing the federal government with an experienced insurance regulator that could better deal with a 2008-type financial crisis than the bank regulators. He also argues that the federal insurance system would substantially eliminate the federal government's contingent liability to intervene to protect the insurance industry in the event of another major national financial crisis.

The editors' objective in this book is to lay out for interested readers the up-to-date positions on the Dodd-Frank Act's Congressional order to produce a plan for "modernizing insurance regulation." The issue of the guarantees, whether state or federal, has been the subject of Congressional debate before. Following a series of major property and casualty insolvencies in the 1960s, Senator Edward Brooke of Massachusetts introduced legislation that included a federal guarantee system. And again, after significant earlier losses from Executive Life and Mutual Benefit, Representative John Dingell introduced a bill in 1993 creating a federal regulatory system for insurers, which also had a prefunded federal guaranty system.

The structure of the insurance business has changed significantly since the guaranty association legislation was finally adopted by most states in the 1970s and 1980s. Since then we have seen the growing sophistication of the state system as it became "national" if not "federal." The question is whether the new issues are of sufficient concern to move away from the largely successful state system. If we may speak for the two sides, we might say for the state advocates, "If it ain't broke, don't fix it." However, others reflecting on the same set of facts might conclude that the state system met limited goals that did not reflect all the needs of policyholders and the industry, and required the federal government to intervene in the financial crisis of 2008.

CONSUMER PROTECTION

The Dodd-Frank Wall Street Reform and Consumer Protection Act created a Consumer Financial Protection Bureau (CFPB). Oddly, from the point of view of this book, the Act specifically excluded products and services provided by insurance companies from regulation by the Bureau. Presumably this was in deference to the existing fact that insurance is regulated at the state level.

The academic literature is fairly light on its analysis of consumer finance protection and especially so in the area of insurance markets. For some analysis of the broader issues related to regulation of consumer financial products, we suggest the reader look at Chapter 3 of *Regulating Wall Street: The Dodd-Frank Act and the New Architecture of Global Finance* (edited by Acharya, Cooley, Richardson, and Walter [2010]).[8] This suggestion aside, Chapter 12 of this book, written by financial economists Santosh Anagol, Shawn Cole, and Shayak Sarkar, provides an interesting perspective.

While there is little substantive academic research on insurance product markets in the United States, Anagol, Cole, and Sarkar (2013) have performed detailed experiments in India's markets.[9] India has a single national regulator of insurance and up until 1999 had only one insurer! Chapter 12 discusses the ethical standard that regulators should impose on "market intermediaries" or "retail sales agents" in the life insurance market or, in U.S. language, on life insurance agents and brokers.

Chapter 12 debates whether the standard for insurance intermediaries' behavior should be a "suitable" or "fiduciary" standard. This legal distinction is currently hotly debated in the United States as to the proper legal standard for stockbrokers. Financial advisers are clearly held to a fiduciary standard but brokers to a suitability one. The national regulator in India in 1913 required a "standardized suitability analysis."

In making an analogy with the Indian insurance markets, Chapter 12 describes the U.S. standard as "caveat emptor." Most state insurance commissioners would dispute such a characterization. They would argue that careful licensing and oversight of agent behavior result in a higher standard, probably close to suitability. However, legally it is difficult to use the words "agent of the company" without suggesting that the agent's primary duty is to the company and not the buyer. Again, U.S. state regulators would respond that the companies are responsible for the behavior of their agents and that their monitoring is reviewed by the state insurance department audits of companies.

State laws in the United States directly attack some particularly unsuitable actions by agents and brokers. For example, selling replacement policies can be very harmful to policyholders. It may be easier to sell a policy to a person who is already paying for an existing policy, and given the complexity of policy provisions, it may not be obvious to the buyer what the disadvantages are (e.g., paying the high acquisition costs a second time, or losing other benefits of the existing policy). States have an elaborate system requiring notification to the first insurer and clear illustrations.

Chapter 12 spends some time describing the experiments performed by Anagol and colleagues. In particular, Anagol et al. (2013) examines the advice given by India's intermediaries as to whether a young family prospect ought to buy the low-commission term policy or the high-commission whole life policy. With a saving feature and high first-year commissions and costs, this problem is a classic issue. One might guess how such a study of American life insurance sales to young families might vary from the Indian experience. One would hope that American buyers, even under a caveat emptor rule, would not buy the preposterous statements that some Indian agents are said to have used to justify the higher-commission policies. But the results might be similar. While Chapter 12 does not provide examples from the American experience of insurance markets, the work of Anagol and colleagues shows the possible need for enhanced consumer protection in some financial markets. It remains an open question whether this is true for insurance markets, and whether this role is better performed at the state versus federal level. (See previous discussion.)

If American insurance commissioners would be asked where they stood on standards for agent/broker performance on the spectrum of caveat emptor, suitability, or fiduciary, they would probably pick something higher than suitability. However, by law, their standard may well be only caveat emptor, which would be the basis on which a policyholder could avail himself or herself of the courts. In Chapter 3, Roger Ferguson argues the merits of an optional federal charter. Clearly, the federal regulator of companies electing such a charter would have to consider whether an explicit suitability standard should be defined.

COMPARISON WITH THE FIO REPORT

As this book goes to press, the Federal Insurance Office (FIO), created by the Dodd-Frank Act (DFA) has released the report, required by DFA, on "How to Modernize and Improve the System of Insurance Regulation in the United States."

The Report includes many specific recommendations on improvements, primarily in how the existing state system should be changed. It also has several changes that would involve additional federal interventions. The Report reframes the federal/state debate to "whether federal involvement is warranted at this time and if so, in what areas." Accordingly, it differs from this book (Book) in approach to the possible federal role. The Report describes its recommendations as creating a "hybrid" federal/state approach.

The changes in state regulation in the Report would eliminate or mitigate existing widely recognized weaknesses in the present 51 jurisdiction regulation. Frequently, the recommendation simply pushes for acceptance by state legislatures of NAIC Model statutes. For example, the significant variation in guaranteed benefits under state guaranty associations could be remedied by all the jurisdictions adopting the model law. In another area, the FIO is concerned about the weakening of capital standards by some states using discretionary accounting and capital rules without the approval of the other states in which a company operates. Another is the seemingly egregious arbitrage in the use of captive reinsurance companies, established in states with weaker capital and reserve standards than the home state of the company.

This Book, on the other hand, approaches the federal/state discussion with an examination of the pros and cons of basic regulation at either the state or federal level. Those papers inclined toward state regulation do not identify the kind of issues raised in the FIO report.

As to the issues of systemic risk, this Book looks at a variety of ways to measure insurers' role in creating systemic risk or in being a "victim" of risk created by other institutions. The Report doesn't take a position on how to determine systemic risk but is concerned more with the regulation of an entity that is deemed systemic. The Report introduces the idea of "Global Systemically Important Insurers" (G-SII) as determined by international standards.

The Report also has a good deal of coverage of the need for state regulatory changes in overseeing a "group," or "non bank holding company" "in DFA language. The Report benefits from the time spent by the FIO since its founding in negotiating international treaties, a responsibility formally assigned to the FIO in the DFA.

This Book explores the guaranty associations in much greater detail than the Report. The only substantive issue in the Report was the concern about uniformity of guarantees—for which it recommends that all states pass the NAIC model statute. This Book, in one paper details the operation of the current system with no recommendations for improvement, and in the other critiques its structure and proposes a federal system similar to the banks' FDIC.

The Report has much more than the Book to say about marketplace regulation. This Book has the one paper on the oversight of producers/agents and pushes for a suitability standard. A specific counter to that issue is the Report's urging compliance with the NAIC Suitability in Annuity Transactions. Also, there are several recommendations for a Federal database for agent licensing.

We hope that the different emphases and approaches in this Book and the Report combine to give Congress useful academic and policy making analyses of the complex issues in creating a Modern Insurance Regulatory System.

CONCLUSION

In Chapter 2, Governor Kempthorne makes the argument for the crucial role life insurance companies play in multiple ways in the U.S. economy. Life insurance companies provide help to widows, parents and children, retirees and businesses, and provide major investment capital to corporations through purchases of corporate bonds and commercial mortgages. These points are only strengthened by the fact that the baby boom generation is approaching retirement age. Most of the authors of the chapters in this book would agree with Governor Kempthorne's view of insurance companies.

The importance of the insurance sector, however, prompts the question: Is the current regulatory system for insurance companies, developed long ago, up to the task of dealing with modern-day insurance companies? And, if not, will this put the economic system in jeopardy if insurance companies can no longer intermediate at their optimal level in times of distress and crisis?

The chapters in this book provide disparate views on these questions. The hope is that this will provide readers with the relevant line of reasoning on all sides of these questions, so they can make their own informed assessment.

NOTES

1. There are two broad types of insurance—life and health and property-casualty—that exhibit substantial differences in how insurers operate and are regulated. Life and health insurers (hereafter, life insurers) sell financial protection against human life contingencies. For example, life insurance protects against financial loss due to unexpected death, annuities protect against financial issues if living longer than expected, and health insurance covers unexpected medical care, disability, and long-term care costs. Many types of life insurance, such as variable annuities, include substantial investment aspects. Property-casualty (P-C) insurers sell insurance protection against a wide and mostly familiar set of risks such as auto, fire, and homeowners insurance. Other major lines of business include tort liability, flood, hurricane and earthquake, medical malpractice, workers' compensation, officers' and directors' liability, marine coverage, and reinsurance.

2. Scott Harrington, "History of Federal Involvement in Insurance Regulation," in *Optional Chartering and Regulation of Insurance Companies*, AEI Study, 2000, ed. Peter J. Wallison; Baird Webel and Carolyn Cobb, "Insurance Regulation: History, Background, and Recent Congressional Oversight," CRS Report for Congress, 2005; Ralph Tyler and Karen Hornig, "Reflections on State Regulation: A Lesson of the Economic Turmoil of 2007–2009," *Journal of Business & Technology Law* 4, no. 2, (2009): 349–370.

3. For a detailed analysis of the systemic risk regulations contained in the Dodd-Frank Act, see Chapters 4 to 9 of *Regulating Wall Street: The Dodd-Frank Act and the New Architecture of Global Finance*, ed. Viral V. Acharya, Thomas Cooley, Matthew Richardson, and Ingo Walter (Hoboken, NJ: John Wiley & Sons, 2010).

4. Globally, too, there are currently nine insurers in the Financial Stability Board (FSB) designated list of global SIFIs.

5. Ralph Koijen and Motoriho Yogo, "Shadow Insurance," working paper, London Business School, 2013.

6. Viral V. Acharya, John Biggs, Hanh Le, Matthew Richardson, and Stephen Ryan, "Systemic Risk and the Regulation of Insurance Companies," Chapter 9 in *Regulating Wall Street: The Dodd-Frank Act and the New Architecture of Global Finance*, ed. Viral V. Acharya, Thomas Cooley, Matthew Richardson, and Ingo Walter (Hoboken, NJ: John Wiley & Sons, 2010).

7. Viral V. Acharya, Lasse Pedersen, Thomas Philippon, and Matthew Richardson, "Measuring Systemic Risk," working paper, NYU Stern School of Business, 2010.

8. Thomas Cooley, Xavier Gabaix, Samuel Lee, Thomas Mertens, Vickie Morwitz, Shelle Santana, Anjolein Schmeits, Stijn Van Nieuwerburgh, and Robert Whitelaw, "Consumer Finance Protection," Chapter 3 in *Regulating Wall Street: The Dodd-Frank Act and the New Architecture of Global Finance*, ed. Viral V. Acharya, Thomas Cooley, Matthew Richardson, and Ingo Walter (Hoboken, NJ: John Wiley & Sons, 2010).
9. See Santosh Anagol, Shawn Cole, and Shayak Sarkar, "Understanding the Advice of Commissions-Motivated Agents: Evidence from the Indian Life Insurance Market," Harvard Business School Working Paper 12–055 (2013), 20.

CHAPTER 2

Life Insurance's Importance to American Families and Industry's Concern about Regulation

Dirk Kempthorne

President and Chief Executive Officer
American Council of Life Insurers

The following are Governor Dirk Kempthorne's NYU Stern School remarks made on March 2, 2012.

The life insurance industry is a venerable institution. It has been playing a significant role in the lives of American families for quite a long time.

Ben Franklin was an early proponent of life insurance. In his Silence Dogood letters, he recommended insurance for widows and orphans that functioned like a current-day pension. Prudential was the first insurer to make coverage affordable to working-class people; MetLife was founded during the Civil War to insure soldiers and sailors against wartime-related disabilities; New York Life covered George Armstrong Custer with a $5,000 policy.

The history of New York companies—indeed, the history of the industry itself—is about helping widows and orphans, parents and children, retirees and businesses. At the same time it is about providing investment capital to help grow the nation's economy and create jobs.

And here's a statistic that opens people's eyes: Life insurers are the number one domestic investor in U.S. corporate bonds.

Through wars, the Great Depression, and now the global financial meltdown—through good times and tough times—the life insurance business has protected families, estates, and businesses.

And now we are entering into a new phase in our history. A big part of this unfolding story is about how the baby boom generation will rely on us for lifetime income when they retire.

That is because people are living longer than ever before. Some 10,000 people reach age 65 every day in the United States, and this trend will continue until the year 2030. Nobel laureate Robert Fogel predicted that one-half of Americans in their 30s today will live to age 100. It is no wonder that some 85 percent of people said in a 2010 survey that Social Security won't be enough to provide them their standard of living in retirement. They need a guaranteed source of income to supplement Social Security. That is what we provide with the annuity. No other private-sector product guarantees people a steady stream of income until they die.

The annuity—the personal pension—addresses the risks and burdens of managing assets over a lifetime. For many retirees, especially older retirees, it can serve as the difference between their independence and dignity, and reliance on children or government.

I can tell you personally: Parents don't like relying on their children for money.

My Dad died recently. He was 95 years old. He never thought he'd live so long. He needed help financially. Believe me, I was proud and happy to help the man who raised me and, among so many other great things, honorably served his country in World War II. But the patriarch of the family did not want to be in that position. He did not want to have to rely on me as his annuity.

So, I'm a believer. I have seen from my Dad's experience and others that an annuity can provide a real and tangible benefit to people. And I know my experience is not unique.

The U.S. Treasury Department recognizes the value of annuities as well. In early 2012, Treasury proposed new regulations that will make it easier for employers to offer annuities in their retirement plans. It sees them as key to helping the baby boom generation solve the retirement income crisis—to earn a paycheck for life; to enjoy dignity and, yes, stability in their retirement years.

Thanks to the stability of the life insurance industry, we will be there for our customers today and 50 years from today. For a business as important as ours, we must have good, smart regulation—regulation that is appropriate for our business. We need a system of regulation that will help us continue providing financial security to families and businesses.

We need a regulatory structure that recognizes the connection between life insurance industry regulation and the cost of capital, our competitiveness, and the well-being of our customers.

Life insurers, like other financial institutions, are facing a storm of new regulation. New accounting standards and solvency requirements are being shaped in the United States and overseas.

Naturally, life insurers are working to influence this process. Before I tell you what we want, let me tell you what we *don't* want. We don't want lax regulation. We *don't* want to get a pass on maintaining strong financial standards. We don't want to avoid regulatory oversight.

So, what is our position on regulation? Let me give another piece of history—more recent history, involving the American Council of Life Insurers (ACLI).

For more than a dozen years now, the CEOs of our member companies have made improved insurance regulation one of the ACLI's top three priorities. A couple of those priority items have changed through the years. But without fail, each January, the CEOs instruct staff to advocate for a system that will better help them serve their customers.

I can't say we are always terribly successful. Progress takes time. But each year the demand is the same. The way our CEOs put it, a reformed regulatory system should have three elements.

First, it should be uniform—consistent standards from jurisdiction to jurisdiction.

Second, the regulations should reflect the unique way we interact with customers, manage our risks, and establish reserves.

Third, it should be efficient—it should eliminate unnecessary and expensive regulations that do nothing but add costs to the system. And let me again emphasize this point: Efficiency is not a euphemism for laxity. Efficiency and effectiveness are not mutually exclusive. To the contrary, efficiency and effectiveness complement each other.

Let me briefly discuss each element.

First, uniformity. This has been a long-standing issue for us, from well before the financial crisis. Back in the 1990s we were pointing to the problems caused by the lack of uniformity of laws, regulations, and interpretations from state to state: the administrative burdens of dealing with 50 states and the District of Columbia, and the excessive time required to get new products to market. In a 1999 survey of ACLI member company CEOs, these were listed as primary problems.

Some 12 years later, in January 2011, we again asked our members to assess the regulatory environment. The responses were virtually unchanged.

What has changed is that regulation has become even more complicated than ever before with the passage of the Dodd-Frank Act and emergence of global regulatory standards.

The problems detailed in 1999 seem almost quaint by comparison to the problems companies face today.

The next element is the appropriateness of regulation. Is it the right fit?

Consider the 25-year-old newlywed who buys a life insurance policy; that policy may remain in force for 50 years, maybe more, before a claim is filed.

Consider a 65-year-old who plans wisely and might purchase a lifetime annuity and collect payments for 30 years or more.

Life insurers set reserves and maintain adequate capital to fulfill promises whenever they occur and for however long they continue. The ongoing, long-term responsibilities of life insurance companies are fundamentally different from those of banks, which typically face more immediate demands on the money they hold.

This ability to plan for the long term is the reason we hold the bonds we purchase for so long—an average of 16 years. These long-term obligations make us a very stable business and provide for America's infrastructure—our nation's roads and bridges—and, yes, jobs.

Here's some interesting data: The National Organization of Life & Health Insurance Guaranty Associations reports that since 2009 it has been called into action 10 times to protect policyholders of insolvent companies. Over the same period, the Federal Deposit Insurance Corporation (FDIC) reports that more than 400 banks have failed.

Now, I know that is an imperfect comparison. Indeed, we stress that life insurers are not banks, so I rightfully admit this is a bit of an apples-to-oranges comparison. Still, it demonstrates that our regulatory system does certain things right. Solvency regulation is one of them.

It keeps our investments in non-investment-grade obligations below 10 percent of assets, ensures sound assets-to-liabilities matching under adverse financial conditions, and serves to make sure our capital levels remain high. In fact, the average industry risk-based capital ratio is now the highest it has been since the Risk-Based Capital Model Act on the topic was established in 1993. In other words, we are well capitalized.

Thanks to smart solvency regulation, in addition to the conservative nature of both our investment strategy and the underwriting risks we assume, life insurers are neither originators nor multipliers of systemic risk.

Still, despite smart solvency regulation, the Dodd-Frank Act created the Financial Stability Oversight Council (FSOC) and directed it to include insurance companies in their evaluation of systemically important financial institutions (SIFIs).

We trust FSOC will understand that life insurers do not pose a systemic risk.

The issue of systemic risk is not for FSOC alone. We hope the Securities and Exchange Commission (SEC), the Commodity Futures Trading Commission, and other federal regulators understand why applying bank-oriented rules on insurance companies would be inappropriate.

We are different from banks. Regulations must be the right fit for what we do.

Third, efficiency. Even if we can all get on the same page in terms of what the regulations should be, can those regulations be implemented without extraneous costs? Will insurance companies be able to bring new and innovative products to market in a timely manner?

That is a major concern of our CEOs. In our surveys, both in 1999 and in 2011, CEOs cited a lack of speed or timeliness in getting new policies to market and the cost of adhering to duplicative regulatory requirements as major concerns.

Efficiency is not a four-letter word; nor is it a code word for abusing consumers. An efficient regulatory system benefits consumers.

Innovative products come to market more quickly. Costs of doing business are reduced, and in a competitive market, those savings are passed on to consumers in terms of lower premiums. Efficient regulation reduces barriers to marketplace entry, and more competition means better products and better prices for consumers.

One of my first appearances after joining the ACLI in November 2010 was at a meeting of our Forum 500 companies. Our Forum 500 companies each have assets of $2 billion or less, or capital and surplus of $200 million or less. In other words, they are small and midsize companies. The ACLI has more than 300 member companies, and 108 participate in the Forum 500.

Very few of these companies do business outside the United States. But when I visited them a few months ago, I reminded them that in a way they are all global companies. That's because the global solvency rules and global accounting standards under development at the G-20, at the Financial Stability Board (FSB), at the International Association of Insurance Supervisors, and at the International Accounting Standards Board will affect how they do business.

They could impact core features of our business—statutory accounting and generally accepted accounting principles (GAAP) accounting, reserving, capital requirements, even taxation.

And I had to stress to these small and midsize companies that it did not matter whether they do business in a single U.S. state, in every state, or overseas.

We put together a PowerPoint presentation showing how a myriad of international organizations—what I sometimes call the alphabet soup—will exert enormous pressure on the U.S. regulatory system to develop standards that are equivalent to the emerging international standards.

Let me give you one quick example. Our stock companies use GAAP accounting for their financial reporting. I'm not an accountant, but I understand that GAAP is highly prescriptive. The GAAP rules number some

25,000 pages. If international standard setters force us to abandon GAAP accounting in favor of International Financial Reporting Standards (IFRS), we will go from 25,000 pages of rules to 2,500 pages.

Now, that might seem like a blessing, but we don't really know. As I noted a second ago, these standards—IFRS standards—are under development. One thing is clear, however: This would be a dramatic change and would require a long adjustment period.

The Federal Insurance Office (FIO) established under Dodd-Frank will have to play a significant role on behalf of the U.S. industry at these international settings.

In coordination with the states and the National Association of Insurance Commissioners (NAIC), the FIO should assure that U.S. interests are represented on an equal basis with those of our global competitors.

The FIO and the state commissioners must work together to define and evaluate the impact of potential changes in global standards and processes on the U.S. markets. And, certainly, they need to assure that these standards and processes do not conflict with state and federal laws.

Bad regulation will stifle growth. Duplicative or unnecessary regulation will raise costs on insurers at a time when our mission is most critical.

Think about the challenges ahead. In its Global Aging Initiative, the Center for Strategic and International Studies found that by the middle of this century, the percentage of the elderly population worldwide will increase from 15 percent today to 25 percent.

In total numbers, that would roughly represent an increase from one billion to more than two billion elders.

In the United States we will likely see the percentage of the elderly population jumping from 13 percent of the population to more than 20 percent between now and the middle of the century.

To avoid human and societal tragedies, we will have to encourage people to save more diligently for retirement. We will have to encourage people to invest part of those savings in lifetime income products.

Regulators in the states, in Washington, D.C., and overseas should partner with the industry in these efforts. Government systems will need help from life insurers to address this budding crisis.

Governments will benefit, but the real beneficiaries will be people.

Industry and regulators will always have differences, but a vibrant industry addressing Americans' financial needs should be a shared goal.

CHAPTER 3

Why Insurance Needs a Federal Regulator Option

Roger W. Ferguson Jr.

President and CEO of TIAA-CREF

The extreme volatility of financial markets in the past decade has drawn increased attention to every part of the financial system, including the insurance industry. A major outcome—the Dodd-Frank Act—proposed changes in the way banks and securities firms are regulated. With respect to insurance companies, the Act's most significant action was to call on the administration to present Congress with a proposal to "modernize insurance regulation." The Act also created a Federal Insurance Office (FIO), whose purpose is limited to advising Congress. While the FIO is a welcome resource to help Congress be more informed about the insurance industry, it has no regulatory authority. As a result, the insurance industry may perceive its activities, such as requests for data and the like, as an imposition by the government—without presenting an alternative regulatory option to the current state-based system.

Congress has, in fact, considered several bills in the past decade to create a federal regulator to oversee insurance issues affecting the banking industry, as well as life and property-casualty insurers. Such legislative attempts at reform have not proven decisive. Life, property-casualty, and health insurers are still regulated by each state individually—a system that has been in place since before the Civil War. This system was designed to oversee local insurers with only a few lines of business, not today's interstate and international commerce by an array of holding companies, and multiline and multinational insurers.

For two decades after World War II, life insurers played a major role in the investment business, primarily through group plans managed for companies and insurance policies sold to individual consumers. The emergence of mutual funds has greatly diminished that role. Today, most employees and consumers think of mutual funds when they have money to invest or are looking to save for retirement. And in virtually all markets—including higher education and the not-for-profit sector—most large insurers compete with large mutual fund companies that are regulated only at the national level. In fact, since banking regulations in the 1980s began to permit all banks to cross state lines, insurance is the only major financial industry regulated primarily at the state level.

THE CONVERGENCE BETWEEN INSURANCE AND FINANCIAL SERVICES

The boundaries between insurance and other financial services have blurred because of convergence among insurance, banking, and securities products. A good example of this convergence is the variable annuity product. Is this an insurance product or a security? The insurance industry engaged in a protracted debate over that question in the 1950s and 1960s, with the Supreme Court ruling, in 1967, that variable annuities were both. This resulted in insurance companies having to meet Securities and Exchange Commission (SEC) registration and prospectus requirements as well as state insurance policy approvals. In addition, insurance agents became subject to oversight by the Financial Industry Regulatory Authority (FINRA), the national securities market conduct regulator, along with existing oversight by state insurance regulators. By contrast, mutual funds and banks found it expedient to wrap their fund products in annuity guarantees and outsource the guarantees to insurance companies. As a practical matter, this allows these institutions to offer insurance-type products while avoiding the time, cost, and effort involved in working with 50 state regulators.

And it isn't only on annuities where the lines have blurred. Consider the efforts that banks are now making to help corporate pension plans protect themselves against longevity risk. The banks are offering derivatives contracts to serve the needs of these customers, which they call the "longevity derisking market." These contracts offset unfavorable deviations from an underlying mortality index in exchange for derivative-based premiums. Like the credit default swaps they resemble, these contracts look a lot like insurance. But, again, banks offering them are regulated at a national level and are not subject to regulation by the 50 states.

The convergence of these industries, without any accompanying change in the insurance regulatory system, has left insurers—at least those with a national footprint—at a competitive disadvantage. Importantly, there are efforts by many state regulators to accommodate the multistate operational needs of most insurers, usually under the auspices of the National Association of Insurance Commissioners (NAIC). The NAIC has been supportive and forward-looking. Its efforts to bring greater uniformity to state regulations are commendable. However, because of the U.S. system of state regulation of insurance, the NAIC has no true enforcement power. It can only develop and recommend model laws; it is up to the states to enact them. The NAIC has tried to overcome this deficit in a variety of ways, including by creating compacts of multiple states that would give the compacts quasi-enforcement powers. However, legislators in some large and important states, perhaps wary of additional oversight and loss of authority within their borders, have refused to join the compacts, limiting their effectiveness.

CHALLENGES OF STATE-BASED REGULATION

In the absence of a federal regulator option, most insurers face two significant challenges with state-based regulation. The first and more important is speed to market. Where mutual funds can respond to a new law or opportunity in weeks, most insurers need months or years. Any new life insurance product requires an insurance policy form that must be filed and approved by all 50 states, and may often need federal securities registration. Some state insurance offices are understaffed and take months to get to a review and approval. Many have peculiar requirements, or interpret model law requirements differently than other states with the same model law, which can require state-specific products and procedures. State insurance regulators and federal securities regulators reviewing the same products operate independently, and often don't understand the needs or requirements of the other.

For most insurance companies doing business in multiple states, this amounts to an increased burden. Despite insurance clearly being "interstate commerce"—a fact the Supreme Court acknowledged back in 1944—U.S. insurance companies too often need legal representation in many, and sometimes most, individual states to move things along. The final result is rarely a uniform national policy. While mutual funds and banks go through an approval process that involves one regulator, many insurance companies are dealing with at least 50, and running into a costly and inefficient process. Importantly, state regulators have recognized this reality and have made significant efforts toward improving the process.

The second problem involves the oversight of insurance sales personnel. This is a vital and important part of insurance regulation and consumer protection. But the states have different rules on licensing, continuing education, and market conduct. Today, consumers and insurance agents often conduct their financial and insurance affairs across state boundaries, so this patchwork of state-specific requirements seems unnecessary. It is also costly for multistate insurers and frustrating for insurers, consumers, and sales personnel.

In many insurance companies, the main servicing staff includes insurance agents operating from call centers around the country. When a call comes in, it can be from a customer in any state. This means that an insurer's call centers need to be staffed with individuals licensed in all 50 states. Call center personnel have a steep learning curve, with much of the training involving nuanced differences among state requirements. The similarity but lack of uniformity from one state to another may even heighten the risk of technical errors. This can greatly increase compliance costs for insurers without providing a commensurate improvement in consumer protection or the consumer experience.

Moreover, having to deal with 50 state regulators does not exempt such insurers from federal regulation. The investment component of variable annuity products requires additional compliance with federal securities rules. Meanwhile, noninsurance competitors in the financial services industry only have to comply with one set of governing rules.

REASONS FOR A FEDERAL REGULATOR OPTION

Giving insurance companies the option of being regulated at the federal level would go a long way toward leveling what is currently a very tilted playing field. It would reduce the resources insurers would need to comply with separate and largely redundant state regulations. It also would provide uniform protection to all consumers no matter where they live, and make oversight regulation more effective.

Why should Congress make a priority of adding a federal regulator option? The first reason is to help insurers continue to offer competitive products. Mutual funds are useful for many individuals. But there is also a place for the kind of investment and mortality guarantees that only insurance companies can offer, and that only annuities can provide. The routine recommendations that advisers make of annuities shows how valuable annuities are and will be to a population that is living longer in retirement. Annuities represent a level of stability and security that traditional mutual fund products can't offer.

A second reason to create a federal regulator option is to give big U.S. insurers the ability to compete globally. Many insurers already have substantial international businesses. Regulators in foreign countries do not understand the idea of 50 regulators in the United States. They would far prefer to know that U.S. insurance companies setting up shop in their countries were complying with rules established by a single federal regulator in Washington. This is equally true for property-casualty insurers.

The U.S. system of state insurance regulation is also a disincentive to foreign insurers looking to offer products in the United States. If a foreign government wanted to retaliate, it could make it harder for U.S. insurers to operate on its territory.

Third, a federal regulator option could help in the event of an industry-wide threat or crisis. The lack of a federal insurance regulator was a gaping hole during the 2008–2009 crisis. Consumers might well have been better protected had there been an experienced federal insurance regulator in place at the time.

CONCLUSION

The arguments against a federal insurance regulator option are not persuasive. One is the idea that it would lead to so-called regulatory arbitrage, where an insurer could choose its regulator, state or federal, and switch to gain advantage or to escape a severe regulator. However, one could make a compelling argument that state and federal banking regulators learn from each other. Indeed, many banking experts think the dual regulatory system covering banks makes all banking regulators more alert and effective. Now, one could use 2008 to poke holes in that theory. But there's a difference between a faulty system and faulty implementation. It's reasonable to think that a dual system of federal and state insurance regulation would raise the overall level of oversight in our industry and would prove beneficial in creating an insurance industry that can compete with other elements of the financial services sector.

There are also objections to creating another Washington bureaucracy, especially given the void of federal experience in insurance matters. But in this case, there's a bigger problem: the bureaucracy that most U.S. insurers already face from the system of state-by-state regulation.

The important thing to remember is that the federal regulator option would be just that, an *option*. Insurers would be free to continue to be chartered and regulated at the state level, and my guess is that many of them would do just that—so that insurance would be a lot like banking in this respect. Still, the federal regulator option is something that would make our industry healthier and more competitive. And that's an outcome that has significant benefits for everyone involved.

CHAPTER 4

Observations on Insurance Regulation—Uniformity, Efficiency, and Financial Stability

Therese M. Vaughan

Regulation is a tricky thing. Markets are constantly changing, as are the operations of the firms, and the products they offer. There are thousands of insurance companies in the world (even just in the United States), and every day, each one is searching for new ways to better meet market demands. New investments, new products, new marketing strategies, new ways of raising capital, new corporate structures, new reinsurance arrangements—all are part of the world regulators must master and oversee. The regulator is expected to set rules to protect policyholders and maintain effective markets, monitor firms and the market to make sure firms are complying and to identify emerging problems, and address problems in a timely and appropriate manner. It is a daunting task. We should not be surprised that regulators make mistakes.

Even if regulators were infallible (which they aren't), it would be a challenge to get the balance right. How much regulation is optimal for the insurance industry to serve its role in society? Overregulation imposes unnecessary costs, stifles market innovations, and drives up consumer costs. The costs of underregulation are self-evident. There is a balance between the level of safety that regulators attempt to provide and the efficiency costs of the regulatory system. What is the right balance?

The catastrophic failures of the banking system during the financial crisis and the regulatory and policy responses are a useful backdrop for a discussion of how to approach supervision of internationally active insurers. At a very simple level, they illustrate two ends of a spectrum. Near one end of the spectrum is the precrisis system of banking regulation. Internationally active banks operated relatively freely through branches supervised by the home supervisor. Uniform international requirements, with particular emphasis on risk-based capital, were the primary means of ensuring a level playing field across jurisdictions. Cross-border information sharing was recognized as weak. There was a strong emphasis on efficiency and designing a regulatory system that interfered minimally with the ability of capital to move freely across borders.[1]

Closer to the other end of the spectrum was the system of regulating internationally active insurance groups (IAIGs).[2] IAIGs operated largely (though not exclusively) through local subsidiaries or branches subject to local requirements. Coordination among supervisors internationally was limited, and no concrete global rules (such as the Basel capital standard) existed. Supervisors applied local rules to firms doing business in their jurisdictions, with an eye toward maintaining viable markets and consumer protection. In short, the main focus of insurance regulators was local.[3] To a large extent, this is still the case. As one banking regulator described it, insurance markets have "balkanized capital."

Just as no regulator is infallible, no regulatory system is perfect. Each of these extremes has strengths and weaknesses, but the strengths and weaknesses are quite different. The precrisis banking system was undoubtedly less costly for firms (and thus consumers and the economy) than the "balkanized" approach in insurance regulation, but there were other problems. In the aftermath of the global financial crisis, banking regulation and supervision have changed significantly. Increased intensity of supervision, higher capital requirements, greater focus on liquidity, renewed focus on risk management and corporate governance, and a tendency toward ring-fencing are all features of the emerging system. Regulators and policy makers have a new appreciation for the challenges of resolving cross-border banks. When an institution is threatened with failure, regulators and policy makers turn inward, focusing on their own markets. Information is shared less freely. This is partly a matter of trust among regulators, but that is only part of the story. It is also the natural result of the incentives and pressures regulators and policy makers face in a crisis.[4] As one policy maker put it, "Global banks are global in life, but national in death."

The postcrisis backlash has increased recognition that regulators can face perverse incentives, that large international financial institutions carry a great deal of influence in some countries, and that regulatory capture can be a problem (even if it is only the less nefarious form of intellectual capture). Cross-border information sharing among supervisors continues to be inadequate postcrisis. The Basel Committee on Banking Supervision (BCBS) and the Financial Stability Board (FSB) recognize that the BCBS's capital requirements for internationally active banks are not implemented uniformly, with some notable differences in the outcomes across jurisdictions. It is not surprising that regulators fail to trust each other. Increased ring-fencing is the logical result of the failure to build truly robust cooperation in international banking regulation. In short, while the precrisis banking regulatory system was arguably *efficient* for internationally active banks, it had serious short-comings.

International insurance regulation, in contrast, tends toward the opposite problem—excessive duplication and inefficiency in regulation. IAIGs must meet the requirements of each local regulator. In the aftermath of the problems of American International Group (AIG), which were largely caused by an unregulated, noninsurance subsidiary, each of these regulators has vowed to place more focus on group supervision. Increasingly, IAIGs face duplicative and inconsistent requirements for group supervision from their legal entity supervisors. Contrary to the world of banking regulation, efficiency and duplication are the main problems in the regulation of IAIGs.

A good question for insurance regulation is this: Can we make the regulatory system more efficient without falling into the traps the banking sector fell into, and, if so, how?

As policy makers consider this question, there is a third model for supervising multijurisdictional groups that merits study: the state-based system of insurance regulation in the United States. Certainly, the challenges in achieving effective international and national regulatory cooperation are not identical, but there are parallels. Like other cases of cross-border supervision, state regulators are subject to local influences and incentives, but their actions can have implications beyond their borders. Like any system, the system is not perfect. It occupies the middle ground between the two extremes: It is neither as efficient as a system that provides near-total deference to a home supervisor nor as inefficient as a fully fragmented system. It provides an example of a system in which information is shared freely, solvency standards are generally uniform, cooperation is strong, and regulators give increasing deference to the home jurisdiction on solvency oversight. The state system has largely been successful at protecting U.S. insurance consumers for nearly 150 years, particularly when compared to the more centralized system of U.S. bank regulation. According to the International Monetary Fund (IMF), in its 2010 Financial Sector Assessment Program (FSAP) report on U.S. financial regulation, strong insurance regulation "contributed to the overall resilience of the insurance sector." A 2013 GAO report noted that the effects of the financial crisis on insurers and policyholders were "generally limited," and gave some of the credit to the actions taken by state regulators and the NAIC.

A BRIEF HISTORY OF U.S. INSURANCE REGULATION

The debate over federal versus state regulation is a long-standing one, going back to the nineteenth century. Through what was arguably a mistake made by the Supreme Court in 1869, the insurance sector developed free from federal influences, and a state-based regulatory system was allowed to thrive. In the absence of the 1869 decision, the insurance sector would likely have developed along the lines of the U.S. banking sector, with larger institutions primarily regulated by a federal regulator and smaller institutions primarily regulated by less influential state regulators. Thanks to 1869's *Paul v. Virginia*, however, the United States has a very different system—a decentralized, state-based system that regulates and supervises a national industry.

It is often stated, incorrectly, that the state regulatory system developed because the insurance industry was largely local, with little activity across state lines. In fact, interstate insurance transactions have been common since the early days of the industry. The National Convention of Insurance Commissioners (NCIC), predecessor to the National Association of Insurance Commissioners (NAIC), was created in 1871 in recognition of the fact that the business of insurance was a national one, and state insurance departments needed to coordinate to reduce the burdens on firms operating across state borders. The NCIC/NAIC Proceedings show an early and ongoing focus on the burdens placed on multistate firms by the state system and on efforts to streamline the system while maintaining its effectiveness.

Over the years, the NAIC and state regulators undertook a number of initiatives to improve the efficiency of the state system. One of the NAIC's earliest projects (in the late 1800s) was the creation of standardized insurance company financial statements to make it easier for companies to file their financial statements in multiple states.[5] These financial statements have grown in size and in importance for the regulatory system. Shared resources for valuing insurance company assets followed in the early part of the next century, as did coordinated financial examinations. The NAIC created a centralized database to enable all states to have access to insurer financial statements, developed a variety of electronic financial analysis tools, built confidential communication systems so states can keep each other informed, and built a variety of databases to track regulator actions. More recently, the states have been working to implement a more coordinated system of group supervision.

To support state solvency oversight, the commissioners created the Financial Analysis Division (FAD), an NAIC staff group that analyzes the financial conditions of nationally significant insurers. The FAD reports its findings to the Financial Analysis Working Group, where top financial regulators engage with the domestic regulators in potentially troubled company situations, encouraging timely action and fostering a coordinated response across the states.

The NAIC's accreditation program has resulted in a largely uniform system of solvency regulation. Where there are differences, they are expected to be transparent to other regulators and to the market in insurer financial statements.[6] Today, most states will defer to an insurer's domestic regulator on financial issues, while maintaining their own watchful eye on the company's financial statements and other information that has been made readily available through NAIC channels. It is perhaps best described as a system of "trust, but verify."

It is often suggested in international circles that the key to increasing regulatory collaboration and deference is to have uniform standards. In its September 2013 report to the G-20 leaders, entitled *A Narrative Progress Report on Financial Reforms*, the Financial Stability Board decried the dislocation of cross-border activities, noting that fragmentation of the international financial system could reduce growth by putting up barriers to the efficient allocation of capital and liquidity in the real economy. The FSB called for timely, consistent implementation of new regulatory standards in order to strengthen confidence in the resilience of national and global financial systems and reverse the fragmentation.

An insurance supervisor once argued to this author that "We need a global capital standard so we can trust each other." The evidence from the history of state regulation suggests, however, that uniform requirements are not the essential element for increased reliance on other supervisors. Indeed, common capital standards occurred relatively late in the evolution of state regulation—not until the 1990s, decades after the creation of more standardized statements, coordinated examinations, centralized databases, and shared analysis tools.

The history of the NAIC suggests two elements that have been successful in encouraging an evolution toward collaboration and deference. First, systems have been built to enable host supervisors to easily monitor nondomestic firms, supporting the "trust, but verify" model. Comprehensive centralized financial data is the backbone of the system. As regulatory problems are identified (for example, AIG's securities lending operations), the solution nearly always involves, at least in part, amending the regulatory financial statements. This is largely driven, not by a desire to impact capital and surplus, but by the fact that regulatory financial statements are a primary tool used by host regulators to monitor their nondomestic firms. It is not uncommon for enhanced financial statement disclosure to be the primary regulatory response.

In its 2010 FSAP report, the IMF called the NAIC's financial databases "world-leading." It is not an accident that they are world-leading; it is a natural result of efforts to make the system more efficient for the regulated firms. Over the years, state regulators have put considerable resources into building their shared data resources to provide a foundation for multistate collaboration. Financial statements include detailed information by line of insurance by state; information on assets owned, bought, and sold (by CUSIP number); and reinsurance arrangements by contract and reinsurer. This information is captured centrally and made available to all states. Coordinated exams, shared analysis tools, and NAIC on-site accreditation reviews provide additional tools for host jurisdictions to monitor the domestic regulator's performance.

The second feature of the U.S. system is that it maintains a strong incentive for the home supervisor to collaborate in times of crisis. In the state regulatory system, nondomestic regulators retain the right to take independent action, seek information directly from the insurer, examine the firm independently at the legal entity and group levels, and fine the company, revoke its license, or order other changes as a condition of maintaining licensure. Any of these actions has the potential to disrupt the home state's plans. The threat of intervention from a host state gives the home regulator both the incentive to collaborate and the cover to take difficult actions in its own state.

Uniform standards can reduce the costs of firms complying with different laws and regulations, but absent a culture of trust and collaboration, the mere existence of uniform standards is unlikely to change the relationship between home and host regulators. Beyond that, there is a danger that an excessive focus on uniform rules will divert attention from other efforts that can have a more dramatic effect.

THE IMPORTANCE OF CHECKS AND BALANCES

One of the lessons of the financial crisis is that regulators can make mistakes. There is no system of regulation that can guarantee an omniscient, perfect regulator. Regulators fail to catch things; they may catch them, but draw the wrong conclusions about what to do, and they may fail to implement policy solutions. Regulatory capture is a recognized problem, as is the potential for local incentives to conflict with the best interests globally. There can be a variety of disincentives for regulators to take action, and regulators get a constant barrage of information from the firms they regulate, tending to lead to a familiarity and overconfidence in the firm's behaviors.

The strength of a well-developed cross-border supervisory system is in its ability to counteract these tendencies. Multiple eyes can increase the probability that problems will be detected.[7] Pressure from host jurisdictions can counter perverse incentives on the home supervisor, increasing the likelihood of timely and appropriate action.

The state regulatory system is best described as a system of constrained discretion. Over time the regulators have gravitated toward increased uniformity in many areas. But there are still areas where the laws are not uniform, and there may be some differences in interpretation. States may deviate, but it is expected that those deviations are fully transparent to other regulators.[8] The ability of other regulators to know what is happening acts as a check on the domestic regulator's ability to get too far out of the mainstream. Some experimentation is allowed, providing for a dynamic and responsive system. Too much deviation will invite questions from others. In short, it is the incentives that make the system work, not the standards.

Other advantages often cited for state insurance regulation include the ability for regulatory mistakes to be localized (diversification of regulatory risk), the ability for states to experiment with alternative regulatory approaches and to learn from each other (the laboratory of the states), and the proximity to consumers, which increases the likelihood consumer problems will be heard and understood. Anyone who has spent time in Washington appreciates the resources spent by large businesses, including large insurers, to have their positions heard. Gaining access to top decision makers can be difficult. It is relatively more difficult for smaller insurers and virtually impossible for the average consumer. State regulators argue that they are more responsive to consumers than a federal regulator would be, with good justification.

Because of the challenges in coordinating multiple actors, the state system tends toward stability in regulation. Changes are largely incremental, and they are typically made in response to identified problems. Gradual implementation of new requirements across the country provides for an opportunity to understand the unintended consequences and adapt. When the NAIC develops model laws and regulations, it tends toward centrist policies, reflecting its traditional history of striving for consensus among the various state viewpoints.

THE OTHER SIDE OF THE PROBLEM

The state regulatory system is best described as a decentralized, bottom-up system, with ongoing efforts to reduce the inefficiencies. The primary advantages of state regulation stem from the decentralized decision making and the potential for tension between the various actors; this is also the source of its primary disadvantages.

At times, the state regulatory system can seem chaotic. New issues constantly emerge, uncovered by a variety of independent actors in the various states. State regulators engage in public debates about the merits of alternative regulatory approaches. Regulated entities, which like predictability and regulatory certainty, are unsurprisingly frustrated.

While some diversity and duplication can be positive, state regulation undoubtedly results in greater diversity and duplication than optimal. This is particularly true in market regulation, where the pressures for collaboration among states are weaker. Market issues tend to receive more public attention than financial regulation, and state regulators, legislators, and governors are accountable first and foremost to their local constituents. The largest states (New York, California, Florida, and Texas) tend to be the most likely to deviate from NAIC standards, likely reflecting their own market and political environments. The inefficiencies in state regulation are particularly problematic for some life insurers who focus on asset management. They see their competition as including other types of financial institutions, and argue that a streamlined federal regulatory system gives their competitors a cost advantage.

The NAIC has made some progress in streamlining some aspects of market regulation. For example, it created an interstate compact to provide multistate approval of life insurance, annuity, and disability products (which currently has 43 member states representing over two-thirds of the premium volume nationwide), and it worked to build a more streamlined producer licensing system. The NAIC recently endorsed the National Association of Registered Agents and Brokers Reform Act (NARAB II), a federal bill that would create a national licensing system for nonresident insurance producers. But more can be done. Most observers agree that it remains unnecessarily difficult for companies to operate on a multistate basis, largely because of variations in market regulation.

Beyond the inefficiencies, it must be recognized that the decentralized decision making is confusing to many outside the system and can be frustrating for those who want to deal with one regulatory authority. In times of crisis, when decisions must be made quickly, the state regulatory system must work harder to be coordinated. Fortunately, it has largely been successful in doing so.

A CLOSING COMMENT

In its August 2013 peer review of the United States, the Financial Stability Board pointed to the importance of insurance regulation for financial stability, identified the primary drawback of the state system as its inability to get to uniformity, and recommended that U.S. authorities confer additional powers and resources at the federal level to promote greater regulatory uniformity. Unfortunately, the FSB did not articulate *why* it believed greater uniformity would enhance financial stability.

State insurance regulators responded with their own critique of the FSB's recommendation, as expressed by Commissioner Tom Leonardi (Connecticut), chair of the NAIC's International Affairs Committee, and posted on the NAIC's website:

> *The authors of the recent FSB peer review acknowledge that the US insurance regulatory system is effective at providing policy-holder protection and ensuring the solvency of individual insurance companies. We can think of no more important and fundamental responsibilities for insurance regulators. However, the authors' opinion that a more federal approach to insurance regulation is necessary fails to identify any credible problem such a shift would solve and offers little factual basis for its conclusions.*

It is puzzling that the FSB has suggested that uniformity in the U.S. regulatory system is essential for financial stability. The FSB did not explain why it saw the need for greater uniformity, but its views may simply reflect its general bias toward uniformity as a means of ensuring a level playing field in the world of open banking markets.[9] Recent experience in the banking sector should have made clear that a uniform federal (or international) regulatory system is not a panacea when it comes to financial stability issues. Uniformity is efficient, but it can be efficiently and catastrophically wrong.

Few would dispute that a lack of uniformity in the existing system of state regulation is unnecessarily inefficient. Furthermore, it is unlikely that the state system will ever achieve the optimal balance of diversity and uniformity, given the importance of local influences. These are fair criticisms. Policy makers should continue to maintain pressure on the state system to correct this deficiency. The problem will never be completely solved, absent federal intervention, but it is important to recognize it for what it is—an efficiency problem, not a financial stability or consumer protection failure.

As the International Association of Insurance Supervisors (IAIS) pursues the development of its Common Framework for the Supervision of Internationally Active Insurance Groups (ComFrame), its greatest fear should be building a system that repeats past mistakes. Robust information sharing and the right incentives for the home supervisor are the preconditions for a more efficient and effective system of international insurance supervision. Getting these right will promote collaboration and trust among supervisors. Without collaboration and trust, ComFrame will be, at best, just another layer of regulation. At worst, it will be the means of replicating the catastrophic mistakes that have been made in other sectors.

NOTES

1. Persaud (2010) provides a critique of the evolution of the supervision of internationally active banks and recommendations for the future.
2. See International Association of Insurance Supervisors (2013) for a discussion of the various ways jurisdictions supervise the cross-border activities of insurance groups.
3. Reinsurance is a global business, but for many years it was largely unregulated on the basis that it was purchased by presumably sophisticated buyers. As reinsurers became regulated, many jurisdictions introduced collateral requirements designed to protect their markets from exposure to the failure of a reinsurer. These requirements are gradually being reduced or eliminated, particularly where the regulator has gained confidence in the quality of the reinsurer's supervision.
4. Beck, Todorov, and Wagner (2012) analyze the incentives for a home country supervisor to intervene when the financial condition of a cross-border bank deteriorates. They find evidence that national supervisors are less likely to intervene in a timely manner when the bank has a higher share of foreign deposits and lower foreign equity ownership. Because the gains of allowing a weak bank to continue operation accrue mainly to shareholders, while the cost is borne by depositors and other debt holders, their findings are consistent with supervisory actions being motivated by local interests.
5. Uniform financial statements were described by the president of the National Convention of Insurance Commissioners (NCIC), predecessor to the NAIC, as "the central idea on which this association was founded." In 1911, the NCIC amended its constitution to create a Standing Committee on Blanks, the only standing committee other than the Executive Committee. Early statements were fairly simple, and there continued to be a lack of uniformity among the states in how various items were reported, which was addressed incrementally. In 1907, the NCIC adopted a resolution calling for uniform valuation of insurer securities, and recommendations were accepted in 1909. The first standard valuation law governing life insurer policy liabilities was adopted in 1943. States were coordinating some of their on-site examinations as early as 1920, and they later formalized the process by creating a "zone" examination system in which a representative from each of the NAIC's four geographic zones was invited to participate in the examination (NCIC Proceedings, various years).
6. There are two main areas of difference in solvency regulation. First, state investment laws vary, with some states offering more flexibility for insurer investments than others. Second, states may permit companies to deviate from statutory accounting principles with "permitted practices."

In both cases, the results are fully transparent to the market and to other regulators. Financial statements contain detailed information on insurer investments (by CUSIP number), and any permitted practices must be disclosed in footnote 1 of the financial statements. Many states granted permitted practices in early 2009, engaging in regulatory forbearance during a time of intense stress in financial markets. The NAIC posted the impact of each permitted practice on its website.

7. For example, the life insurance fraud perpetrated by Martin Frankel began at about the same time period as Bernie Madoff's investment fraud (in the early 1990s). In both cases, regulators missed early warnings. Early warnings that the Madoff funds were a Ponzi scheme were ignored by the Securities and Exchange Commission (SEC) until the funds imploded in 2008. In contrast, early warning signs related to Frankel's Ponzi scheme were ignored by several states, but Mississippi intervened in 1999 and brought the fraud to light.

8. More recently, problems have emerged with the transparency of captive insurance arrangements used by some life insurance companies to reduce their reserves. The Dodd-Frank Act, which preempted extraterritorial oversight of a ceding company's reinsurance arrangements, have made resolution of this issue more difficult, but the NAIC is working on standards to resolve the problem.

9. The FSB is dominated by central bankers, banking supervisors, and other policy makers generally more experienced with the banking sector than with the insurance sector.

REFERENCES

Beck, Thorsten, Radomir Todorov, and Wolf Wagner. 2012. "Supervising Cross-Border Banks: Theory, Evidence, and Policy." European Banking Center Discussion Paper No. 2012-015.

International Association of Insurance Supervisors. 2013. "Issues Paper on Supervision of Cross-Border Operations through Branches," October 30.

International Monetary Fund. 2010. *United States: Publication of Financial Sector Assessment Program Documentation—Detailed Assessment of Observance of IAIS Insurance Core Principles.* IMF Country Report No. 10/126.

Persaud, Avinash. 2010. "The Locus of Financial Regulation: Home versus Host." *International Affairs* 86 (3): 637–646.

U.S. Government Accountability Office. 2013. *Insurance Markets: Impacts of and Regulatory Response to the 2007–2009 Financial Crisis.* GAO-13-583, June 27.

CHAPTER 5

Lessons Learned from AIG for Modernizing Insurance Regulation

Eric R. Dinallo*

Insurance Superintendent for New York

As we now know, the crisis for American International Group (AIG) did not come from its state-regulated insurance companies. The primary source of the problem was AIG Financial Products, which wrote credit default swaps (CDSs), derivatives, and futures with a notional amount of about $2.7 trillion, about $440 billion of which were credit default swaps. Collateral calls by global banks, broker-dealers, and hedge funds that were counterparties to these credit default swaps were the main source of AIG's problems. To understand the crisis, it is essential to understand why AIG Financial Products was able to make such huge bets with its credit default swaps with essentially nothing backing up its promise to pay if the bet went against it. In general, AIG took advantage of the general tide of deregulation, but there are three specific aspects of deregulation that, working together, created a perfect storm of financial disaster: (1) allowing financial institutions to select their own regulator; (2) creating financial conglomerates after the elimination of the divisions between financial institutions

---

* I was the Insurance Superintendent for New York from January 2007 through July 2009, including the period of the financial crisis. Most of the following article is adapted from testimony I gave before Congress's Financial Crisis Inquiry Commission on July 1, 2010. As a note, when I refer to AIG throughout these remarks, I mean the parent company. When I discuss AIG's insurance companies, I say so explicitly. Also, when I use "us" or "we" or "our," I am referring to the New York State Insurance Department during the period when I was its superintendent. These comments are largely derived from testimony I gave before Congress' Financial Crisis Inquiry Commission in 2009.

previously required by the Glass-Steagall Act; and (3) deregulating credit default swaps.

By purchasing a small savings and loan in 1999, AIG was able to select as its primary regulator the Office of Thrift Supervision (OTS), the federal agency that was at that time charged with overseeing savings and loan banks and thrift associations. Clearly, OTS's expertise was in savings and loans, not complicated international financial institutions conducting a huge derivative business. The net effect was that AIG Financial Products was not effectively regulated on a liquidity basis, as OTS itself later explained in testimony to Congress.

Financial modernization of the later 1990s made it possible for AIG to combine its various operations in a single company, and to engage a broad variety of regulated and unregulated activities within the same parent company. The Glass-Steagall Act had since the Depression separated financial services businesses that provided guarantees, such as insurance policies or bank deposits, from businesses that took on risk, such as investment banking. But the Gramm-Leach-Bliley Act of 1999 overturned that separation, permitting AIG to combine its insurance businesses with other financial services businesses in the same company. Had AIG Financial Products been a stand-alone company, it is unlikely that its counterparties would have been willing to do business with it, because its commitments would never have carried AIG's triple-A credit rating. Finally, the decision to exempt credit default swaps from regulation in the Commodity Futures Modernization Act (CMFA) of 2000, against the advice of the chair of the Commodity Futures Trading Commission (CFTC), proved catastrophic for AIG and other companies heavily involved in swaps trading.

In sum, this combination meant that AIG could operate an ineffectively regulated hedge fund selling billions in unregulated securities making billions in promises with insufficient reserves to back up those promises. Clearly that was a recipe for disaster.

As Federal Reserve Chairman Ben Bernanke said, "AIG had a financial products division which was very lightly regulated and was the source of a great deal of systemic trouble." Chairman Bernanke accurately called the Financial Products unit "a hedge fund basically that was attached to a large and stable insurance company that made large numbers of irresponsible bets, and took huge losses."

Proponents of deregulation argued that financial innovation was essential and if the United States did not allow activities here, the market and the profits would go elsewhere. Sadly, it is clear that not all financial innovation is positive, not all reduces risk, and not all promotes economic growth. A major international competitive advantage for the United States is its stable, secure, and transparent financial system. If we allow that to be damaged or destroyed, the cost for all Americans will be steep.

Just as AIG was overly aggressive in seeking profits from credit default swaps in its Financial Products unit, it was equally aggressive in its securities lending program, which was operated centrally by the parent company for its insurance companies. Many insurance companies and other financial institutions use securities lending, but none had the severe problems that AIG had.

State regulators identified the problems in the securities lending program well before the crisis, and were working with the company to unwind the program in an orderly fashion. It was the crisis caused by collateral calls on the credit default swaps at Financial Products that made a continuation of an orderly reduction impossible. While there is no question that the insurance subsidiaries would have had losses from the program, the losses would have been manageable and would not have made the insurance subsidiaries as a group insolvent.

The federal rescue of AIG was possible precisely because there were strong operating insurance companies to repay the federal government and taxpayers. The reason that those insurance companies were strong was because regulation walled them off from nonrelated activities in the holding company and at Financial Products.

In most industries, the parent company can reach down and use the assets of its subsidiaries. With insurance, that ability is greatly restricted. State regulation requires that insurance companies maintain healthy reserves for policyholders' claims backed by investments that cannot be used for any other purpose. That is why policyholders were and continued to be protected.

Now, let me provide some background. Before the crisis, AIG was a huge, global financial services holding company that did business in 130 countries. In 2008, AIG had 71 U.S.-based insurance companies. In addition to those U.S.-based insurance entities, AIG had 176 other financial services companies, including non-U.S. insurers.

State insurance departments have the power and authority to act as the primary regulator for the insurance companies domiciled in their state. So the New York State Insurance Department (NYSID) was the primary regulator for only those AIG insurance companies domiciled in New York. At the time of the crisis, the NYSID was the primary regulator for 10 of AIG's 71 U.S. insurance companies. AIG's New York life insurance companies were relatively small. The New York property insurance companies were much larger. Other states act as primary regulator for the other U.S. insurance companies.

State insurance regulators are not perfect. But one thing they do very well is focus on solvency—on the financial strength of insurance companies.

State regulators require insurers to hold conservative reserves to ensure that they can pay policyholders. That is why insurance companies performed relatively well during the crisis. One clear lesson of the financial crisis is the importance of having plenty of capital and not having too much leverage.

As noted, by purchasing a savings and loan in 1999, AIG was able to select as its consolidated supervisor the federal Office of Thrift Supervision, the federal agency that was charged with overseeing savings and loan banks and thrift associations. OTS, of course, was dissolved by the Dodd-Frank Wall Street Reform and Consumer Protection Act of 2010, and its functions were sent largely to the Federal Reserve.

When companies are permitted to pick their regulator, the opportunity for regulatory arbitrage is created. The whole purpose of financial services regulation is to appropriately control risk. But regulatory arbitrage increases risk because it creates the opportunity for a financial institution to select its regulator based on who might be more lenient, who might have less strict rules, and who might demand less capital.

This is not a theoretical contention. I referred the Financial Crisis Inquiry Commission to a January 22, 2009, article in the *Washington Post* titled "By Switching Their Charters, Banks Skirt Supervision." The article reports that since 2000 at least 30 banks had switched from federal to state supervision to escape regulatory action. The actual number is likely higher because the newspaper was only able to count public regulatory actions. The reporters could not discover whether banks acted to preempt action when they saw it coming. In total, 240 banks converted from federal to state charters, while 90 converted from state to federal charters. The newspaper was unable to discover if any of those formerly state banks were avoiding state action.

One of the most important aspects of regulating financial services institutions is the setting of appropriate capital and reserve requirements. Were AIG's capital and capital requirements sufficient from 2005 to 2008? The New York Insurance Department is not in a position to know about the capital requirements for AIG's holding company or its Financial Products unit. I can assure you that the capital of the AIG group's licensed U.S. insurers was certainly sufficient to ensure the orderly operation of the AIG insurance companies. What's more, it is clear that the AIG holding company's top triple-A credit rating was based on the strength of its insurance companies. But since the assets of the insurance companies cannot be used for the obligations of the holding company, AIG Financial Products' counterparties were mistaken if they thought AIG's strength protected them. The use of insurance company funds to support the operations of Financial Products would have been improper and disallowed under the insurance law. Had AIG Financial Products been given a credit rating based on its own resources, it is unlikely that it would have been perceived as strong enough to keep the promises it was making.

This is one of the important lessons of the financial crisis: the problem of illusory credit ratings. Let me be clear what I mean by *illusory*. Unlike the credit ratings for securities based on subprime mortgages, there was a solid basis for the top triple-A credit rating for AIG's parent company. But that was based on the strength of its core insurance companies, and the assets of those companies could essentially be used only to support the insurance operations.

AIG was probably not the only company to take its strong credit rating from its core business and monetize that presumed financial strength to go into another line of business, where that strong credit rating was meaningless because the assets of its core business were protected by regulation. Thus, AIG used its perceived strength to have its Financial Products unit sell credit default swaps, though it was an illusion that the holding company's strength could be applied to the promises Financial Products was making, at least on a liquidity basis.

The primary source of AIG's problem was AIG Financial Products, which had written credit default swaps, derivatives, and futures with a notional amount of about $2.7 trillion, including about $440 billion of credit default swaps. For context, that was roughly equal to the gross national product of France. It is worth noting what AIG was doing with those credit default swaps. The focus has been on swaps guaranteeing bonds backed by subprime residential mortgages. There were plenty of those. But AIG was also selling credit default swaps to help banks manage their own regulatory requirements for reserves in two ways. First, thanks to AIG's credit default swaps, the banks could use the AIG bonds they held, backed by subprime mortgages, to lower reserves held against them because of AIG's stellar credit rating. Second, the banks also used swaps directly to lower their own reserve requirements.

I would like to quote from a March 6, 2009, story in the *Financial Times* by Henny Sender titled "AIG Saga Shows Dangers of Credit Default Swaps":

> *In retrospect, a glance at AIG's second quarter 2008 financial statement makes for an interesting read. Buried in that report is a cautionary tale showing just how dangerous credit derivatives can be when combined with insufficient risk management and regulatory oversight—or both sides of these transactions. Unfortunately, few people read the report when it would have been relevant.*
>
> *The report fully discloses the $446bn in credit insurance AIG sold. The swaps were written out of AIG Financial Products, a*

non-bank hidden at the heart of the insurance giant. But because AIG wasn't regulated as a bank, it wasn't saddled with any requirements to hold capital against these massive potential liabilities.

A large part of those credit default swaps, about $307bn worth, was bought by European banks in endearingly named "regulatory capital forbearance" trades. By buying such insurance, these banks didn't have to hold capital against their long-term holdings of securities. Another large chunk went to Wall Street firms to hedge their holdings of complicated securities backed by subprime mortgages.

By the end of the year, just this part of this massive book of credit default swaps would cause almost $30bn in losses and trigger what is likely to prove one of the most costly bail-outs ever. Meanwhile, the $307bn "forbearance" book produced a mere $156m in revenue for the first half of last year. These exposures probably represent one of the most skewed risk-reward equations of all time.

AIG did such a booming business selling credit protection because it offered to post generous collateral if the value of the insured securities dropped or if its own credit rating fell. (Other providers, such as the monoline insurers, balked at such terms.) That collateral was meant to give AIG's clients assurance that they were safely hedged. In fact, that sense of safety was always an illusion. Clients hadn't reduced their risk; they had increased it.

To quote Chairman Bernanke again, Financial Products "took all these large bets where they were effectively, quote, 'insuring' the credit positions of many, many banks and other financial institutions."

In sum, an essentially unregulated institution (AIG Financial Products) sold unregulated securities (credit default swaps), which were used to help regulated banks hold less capital in reserve than they apparently should have.

That leads us to a discussion of credit default swaps. Let me first establish why the insurance regulator for New York was a relevant authority on credit default swaps. I will expand on these issues at greater length, but to provide a context, I will start with a brief summary.

As credit default swaps were developed, there was a question about whether or not they were insurance. Since initially they were used by owners of bonds to seek protection or insurance in the case of a default by the issuer of the bonds, this was a reasonable question. In 2000, the New York Insurance Department was asked to determine if certain swaps were insurance and said "no."

After I took office in January 2007, the impact of credit default swaps was one of the major issues we had to confront. First, we tackled the problems of the financial guaranty companies, also known as bond insurers or monolines. Credit default swaps were a major factor in their problems. Afterward, we were involved in the rescue of AIG. Again, credit default swaps were the biggest source of that company's problems. Through these experiences, we needed to study carefully the history and issues surrounding credit default swaps. And we learned the hard way about their impact on markets and companies.

A credit default swap is a contract under which the seller, for a fee, agrees to make a payment to the protection buyer in the event that the referenced security, usually some kind of bond, experiences any number of various "credit events," such as bankruptcy, default, or reorganization. If something goes wrong with the referenced entity, the protection buyer can put the bond to the protection seller and be made whole, or a net payment can be made by the seller to the buyer.

Originally, credit default swaps were used to transfer and thus reduce risk for the owners of bonds. If you owned a bond in company X and were concerned that the company might default, you bought the swap to protect yourself. The swaps could also be used by banks that loaned money to a company. This type of swap is still used for hedging purposes.

Over time, however, swaps came to be used not to reduce risk, but to assume it. Institutions that did not own the obligation bought and sold credit default swaps to place what Wall Street calls "a directional bet" on a company's creditworthiness.

In May 2008, I began to refer to swaps bought by speculators as "naked" credit default swaps both to draw the analogy to naked shorting in stocks, which ironically was regulated, and to make clear that the swap purchasers did not own the underlying obligation. This type of protection becomes more valuable as the company becomes less creditworthy. I have argued that these naked credit default swaps should not be called "swaps" because there is no transfer or swap of risk. Instead, risk is created by the transaction. For example, you have no risk on the outcome of the third race until you place a bet on horse number five to win.

I explained that the first type of swap (let's call it the covered swap) is arguably insurance. The essence of an insurance contract is that the buyer has to have a material interest in the asset or obligation that is the subject of the contract. That means the buyer owns property or a security and can suffer a loss from damage to or the loss of value of that property. With insurance, the buyer only has a claim after actually suffering a loss. With the covered swaps, if the issuer of a bond defaults, then the owner of the bond has suffered a loss and the swap provides some recovery for that loss. The second type of swap—naked swaps—contains none of these features.

One problem is that with swaps, identifying covered and naked swaps can be very complicated. For example, company A that does business with company B may seek to protect itself from not being paid by company B by buying a credit default swap on company B's debt. Clearly here the buyer has a material interest, but not directly in the bond. Or the buyer of a credit default swap may own the underlying bond when it buys the swap, but then sell the bond but keep the swap.

At the time of the crisis at AIG, because the credit default swap market was not regulated, there was no valid data on the number of swaps outstanding and how many were naked. At that time, estimates of the market were as high as $62 trillion. By comparison, at that time there was only about $6 trillion in corporate debt outstanding, $7.5 trillion in mortgage-backed debt, and $2.5 trillion in asset-backed debt. That's a total of about $16 trillion in private-sector debt.

Now, I think it would be useful to go into some of the old but highly relevant history.

Betting or speculating on movements in securities or commodities prices without actually owning the referenced security or commodity is nothing new. As early as 1829, "stock jobbing," an early version of short selling, was outlawed in New York. The Stock Jobbing Act was ultimately repealed in 1858 because it was overly broad and captured legitimate forms of speculation. However, the issue of whether to allow bets on security and commodity prices outside of organized exchanges continued to be an issue.

"Bucket shops" arose in the late nineteenth century. Customers "bought" securities or commodities on these unauthorized exchanges, but in reality the bucket shop was simply booking the customer's order without executing on an exchange. In fact, they were simply throwing the trade ticket in a bucket, which is where the name comes from, and tearing it up when an opposite trade came in. The bucket shop would agree to take the other side of the customer's bet on the performance of the security or commodity.

Bucket shops sometimes survived for a time by balancing their books, but were wiped out by extreme bull or bear markets. When their books failed, the bucketeers simply closed up shop and left town, leaving the "investors" holding worthless tickets. The Bank Panic of 1907 is famous for J. P. Morgan, the leading banker of the time, calling other bankers to a meeting and keeping them there until they agreed to form a consortium of bankers to create an emergency backstop for the banking system. At the time there was no Federal Reserve, no FDIC.

A more direct and immediate result of the 1907 Bank Panic was passage of New York's anti–bucket shop law in 1909. The law, General Business Law Section 351, made it a felony to operate or be connected with a bucket shop or "fake exchange." Because of the specificity and severity of the much-anticipated legislation, virtually all bucket shops shut down before the law came into effect, and little enforcement was necessary. Other states passed similar laws.

Section 351 prohibited the making or offering of a purchase or sale of security, commodity, debt, property, options, bonds, and so on without intending a bona fide purchase or sale of the security, commodity, debt, property, options, bonds, and so on. If you think that sounds exactly like a naked credit default swap, you are correct. What this tells us is that back in 1909, 100 years ago, people understood the risks and potential instability that come from betting on securities prices, and outlawed it.

With the growth of various kinds of derivatives in the late twentieth century, there was legal uncertainty as to whether certain derivatives, including credit default swaps, violated state bucket shop and gambling laws.

The Commodity Futures Modernization Act of 2000, signed by President Clinton on December 21, 2000, created a "safe harbor" by (1) preempting state and local gaming and bucket shop laws except for general antifraud provisions, and (2) exempting certain derivative transactions on commodities and swap agreements, including credit default swaps, from CFTC regulation.

The CFMA also amended the Securities Act of 1933 and the Securities Exchange Act of 1934 to make it clear that the definition of *security* did not include certain swap agreements, including credit default swaps, and that the SEC was prohibited from regulating those swap agreements, except for its antifraud enforcement authority.

So by exempting credit default swaps from state laws, SEC regulation, or CFTC regulation, the way was cleared for the growth of the market. But there was one other issue. If swaps were considered insurance, then they could be regulated by state insurance departments. The capital and underwriting limits in insurance regulation could threaten the rapid growth in the market for these derivatives.

So, in 2000, the New York Insurance Department was asked a very carefully crafted question: "Does a credit default swap transaction, wherein the seller will make payment to the buyer upon the happening of a negative credit event and such payment is not dependent upon the buyer having suffered a loss, constitute a contract of insurance under the insurance law?"

Clearly, the question was framed to ask only about naked credit default swaps. Under the facts as presented, the swap was not insurance, because the buyer had no material interest and the filing of a claim did not require a loss. The Insurance Department therefore answered "no." But the entities involved were careful not to ask about covered credit default swaps. Nonetheless, the market took the Insurance Department's opinion on a subset of credit default swaps as a ruling on all swaps.

It bears repeating. The fear in 2000 was that if the United States or New York regulated credit default swaps and required holding sufficient capital against the swap, the market would go where unregulated sellers could make more money. We forgot that the biggest competitive advantage of the U.S. financial system has always been that we offer safety, security, and transparency. If we destroy that perception, the long-term cost to our society is incalculable.

Why did that matter? As we have seen, the financial system was placed in peril because there was no comprehensive management of counterparty risk. Deals were made privately between two parties. These bilateral arrangements meant that there were no standards for the solvency of the counterparties. The buyer did not know how much risk the seller was taking on. And there were no requirements for the seller to hold reserves or capital against the risks it was taking on by selling swaps.

None of this was a problem as long as the value of everything was going up and defaults were rare. But the problem with this sort of unregulated protection scheme is that when everyone needed to be paid at once, the market was not strong enough to provide the protection everyone suddenly required.

Unlike insurance, credit default swaps are marked to market. That means the value of the swap reflects the current market value, which can swing sharply and suddenly. Value changes require the sellers to post collateral. Sudden and sharp changes in the credit rating of the issuer of the bonds or of the bonds themselves can produce large swings in the value of the swaps and thus the need to post large and increasing amounts of collateral. That capital strain can produce sudden liquidity problems for sellers. The seller may own enough assets to provide collateral, but the assets may not be liquid and thus not immediately accessible. When many sellers are forced to sell assets, the prices of those assets fall and sellers are faced with taking large losses just to meet collateral requirements. As the prices of the assets are driven down by forced sales, mark-to-market losses increase and the collateral posting cycle continues. Meanwhile, the underlying assets may continue to perform, paying interest and principal in full.

The aforementioned was a substantial part of the problem at AIG. A ratings downgrade on September 15, 2008, produced immediate collateral calls. The company did not have sufficient liquid assets at Financial Products or at the holding company to satisfy these calls.

Did New York have the ability to regulate credit default swaps? While the CFMA preempted state gambling laws, it did not preempt state insurance law. Apparently the market felt that New York's letter put that possibility to rest.

But given the temper of the deregulatory times, it is fair to assume that if New York had tried to unilaterally regulate credit default swaps in 2000, it would have been overruled one way or another.

However, when the Insurance Department understood the impact of credit default swaps, New York chose to act. In May 2008, we publicly warned of the scale of the problem and explained that some credit default swaps were clearly insurance. Thereafter, I published opinion articles making this case. On September 22, 2008, we announced that New York State would, beginning in January 2009, regulate the insurance, or covered, part of the credit default swap market that had been unregulated—the part that the Insurance Department had jurisdiction to regulate. That announcement played an important role in spurring national discussion about a comprehensive regulatory structure for the CDS market.

Ultimately, of course, Congress agreed that credit default swaps needed to be regulated, and as part of the Dodd-Frank Act, gave that responsibility jointly to the SEC and the CFTC. The era of unregulated credit default swaps is over, but at a tremendous price.

Does requiring adequate capital mean the end of financial innovation? Of course not; it just means that most institutions will operate with less leverage. Risk and reward are integral to capitalism. But innovators should risk their own capital, not the entire financial fabric. Setting that balance is where effective regulation comes in.

We have looked at the history of credit default swaps. It is also worth noting the history that allowed AIG to set up a unit, Financial Products, that could conduct this business.

By 1933, those who lived through the 1907 credit crisis and the 1929 stock market crash had recognized two things: There were certain sacred financial services products, such as bank deposits and insurance policies, that had to be protected at all costs, and those products should never be exposed to the possible excesses of leveraged investment banking. The wall between those businesses was institutionalized in the form of the Glass-Steagall Act of 1933, which kept commercial banks, insurance companies, and investment banks out of each other's lines of business. Underlying the inherent wisdom of Franklin Roosevelt and his advisers was the fundamental principle that guaranteed consumer deposits—whether bank deposits or insurance premiums—must be kept separate from high-risk investment vehicles such as investment banks and their modern equivalents, hedge funds and private equity. The goal was to encourage the benefit to the economy of risk taking by some financial institutions, without creating the risk of runs on commercial banks or insurance companies, by keeping those activities behind solid walls.

Those walls were removed in 1999 by the Gramm-Leach-Bliley Act. The theory was that large financial institutions able to do commercial and investment banking and insurance would diversify risk and thus be stronger and less risky.

How has that turned out? Reconsider AIG, an excellent insurance company, which became a financial services conglomerate. AIG's Financial Products unit was able to sell hundreds of billions of dollars of credit default swaps and run up $2.7 trillion in notional exposure because rating agencies and counterparties wrongly assumed that AIG's triple-A rating and $1 trillion balance sheet stood behind it. In fact, AIG's insurance company reserves were still protected by the moat of state insurance regulation and not available to bail out Financial Products' bad bets.

The point is that standing alone, AIG Financial Products, looking like a recklessly run hedge fund, could not have taken on all that risk. Only being part of a financial conglomerate made that possible. Even though AIG's healthy insurance companies and their reserves were protected, those companies took a substantial hit from the reputational damage. The outcome was the worst of both worlds. AIG Financial Products did not diversify risk but, instead, concentrated and correlated risk. So we discovered that an undercapitalized and underregulated unit of a huge financial services conglomerate could risk not only that entire enterprise but also the many banks with which it did business. It was those risks of a broad market impact that made the government rescue of AIG necessary.

To prevent cascading damage to the economy, the regulators not only require commercial banks and insurance companies to hold sufficient reserves to deliver on their guarantees, but also guarantee they will act to stop runs on commercial banks through the FDIC, or on insurance companies through state resolution bureaus and guaranty funds. Through the financial supermarkets, regulators' guarantees to act were effectively extended to risk-taking activities where there were no clearly available reserves or liquidity. Thus the risk-taking parts of a company could both use high leverage to boost profits and also benefit—without paying the cost—from the protections of the guaranteed section of the company. If that is not moral hazard, what is?

Thanks largely to Gramm-Leach-Bliley, financial supermarkets were arguably allowed to grow "too big and too interconnected" to fail, putting policyholder and bank depositor money at direct or indirect risk. Instead of reducing risk, the new law created a new, systemic risk that could bring down an entire institution or the entire marketplace—and leave governments no choice but to intervene. The Dodd-Frank Act, obviously, sought to reverse this trend by requiring greater supervision of financial institutions, and, in particular, higher solvency standards for the financial supermarkets. Ironically, the Federal Reserve, in applying these heightened supervisory standards, will require an even greater level of group consolidation than many of these firms have already.

Let me turn to AIG's securities lending program. It is important to understand that securities lending did not cause the crisis at AIG. AIG Financial

Products did. If there had been no Financial Products unit and only the securities lending program as it was, there would not have been the crisis there was at AIG. Financial Products' trillions of dollars of transactions created systemic risk. Securities lending did not.

If not for the crisis caused by Financial Products, AIG would be just like other insurance companies, dealing with the stresses caused by the financial crisis, but because of its size and strength, most likely weathering them well.

Although we could question it on a cost-benefit basis, securities lending is an activity that has been going on for decades without serious problems. Many, if not most, large financial institutions, including commercial banks, investment banks, and pension funds, participate in securities lending.

Securities lending involves financial institution A lending a stock or bond it owns to financial institution B. In return, B gives A cash collateral worth generally about 102 percent of the value of the security it is borrowing. A then invests the cash. A still owns the security and will benefit from any growth in its value. And A invests the cash collateral to gain a small additional amount.

If B decides it wants to return the security it borrowed from A, A is then required to sell its investment to obtain the cash it owes B. Generally, in a big securities lending program, A will have either some assets it can easily sell or sufficient cash to handle normal returns. But if there is a run—if many of the borrowers return the securities and demand cash—A may not be able to quickly sell enough assets to obtain the cash it needs or may have to sell assets at a loss before they mature.

As early as July 2006, the New York Insurance Department and other state regulators were engaged in discussions about the securities lending program with AIG. Those discussions at first related to the issue of risk-based capital and how the companies were reporting their securities lending program on their financial statements. It was in the course of those discussions that we learned about the details of AIG's securities lending program.

AIG securities lending was consolidated by the holding company in a special unit it set up and controlled. This special unit was not a licensed insurance company. In theory, having the parent company operate securities lending centrally was not inappropriate. The insurance companies could have benefited from reduced operational costs, increased expertise, and reduced risk from sharing any losses. That, of course, assumed that the securities lending program was run prudently.

AIG maintained two securities lending pools, one for U.S. companies and one for non-U.S. companies. At its height, the U.S. pool contained an outstanding balance of $76 billion. The majority of the U.S. security lending program was concentrated with 12 life insurers, three of which were from

New York. Those three New York companies contributed about 8 percent of the total assets in the U.S. securities lending pool.

The program historically maintained sufficient liquidity to meet cash demands, and the remaining funds were invested almost exclusively in the highest-rated securities. Even the few securities that were not rated at the top level of triple A were either double A or single A. Today, with the perfect clarity of hindsight, we all know that those ratings were not aligned with the market value of many mortgage-backed securities, which made up 60 percent of the invested collateral pool.

In addition, there was an arguable mismatch in maturity between the mortgage-backed securities and the short-term lending. As state regulators monitored the program, we became increasingly concerned about the market value and liquidity of the mortgage-backed securities and about the maturity mismatch. AIG officials did not agree with our concerns and continued to defend the choice of investments, even as they were winding down the program.

In 2007, because of those concerns, and as the problems in the subprime mortgage market began to affect the prices of the securities, state regulators began working with the company in winding down the program. Unfortunately, the securities lending program could not be ended quickly because, beginning in 2007, some of the residential mortgage securities could not be sold for their full value. At that time there were still relatively few defaults, and the securities were still paying off. But selling them would have involved taking a loss.

Still, we insisted that the program be wound down and that the holding company provide a guarantee to the life insurance companies to make up for any losses that were incurred during the process. In fact, the holding company provided a guarantee of first $500 million, then $1 billion, and finally $5 billion.

Neither the NYSID nor any other state regulator issued a written directive to AIG to wind down the securities lending business. The lack of a directive was not unusual. First, regulators are usually able to ask for and obtain even substantial changes in insurers' behavior without having to make a formal, written demand. Insurers recognize that state regulators have substantial power and usually prefer to cooperate. Second, a written request that would be disclosable to the public asking a company to sell a large quantity of securities would alert others to the insurer's plans, thus making sales more difficult and expensive. Also, in the case of securities lending, raising written (and thus public) questions about the program could cause counterparties to contractually end the loans (versus continuing to roll over the loans) and cause forced sales and losses. The state regulators were successfully working with AIG to expeditiously reduce the size of the program in an orderly manner to reduce losses without the complications of a written request.

In 2008, New York and other states began quarterly meetings with AIG to review the securities lending program. Meanwhile, the program was being wound down in an orderly manner to reduce losses. From its peak of about $76 billion, it had declined by $18 billion, or about 24 percent, to about $58 billion by September 12, 2008.

At that point, the crisis caused by Financial Products caused the equivalent of a run on the AIG securities lending program. Borrowers that had usually rolled over their positions from period to period began returning the borrowed securities and demanding their cash collateral. From September 12 to September 30, borrowers demanded a return of about $24 billion in cash.

There are two essential points about AIG and its securities lending program. First, without the crisis caused by Financial Products, there is no reason to believe there would have been a run on the securities lending program. We would have continued to work with AIG to unwind its program, and any losses would have been manageable.

Second, even if there had been a run on the securities lending program with no federal rescue, our detailed analysis indicates that the AIG life insurance companies would have been solvent. Certainly, there would have been losses, with some companies hurt more than others. But we believe that there would have been sufficient assets in the companies and in the parent to maintain the solvency of all the insurance companies. Indeed, before September 12, 2008, the parent company contributed slightly more than $5 billion to the reduction of the securities lending program.

But that is an academic analysis. Whatever the problems at securities lending, they would not have caused the crisis that brought down AIG. And without Financial Products and the systemic risk its transactions created, there would have been no reason for the federal government to get involved. State regulators would have worked with the company to deal with the problem and protect policyholders.

I would like to also review briefly what the New York Insurance Department did during the crisis about securities lending in the insurance industry.

Based on what we were seeing at AIG, but before the crisis in September 2008, the NYSID warned all licensed New York companies that we expected them to manage prudently the risks in securities lending programs. On July 21, 2008, New York issued Circular Letter 16 to all companies doing business in New York, which expressed the NYSID's concerns about security lending programs. We cautioned them about the risks, reminded them of the requirements for additional disclosure, and told them we would be carefully examining their programs.

On September 22, 2008, the NYSID sent a Section 308 letter to all life insurance companies licensed in New York requiring them to submit information relating to security lending programs, financing arrangements, security impairment issues, and other liquidity issues. (Section 308 is the provision of the New York State insurance law that gives the NYSID the authority to request additional information between periodic examinations.) The New York Insurance Department staff then conducted a thorough investigation of the securities' lending programs at life insurance companies that were licensed in New York. The results were reassuring. Almost all of the companies had modest-sized programs with highly conservative investments, even by today's standards. Companies with larger programs had ample liquidity to meet redemptions under stress. What became clear was that AIG was in a uniquely troubling situation.

Was AIG able to take advantage of a regulatory gap by having its holding company operate its securities lending program? I believe the answer is no. It is true that the company was able to take risks with the program. But, by the same token, it could have directed all its insurance companies to take similar risks if they were all operating their own programs.

The key point is that while state regulators did allow AIG to be aggressive, we came to understand the problem through our normal regulatory activities and forced the company to change. Regulation, like all human activities, is a process of learning. The state insurance departments have learned about the need to keep a much closer watch on securities lending and have set clear standards. And it is worth noting that it was only AIG that was using securities lending in such a risky manner. Like everyone else, we learned a hard lesson about the value of credit ratings, an issue the National Association of Insurance Commissioners (NAIC) and the federal government are still working to resolve. Indeed, AIG's program was invested in triple-A-rated securities, as required. State insurance regulators, like almost everyone else at the time, relied on those ratings.

Our involvement with AIG changed dramatically on Friday, September 12, 2008. The immediate spark for the crisis was the sudden decision by the credit rating agencies to downgrade AIG without waiting to see the results of its restructuring, then only two weeks away. The downgrade required AIG to post additional collateral against its credit default swaps and against its guaranteed investment contracts. AIG's initial estimates were that it needed about $18 billion in cash to post collateral. While AIG had assets, including its insurance companies, worth many times this amount, the assets were not liquid and could not be used to solve the collateral problem. Thus it appeared initially that the company had a liquidity problem. That is, it was not short of capital, but it was short of cash because it could not turn most of its assets into cash quickly enough.

The Insurance Department received a call from two AIG senior executives informing us of the company's serious and immediate liquidity problem, and asking for assistance. We had conference calls with AIG leaders Saturday morning and then went over to their office for the remainder of the weekend to provide assistance and be in a position to expedite the consideration of any regulatory actions that might be needed to get through the crisis.

The Insurance Department worked with AIG to develop solutions, vet proposals, and find transactions that would stabilize AIG while protecting policyholders. As a result, we developed a proposal that the governor announced on Monday, September 15. This plan would have allowed AIG to temporarily access about $20 billion of excess surplus assets in its property-casualty insurance companies while fully protecting policyholders.

There are some key points that are important to understand. The proposal was just that: a proposal that we agreed to consider. It was never finalized. Agreement was dependent on conditions that would have guaranteed the protection of policyholders, including a substantial investment from capital providers and a restructuring of AIG's U.S. operations that would essentially have made the life insurers subsidiaries of the property-casualty operations. Thus the $20 billion liquidity provided would have been one part of a total solution of the company's problems. At the point at which we were discussing this proposal, everyone thought that AIG only had a temporary cash flow problem. When it became clear after a few days that the problem was much bigger, our proposal was dropped and replaced by the federal government's extension of assistance.

When it became clear that the company needed more money and that the NYSID plan was not feasible, the Federal Reserve asked two banks to try to form a private bank group to raise the necessary funds. Eventually, it became clear that no private-sector rescue was possible. At that point, the U.S. Treasury and Federal Reserve proposed the $85 billion bridge loan, and the NYSID proposal was no longer needed.

Staff of the Insurance Department participated in meetings at AIG over the weekend of September 12 through 14 and then in the meetings at the Federal Reserve that eventually resulted in the rescue. We were involved in meetings and informal discussions about different ideas and provided expertise on insurance issues.

Following the rescue, New York's involvement with the parent company was substantially reduced. Those issues were handled by the Federal Reserve and the Treasury. However, the New York Insurance Department co-chaired a 50-state task force created by the National Association of Insurance Commissioners to monitor the financial condition of the insurers, oversee and facilitate the sale of any insurance operations, and coordinate state regulatory responses. One of the main purposes of the task force was to protect policyholders by ensuring that insurance operations were purchased by stable, responsible entities capable of operating them successfully. And the Insurance Department also worked closely with the Federal Reserve and with Treasury to ensure that the regulatory approval process was efficient and did not hold up transactions.

To sum up, what happened at AIG arguably demonstrates the strength and effectiveness of state insurance regulation, not the opposite. The only reason that the federal rescue of AIG was possible was because there were strong operating insurance companies that provided the possibility that the federal government and taxpayers would be paid back. And the reason why those insurance companies were strong was because state regulation walled them off from nonrelated activities in the holding company and at Financial Products.

In most industries, the parent company can reach down and use the assets of its subsidiaries. With insurance, that ability is greatly restricted. State regulation requires that insurance companies maintain healthy reserves backed by investments that cannot be used for any other purpose. I've said that the insurance companies were the bars of gold at AIG. There are activities that the states need to improve, such as licensing and bringing new products to market. But where they are strong has been in maintaining solvency.

I would note that at a time when financial services firms were in trouble because they did not have adequate capital and were too highly leveraged, at a time when commercial banks and investment banks had very serious problems, insurance companies remained relatively strong. Clearly a lesson from this crisis is that all financial institutions should be required to hold sufficient capital and reserves to meet their promises and liquidity needs. As the crisis becomes a memory, regulators of all types are well-served by looking at not only what failed in 2008 but also at what worked.

CHAPTER 6

Assessing the Vulnerability of the U.S. Life Insurance Industry

Anna Paulson, Thanases Plestis, Richard Rosen,
Robert McMenamin, and Zain Mohey-Deen

Federal Reserve Bank of Chicago[1]

This chapter explores the vulnerability of the U.S. life insurance industry to hypothetical asset valuation and policyholder redemption shocks. Life insurance companies are important to analyze for several reasons. First, life insurance companies make up a substantial share of the U.S. financial sector.[2] As of June 2013, they held $5.7 trillion in assets, which is about one-third the size of the $15.2 trillion banking sector.[3] Life insurance companies play an important role in financing corporations, holding 17 percent of all outstanding corporate and foreign bonds in the United States.[4] Households rely on the life insurance industry for products that protect against mortality risk and longevity risk, and provide opportunities to save and invest. Sixty-four percent of U.S. households own some form of life insurance.[5] In addition, certain U.S. life insurance companies have been recently determined to be systemically important, either by the Financial Stability Board or by the Financial Stability Oversight Council, or both, meaning that they could pose a risk to the broader financial system if they were to fail. According to several measures of systemic risk that have been developed by researchers, some large insurance companies also have measures of systemic risk in the neighborhood of large banking organizations that are typically considered systemically important (see, for example, Billio et al. 2012 and Acharya et al. 2010).[6]

To provide context for our exploration of the vulnerability of insurers, we begin by comparing life insurer balance sheets to those of banks, who are vulnerable to depositor runs. Banks fund themselves with highly liquid demand deposits, which make up over 70 percent of banks' liabilities (see Table 6.1), and illiquid and difficult-to-value loans make up a large share of their assets. It is this combination of liquid liabilities and illiquid and opaque assets that makes banks vulnerable to runs (see Diamond and Dybvig 1983, for example). While life insurers offer some demand-deposit-like products and many life insurance products allow customers to access the accumulated cash value of their policies, there are often penalties for doing so, making life insurer liabilities less liquid than those of banks. In addition, life insurers tend to invest in corporate bonds and equities, which are relatively liquid and easy to value. This makes life insurers less vulnerable to runs than banks.

However, life insurers are not immune to runs. For example, General American Life Insurance Company (GA Life) experienced a run in 1999.[7] GA Life had issued funding agreements[8] with a clause that gave customers the option to withdraw the value of their investments with seven days' notice. In other words, GA Life possessed highly liquid liabilities. After a ratings downgrade, institutional investors began to exercise their option to cash out, and within a week GA Life, a company with about $14 billion in assets, had received redemption requests, mostly from money market funds, totaling $4.4 billion (Lohse 1999). GA Life did not have enough liquid assets that it could sell to raise cash quickly enough to meet these redemption requests, and the company was placed under supervision by the Missouri Insurance Department.

More generally, the financial crisis of 2008 provided a powerful demonstration that a variety of financial entities can be vulnerable to runs. A run on uninsured Wachovia deposits by institutional investors eventually forced

TABLE 6.1   Stylized Bank and Life Insurance Balance Sheets (June 2013)

	Primary Assets	Primary Liabilities/Funding
Banks	Loans (53% of total assets) Relatively illiquid and opaque	Customer deposits (71% of total liabilities) Very liquid
Life insurers	Bonds and stocks (91% of total assets) Relatively liquid and transparent	Policyholder liabilities (80% of total liabilities) Less liquid than deposits

Source: Based on data from the Board of Governors of the Federal Reserve System, *Flow of Funds Accounts of the United States*, Z.1 statistical release, June 6, 2013, available at www.federalreserve.gov/releases/z1/Current/z1.pdf. The banking sector is defined as all "private depository institutions," which include U.S.-chartered depository institutions, foreign banking offices, banks in U.S.-affiliated areas, and credit unions.

the sale of the company to Wells Fargo (Acharya et al. 2009). In addition to runs by bank depositors, other financial entities also experienced runlike behavior. For example, after Lehman Brothers failed and the Reserve Fund "broke the buck," there was a large-scale run on money market mutual funds (MMMFs) (Covitz, Liang, and Suarez 2012). With the prominent exception of American International Group (AIG), many have argued that the life insurance industry was relatively peripheral to the financial crisis (see Harrington 2009, for example); however, the wide swath of financial institutions that were swept up in the crisis suggests that no institution is immune to financial instability.

When a financial institution faces a run, it typically attempts to liquidate assets to raise the cash necessary to satisfy withdrawal requests. This can lead the institution to sell assets at a loss (a fire sale), which may in turn depress other asset prices and thereby impact the stability of other financial institutions. This sequence of events demonstrates the important relationship between the liquidity of liabilities and the liquidity of assets. Institutions with a large supply of liquid assets will be able to meet redemption requests without having to resort to fire sales. Fire sales and fire-sale externalities are critical elements of the 2008 financial crisis (see Brunnermeier 2009, for example). The values of many financial asset classes changed quickly during the financial crisis. Subprime mortgage-backed securities (MBSs), which were issued in large volumes leading up to the crisis, experienced significant declines in value during the crisis, as measured by the ABX.HE index (Gorton 2008).[9] In addition, high-yield corporate bond spreads increased as liquidity in the secondary market worsened and investors sought high-quality assets (Acharya, Amihud, and Bharath 2010). The S&P 500 index fell 56.8 percent from its peak in October 2007 to a low point in March 2009 (Dwyer 2009). These movements in asset prices had negative impacts on many financial institutions, including life insurers, particularly those with large holdings of nonagency MBSs.

We have argued that the liquidity of both liabilities and assets is important for assessing an institution's vulnerability to a financial shock. In the rest of this chapter, we analyze the liquidity of the liabilities and the assets of the life insurance industry in an effort to better understand the ability of the industry to withstand two scenarios: one where many policyholders seek to withdraw funds from the industry at once and another where the various assets held by the industry suffer a severe negative shock.[10] These exercises are intended to be illustrative rather than realistic. Indeed, they are deliberately extreme, so that we can better understand the resilience of the life insurance industry.

Following a brief overview of the life insurance business model, we characterize the liquidity of life insurer liabilities based on how easy it is for policyholders to withdraw funds from various product classes. We then use this characterization to conduct a hypothetical exercise to quantify the total amount of funds that might be withdrawn from the industry in episodes of moderate and extreme stress. The next section describes life insurer asset holdings and uses historical price data to consider what would happen to the value of life insurer assets if these assets were to suffer a severe shock (a decline in value that happens one month out of 60). We then compare life insurer holdings of liquid assets to the demands for cash estimated under the moderate and extreme withdrawal shock scenarios. The final section offers conclusions.

LIFE INSURANCE BUSINESS MODEL

Life insurance is often described as a liability-driven business. Life insurers take in funds today in exchange for the promise to make conditional payments in the future. The products they sell, which make up the vast majority of their liabilities, meet several policyholder objectives, but we focus on the two most prominent ones. The first objective—protection—compensates the policyholder or beneficiaries following an adverse event, such as loss of life. For example, a life insurance policy pays out money to the policy's beneficiaries upon death of the policyholder. The second objective—savings—allows the policyholder to accumulate wealth over time. Policies that fulfill the savings objective generally allow the policyholder to accumulate savings that may later be withdrawn, following a period of buildup.

Life insurance companies generally sell three types of products: life insurance, annuities, and deposit-type contracts. Life insurance offers protection for beneficiaries against the financial consequences of the policyholder's early death. Annuities offer protection against the consequences of outliving one's financial resources. Deposit-type contracts offer no insurance-like features; they are similar to bank certificates of deposit and are purely investment vehicles.

Typically, insurers collect premiums from customers before, and in some cases well before, they have to pay out funds. For example, a customer may pay premiums for many years on a life insurance policy before there is a claim on the policy. To account for the possibility that an insurance or annuity policy might have to pay out funds, insurers set aside reserves. Reserves comprise the vast majority of liabilities on insurers' balance sheets. Insurance companies invest reserves in assets such as corporate bonds. Their objective is to increase profits while retaining sufficient liquidity to meet potential payouts. Over half of life insurers' assets are invested in corporate, foreign, and government bonds and another 6 percent of assets are invested in mortgages.[11] Most of these fixed-income investments have long durations, reflecting the long duration of insurance liabilities.

Life insurers segregate their assets (and, by extension, their liabilities) into two independent accounts on their balance sheets—the general account (GA) and the separate account (SA). General-account assets support liabilities that feature guaranteed returns to customers from the insurer. In contrast, separate-account assets support pass-through products, in which investment gains and losses are passed on to the customer and no more than a minimum return may be guaranteed.[12] Typical general-account products include term life insurance, whole life insurance, fixed annuities, and disability insurance. Products whose payouts fluctuate based on the investment environment include variable annuities and variable life insurance. The assets that back these products are recorded on the separate account. In this chapter, we focus our attention on general-account assets and liabilities because life insurers typically do not pass on investment gains and losses on general-account products to their customers, so they must manage the associated liquidity and valuation risks of these assets and liabilities.

CHARACTERIZING THE LIQUIDITY OF INSURER LIABILITIES

Products sold by life insurers are said to be liquid if policyholders can easily extract cash from them. The act of extracting cash from a policy is known as a *surrender* or a *withdrawal*. Three key product features limit policy surrenders and withdrawals. First, only policies that feature a cash value can be surrendered.[13] Otherwise, there is no tangible dollar value to extract. Second, cash value growth is typically slow early in the life of a policy and accelerates in later periods.[14] This means that only a small amount of cash (relative to contributed premiums) can be extracted from newly issued policies. Third, some policies with cash values contain contractual features that limit or even prohibit the amount of cash that can be extracted. One feature that limits the amount of cash that can be surrendered is the *surrender charge*, which is paid by the policyholder upon surrender.[15] Surrender charges are typically high in early periods and decrease over time. For example, the surrender charge of a fixed annuity might start at 10 percent of the accumulated cash value and decline to zero after seven years. For this reason, policyholders usually find it undesirable to extract cash from newly issued policies.[16]

Life insurer liabilities can be segmented into four buckets based on their liquidity or ease of withdrawal (see Table 6.2).[17] The buckets are based on the ability to cash in a product, the cost of cashing in from the policyholder

TABLE 6.2 Categorizing the Liquidity of Life Insurer Liabilities

Liability Bucket	Bucket Description	Product Examples
Zero liquidity	Liabilities with no redemption rights	Immediate annuities Term life
Very low liquidity	Stable redemption profile and low surrender value	Accident and health
Low liquidity	Stable redemption profile	Whole life Universal life
Moderate liquidity	Redeemable at book value with significant penalties	Deferred annuities
High liquidity	Retail liabilities with little impediment to surrender	Deferred annuities
	Redeemable/putable institutional liabilities	GICs Funding agreements

Note: Adaptations of buckets in "Special Report: Moody's Global Liquidity Stress Test for Life Insurance Operating Companies" by Joel Levine (Report No. 121220, Moody's Investors Service, March 2010).

perspective, and the likelihood that the need to satisfy surrenders would lead to cash outflows from the insurer.

1. *Zero liquidity.* On one end of the spectrum, life insurance products with almost no liquidity are those with no provisions for policyholders to extract cash immediately or to surrender the policy for a cash value. These include annuities that are already in the payout phase of the contract (annuitized), term life insurance (which has no savings component), and most disability insurance.
2. *Low liquidity.* Low-liquidity products feature a cash value, but policyholders are likely to face high costs to replace these products and must pay penalties for early withdrawal. Products that are protection-oriented with some embedded savings elements, like whole life and universal life insurance, typically fall into this category. These products may allow the savings portion to be withdrawn at the policyholder's discretion, but they have experienced relatively low and consistent historical surrender rates. The costs of replacing the policies and the penalties for extracting value mean policyholders are unlikely to withdraw funds en masse.[18]
3. *Moderate liquidity.* Moderate-liquidity products have contract terms that allow for some liquidity, but restrict the timing of withdrawals or impose surrender charges on withdrawals. Deferred annuities are

examples of products that may have these features. In addition to providing protection and savings features, these products are also intended to provide liquidity for the policyholder.

4. *High liquidity.* High-liquidity products impose few limitations on or penalties for early withdrawal. These highly liquid liabilities include guaranteed investment contracts (GICs) and funding agreements.[19] In addition, deferred annuities that offer low surrender charges and enable policyholders to determine the timing of withdrawals are classified as having high liquidity. In general, the most liquid life insurance products allow policyholders to withdraw cash at will and at book value, similar to bank demand deposits.

To quantify the share of liabilities that falls into each of these liquidity buckets, we examine insurers' statutory filings, which report the reserves held against various product categories. We supplement this with statutory information on the likely contractual terms of these products, such as the cost to withdraw funds. Zero-liquidity liabilities consist of accident and health (A&H) reserves, plus annuity and deposit-type liabilities that do not allow discretionary withdrawals. Low-liquidity liabilities consist of life contract reserves, or the reserves that do not back annuities, deposit-type contracts, or A&H. The moderate-liquidity bucket contains annuity and deposit contracts that allow discretionary withdrawals with penalties or withdrawals at fair value. Finally, the high-liquidity bucket is made up of reserves for annuity and deposit contracts that allow discretionary withdrawals at book value. The methodology classifies liabilities based on common characteristics across the product groups, rather than aggregating product-level information.

Our analysis of the data indicates that life insurers had about 46 percent of liabilities in the zero- to low-liquidity categories and 54 percent in the moderate- to high-liquidity categories at the end of 2012 (see Table 6.3). This shows a slight shift toward more liquid liabilities since 2007, when zero- and low-liquidity liabilities represented about 50 percent of the total. Looking at the riskiest bucket, high liquidity, we see a rise to an 11 percent share in 2012 from 9 percent in 2007. These aggregate data mask considerable firm-level heterogeneity. For example, two of the largest 10 life insurers, by assets, have more than 20 percent of liabilities in the high-liquidity category.

To facilitate comparisons across firms and over time, a composite score is created, which is the weighted sum of the share of liabilities in each bucket. Zero-liquidity liabilities get a weight of 0, low-liquidity liabilities get a weight of 3.33, moderate-liquidity liabilities get a weight of 6.67, and high-liquidity liabilities get a weight of 10. From 2007 to 2012, the industry average composite liquidity score rose from 4.66 to 4.90, consistent with a modest increase in the liquidity of liabilities (see Table 6.3).

TABLE 6.3   Liquidity Profile of Life Insurance Industry Liabilities

	2007	2008	2009	2010	2011	2012
Zero liquidity	19.5%	22.6%	19.8%	18.8%	18.6%	18.6%
Low liquidity	30.4%	30.0%	28.0%	27.9%	28.3%	27.2%
Moderate liquidity	41.1%	37.2%	41.9%	43.3%	42.1%	42.9%
High liquidity	9.1%	10.2%	10.3%	9.9%	11.0%	11.3%
Composite score	4.66	4.50	4.76	4.81	4.86	4.90

Note: Numbers indicate percentage of total during a given year, except composite score.
Source: Authors' calculations based on insurance statutory filings data from SNL Financial.

The liquidity measures presented here are indicative approximations for the liquidity of the reserves of insurers. However, these measures have important limitations. As mentioned earlier, we are not looking directly at the liquidity of specific products when assessing liquidity characteristics. We also use aggregate data about withdrawal characteristics of certain products to classify liquidity, which is likely to obscure some information.

WITHDRAWAL SCENARIOS

In addition to classifying insurer liabilities by their liquidity characteristics, it is useful to estimate the fraction of life insurer general-account liabilities that may be susceptible to mass withdrawals in a stress scenario. During a stress scenario, a large number of policyholders collectively withdraw from the cash values of their policies, forcing life insurers to liquidate assets in a process akin to a bank run by depositors. Withdrawals may be triggered by company-specific factors or by a combination of macroeconomic factors that may impact the industry as a whole. Company-specific factors are likely to center around concerns about the solvency of the insurer. Policyholders tend to withdraw funds when they fear that their insurer is becoming insolvent. For example, after news about the losses and risks associated with junk bond holdings spread in 1990, policyholders began to withdraw funds from Executive Life and Executive Life of New York, which were heavily invested in junk bonds. That year, policyholders withdrew a total of $4 billion from the two companies, which had approximately $14 billion in total combined assets at the time (U.S. Government Accountability Office 1992).

Aspects of the macroeconomic environment could trigger policy surrenders as well, and surrenders triggered by macroeconomic events would be likely to affect many life insurers at the same time. For example, rising interest rates, particularly following a low interest rate period, create an incentive for policyholders to tap into the liquidity of their policies to reinvest at higher rates (Berends et al. 2013). In an environment of *gradually* increasing rates, insurers may be able to alter product features to retain some current policyholders and attract new ones. However, a *rapid, sharp* increase in interest rates might cause problems that a gradual increase in rates would not. Policyholders might redeem their policies en masse. If the volume of redemptions forced insurers to liquidate assets quickly, and if the volume of redemptions exceeded insurers' holdings of highly liquid assets, asset fire sales could trigger solvency concerns for the insurer that could spark further policy redemptions. Therefore, a period of rapidly rising interest rates could act as a source of stress for life insurance companies.

Two cases of stress—extreme stress and moderate stress—are analyzed (see Table 6.4). These cases are not intended to be realistic but merely to serve as benchmarks for understanding the liquidity characteristics of the life insurance industry. A larger share of policy reserves is assumed to be withdrawn in the extreme stress scenario.[20] For example, 20 percent of total life insurance reserves are assumed to face withdrawals in the extreme scenario versus 10 percent in the moderate scenario. For annuities and deposit-type contracts, withdrawal assumptions are made based on each product's characteristics. In the extreme stress scenario, policies that prohibit withdrawals are assumed to have zero withdrawals, while all policies that do allow withdrawals are assumed to experience full withdrawals. In the moderate stress scenario, withdrawals for policies that allow withdrawals with a penalty are assumed to experience withdrawals equal to 50 percent of reserves. Note that the category for "Other liabilities" includes some important items that contribute to liquidity risk. Reinsurance liabilities, which account for 30 percent of other liabilities, are very liquid.[21] Derivatives, contract claims, and other miscellaneous items may also be liquid. For this reason, withdrawal percentages of 40 percent and 30 percent are assigned to the "Other liabilities" category for the extreme and moderate stress scenarios, respectively.

Overall, 43 percent of the life industry's total general-account liabilities are estimated to be subject to withdrawals in an extreme stress scenario, while 31 percent would be subject to withdrawals in a moderate stress scenario. This corresponds to $1.4 trillion of "runnable" liabilities (liabilities that may be withdrawn under stress) in the extreme stress scenario (which is 4.3 times industry capital) and $1.0 trillion in the moderate stress scenario (which is 3.1 times industry capital).

TABLE 6.4 Composition and Liquidity of the Life Insurance Industry's Aggregate General Account Liabilities (2012 Q4)

Liability Category	Liabilities ($ Billions)	Percent of Total Liabilities	Percent of Liabilities Withdrawn during Extreme Stress	Percent of Liabilities Withdrawn during Moderate Stress
General account liabilities	3,266	100.0	43*	31*
Accident and health	219	6.7	2	1
Life insurance	978	30.0	20	10
Annuities	1,304	39.9	—	—
No discretionary withdrawal	467	14.3	0	0
Discretionary withdrawal with penalty	408	12.5	100	50
Discretionary withdrawal, no penalty	430	13.2	100	100
Deposit-type contracts	271	8.3	—	—
No discretionary withdrawal	97	3.0	0	0
Discretionary withdrawal with penalty	85	2.6	100	50
Discretionary withdrawal, no penalty	89	2.7	100	100
Other liabilities	494	15.1	40	30

*Value based on the percentages displayed underneath for each liability category.
Source: Authors' calculations based on insurance statutory filings data from SNL Financial.

ASSET HOLDINGS AND ASSET RISK

In this section, we describe life insurer asset holdings and consider the implications of an extreme drop in value of an asset class held by the industry or of asset values generally. The life insurance industry's aggregate general account held $3.59 trillion in assets at the end of 2012, roughly double the $2.05 trillion in assets held in the separate account (see Table 6.5).[22]

TABLE 6.5 Life Insurance Industry Aggregate Assets (2012 Q4)

	General-Account (GA) Assets		Separate-Account (SA) Assets	
	Dollars in Billions	Percent of GA Investments	Dollars in Billions	Percent of SA Investments
Bonds	2,547.3	74.8	298.7	14.7
Treasury and federal government bonds	178.0	5.2	—	—
State, municipal, and agency	126.4	3.7	—	—
Agency MBSs	229.8	6.7	—	—
Nonagency MBSs	237.6	7.0	—	—
ABSs	170.9	5.0	—	—
Corporate and foreign bonds	1,581.1	46.4	—	—
Affiliated bonds	23.6	0.7	—	—
Stock	77.5	2.3	1,627.0	80.0
Mortgages	335.6	9.9	8.5	0.4
Real estate	21.4	0.6	10.0	0.5
Policy loans	127.5	3.7	0.4	0.0
Cash	106.6	3.1	19.8	1.0
Derivatives	41.6	1.2	0.4	0.0
Other investments	149.2	4.4	68.8	3.4
Total invested assets	3,406.7	100.0	2,033.5	100.0
Total assets	3,592.6	—	2,054.3	—

Source: Authors' calculations based on insurance statutory filings data from SNL Financial.

The assets held in the two accounts are very different. In the general account, fixed-income assets like bonds and mortgages constitute the largest share of invested assets, at 74.8 percent and 9.9 percent, respectively. Separate-account assets comprise primarily equities. Only 14.7 percent of separate-account invested assets are bonds, and mortgages make up only 0.4 percent.[23]

Corporate bonds make up the largest share of general-account assets. Insurers had $1.6 trillion of corporate bonds at the end of 2012, and corporate bonds accounted for 46.4 percent of all general-account invested assets (see Table 6.5). As a major corporate bond investor, the life insurance industry represents an important source of funding for U.S. corporations. Corporate bonds issued by industrial and manufacturing firms and by financial firms comprised 28.7 percent and 25.4 percent, respectively, of all corporate bonds held by insurers (see Figure 6.1). No other industry accounted for more than 10 percent of insurer corporate bond holdings.

The recent global financial crisis was characterized by problems with financial firms and real estate. To measure the life insurance industry's exposure to these areas, we compare their holdings with the total credit

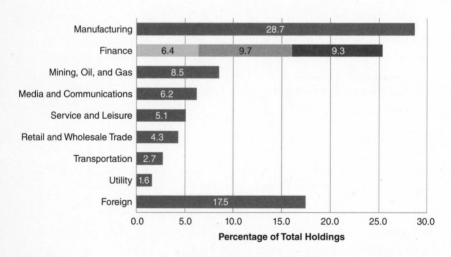

FIGURE 6.1 Life Insurance Corporate Bond Holdings by Industry (2012 Q4)
Note: Bonds that are missing an industry classification are excluded.
Source: Authors' calculations based on insurance statutory filings data from SNL Financial as well as data from Mergent Financial and Standard & Poor's.

market instruments outstanding in these sectors. Overall, 24.8 percent of corporate bonds in 2012 were issued by financial firms.[24] This share is comparable to the sector's share of insurers' holdings at 25.4 percent.

Insurers' exposure to real estate comes through mortgage-backed securities (13.7 percent of insurers' invested assets), mortgage loans (9.9 percent), and real estate owned (0.6 percent).[25] The 24.2 percent of total real-estate-related holdings on insurers' general account is somewhat less than the real estate sector's 36.3 percent share of all outstanding credit market instruments.[26] This suggests that insurers are not overexposed to this market sector. However, it is important to keep in mind that different real-estate-related investments have different risk profiles. For example, mortgage loans have direct real estate risk, whereas MBS investments have indirect exposure. Mortgage-backed securities issued by government-sponsored agencies, such as Fannie Mae or Freddie Mac, or guaranteed by Ginnie Mae, are guaranteed against defaults, so they are subject to prepayment risk (the risk that loans are paid off early). Nonagency MBSs have default risk as well as prepayment risk.

The value of the life insurance industry's assets fluctuates with asset valuations generally. The financial crisis provided a powerful demonstration that asset values can change quickly. In addition, the value of the industry's large fixed-income holdings will vary with interest rates, rising when interest rates fall and declining when interest rates increase. Using asset price data from October 2002 to December 2012, one can quantify the potential impact of an extreme downturn in asset prices on the value of insurer-owned general-account assets. First, insurance asset classes are matched to asset price indexes that are likely to track the value of those asset classes closely (see Appendix 6A for details on the matching process). The performance of the indexes is used to estimate the performance of the matched asset classes.[27] For each day in the sample period, the change in price for all indexes over the past month is calculated. The change for a weighted average of the indexes is also calculated, where the weights are equal to the shares of the matched asset classes from the insurer's general-account balance sheet. The standard deviation of these changes is computed and used to estimate the loss in asset value that occurs with a particular frequency. Our analysis focuses on a loss that would occur one month in every 60 months—or once in five years—which corresponds to a 2.13 standard deviation price change. It is important to note that the analysis estimates a loss in market value, not in book value.

The one-month-in-60 losses, when calculated for the life insurance industry's aggregate general-account portfolio, vary across asset classes (see Table 6.6). At the high end, nonagency MBS are estimated to lose

TABLE 6.6   Estimated One-Month-in-60 Losses for the Life Insurance Industry Aggregate General-Account Portfolio, by Asset Class (2012 Q4)

Asset Category	Assets ($ Billions)	One-Month-in-60 Asset Loss	One-Month-in-60 Asset Loss ($ Billions)
Bonds	2,547	5.8%	147
Corporate and foreign bonds	1,581	7.0%	110
Agency MBSs	230	2.7%	6
Nonagency MBSs	238	16.0%	38
ABSs	171	8.0%	14
Treasury and federal government bonds	178	5.6%	10
State, municipal, and agency	126	4.2%	5
Affiliated bonds	24	17.0%	4
Stock	77	9.9%	8
Mortgage loans	336	15.5%	52
Cash and equivalents	107	0.0%	0
Policy loans	127	0.0%	0
Derivatives	42	17.0%	7
Real estate	21	15.5%	3
Other investments	149	17.0%	25
Total investments	**3,407**	**5.7%**	**196**
Other assets	186	—	—
Separate-account assets	2,053	—	—
Total assets	**5,646**	—	—

Notes: Values for the nonindented asset categories are reported directly from the filings. Values for the indented asset categories are constructed using the summary investment schedule, which is available annually. The values of these categories are adjusted to sum to the value of "Bonds" based on their annual relative distribution. In addition, data from Schedule D is used to segment "Corporate and foreign bonds" from "ABSs," since these are reported together in the summary investment schedule.

Source: Authors' calculations based on statutory filings data from SNL Financial.

16 percent in market value once every 60 months. In contrast, the corporate bond portfolio is estimated to lose 7 percent. Overall, the industry's entire general-account portfolio is estimated to lose 5.7 percent in value, reflecting some benefits from diversification. Note that, on one hand, the historical period that is analyzed includes the financial crisis, so the estimates of potential losses may somewhat overstate the risk going forward. On the other hand, the period leading up to the crisis, which is also included in the analysis, was a period of unusual calm in financial markets.

Back-of-the-envelope calculations suggest that a severe shock to asset prices could reduce the value of the life industry's general-account investments by 5.7 percent, or $196 billion, using fourth-quarter 2012 data. This corresponds to a 59 percent loss in total industry equity, which was $329 billion in that quarter. However, because insurers make investments to match liabilities, these asset losses would be partially offset by gains on insurance liabilities. Consider a scenario in which interest rates increase. Because fixed-income securities constitute the bulk of insurers' general-account assets, the market value of the industry's overall asset portfolio would likely decrease. However, gains on insurance liabilities would likely offset some of that decrease. Because insurance liabilities tend to be long-term, rising interest rates would likely cause significant declines in the present value of future expected policyholder payments; therefore, the decreased value of policy liabilities would offset the decreased value of general-account assets, and equity would be preserved.

The extent to which one-month-in-60 asset losses would be offset by liability gains can be roughly estimated using insurance stock price data.[28] The one-month-in-60 loss for the SNL Life Insurance stock index is calculated and used to derive the one-month-in-60 loss for the life industry's total equity.[29] Twenty-two percent of industry equity, or $73 billion, is estimated to be lost once in 60 months. Recall that the one-month-in-60 losses for the industry's total asset portfolio is 5.7 percent, or $196 billion. This implies that liability gains of $123 billion ($196 billion less $73 billion) would have occurred to offset this hypothetical loss in assets. According to this back-of-the-envelope calculation, 63 percent of a one-month-in-60 loss in asset value would be made up for by a gain on liabilities. Of course, this industry perspective may mask considerable variation at the individual firm level. Some insurance companies will have greater exposure to riskier asset classes and others will have less. Firms will also vary in the extent to which their liability gains would offset their losses on investments. Similarly, equity cushions differ across firms.

ASSET AND LIABILITY RISK

In addition to asset valuation risk, insurers must consider the liquidity risk of their asset holdings. For example, in the event of a sudden redemption of liabilities by policyholders or depositors, a firm's ability to respond will depend on whether it has sufficient liquid assets that it can sell quickly and with little impact on the value of the assets—in other words, assets that can be sold without a price concession. One way firms can offset the risk of offering liquid liabilities is by increasing their share of liquid assets. The following analysis compares the industry's holdings of very liquid assets to estimated withdrawals under the moderate and extreme scenarios described earlier.

We consider two definitions of liquid assets. The first, which we refer to as "very liquid" assets, includes all Treasury securities, agency mortgage-backed securities, short-term investments, and cash. Historically, these assets have had relatively stable prices (see Table 6.6). The second definition is somewhat less stringent and also includes high-quality public corporate bonds with a rating of A or higher. We refer to this set of assets as "liquid" assets. At the end of 2012, the industry held very liquid assets of $0.5 trillion and liquid assets of $1.1 trillion (see Table 6.7).

We next compare the value of very liquid and liquid assets to withdrawals estimated under the moderate and severe scenarios. Total withdrawals were estimated to be $1 trillion and $1.4 trillion under the moderate and severe scenarios, respectively. When we restrict attention to only very liquid assets, the difference between withdrawals and very liquid assets is $0.5 trillion in the moderate withdrawal scenario and $0.9 in the extreme withdrawal scenario (see Table 6.7). In both of these scenarios, life insurers face a liquidity shortfall scenario. As of the fourth quarter of 2012, these shortfalls correspond to 1.5 and 2.7 times industry capital, respectively. However, when we include high-quality corporate bonds and look at liquid assets, rather than just very liquid assets, the industry has a liquidity cushion in the moderate stress scenario and the liquidity shortfall drops to $0.3 trillion in the extreme stress scenario, which corresponds to 0.9 times industry capital.

We reiterate that this analysis is intended to serve as a useful summary measure of the liquidity of the industry, taking into account both assets and liabilities. However, it is not meant to describe what might actually happen in an actual stress scenario. Nor do we consider the scenarios we analyzed likely. Indeed, the asset valuation scenarios are estimated to occur only one month in 60. Should the life insurance industry be faced with an actual stress scenario, the liquidity of assets would depend on financial market conditions at the time, and withdrawals from life insurance companies would likely vary considerably by firm and as a function of the events that triggered the withdrawals.

TABLE 6.7 Liquid Liabilities and Liquid Assets in the Extreme and Moderate Stress Scenarios (2012 Q4)

Stress Scenario	Liabilities Withdrawn ($ Billions)	Very Liquid Assets (Excludes Public, A-Rated Corporate Bonds)			Liquid Assets (Includes Public, A-Rated Corporate Bonds)		
		Assets ($ Billions)	Difference (Shortfall)	Assets Divided by Runnable Liabilities	Assets ($ Billions)	Difference ("Shortfall")	Assets Divided by Runnable Liabilities
Moderate	1,014	514	499	51%	1,109	-96	109%
Extreme	1,409	514	895	36%	1,109	300	79%

Notes: Runnable liabilities represent the dollar value of liabilities that may be withdrawn under a stress scenario. Liquid assets are defined to include all Treasury securities, agency mortgage-backed securities, short-term investments, and cash. Corporate bonds with a rating of A or higher are also included in the columns at right. Shortfall represents the difference between runnable liabilities and liquid assets. A negative value indicates that liquid assets are sufficient to cover runnable liabilities. Liquid assets divided by runnable liabilities is another measure of coverage. Values of 100 percent or more indicate sufficient coverage.

Source: Authors' calculation based on statutory filings data from SNL Financial.

CONCLUSION

This chapter has characterized the life insurance industry's vulnerability to extreme and hypothetical shocks to either assets or liabilities. The results of this exercise point to the importance of the industry's large holdings of high-quality corporate bonds as a potential liquidity buffer. Were the industry to be in a situation where many life insurers needed to raise cash quickly and they chose to sell corporate bonds in an effort to do so, these sales might have negative ramifications for corporate bond valuations generally and for other investors in this asset class.

The analysis presented here is intended to serve as a useful summary of the liquidity of the industry, taking into account both assets and liabilities. However, it is not meant to describe what might actually happen in an actual stress scenario. Nor do we consider the scenarios we analyzed likely to occur. Indeed, the asset shocks are estimated to occur only one month in 60, and the chance of something like the withdrawal scenarios that we discussed is likely to be considerably more remote. Should the life insurance industry be faced with an actual stress scenario, the liquidity of assets would depend on financial market conditions at the time, and withdrawals from life insurance companies would likely vary considerably by firm and as a function of the events that triggered the withdrawals.

APPENDIX 6A: DETAILS ON ESTIMATING ASSET RISK

For each asset class, the following indexes were matched:

Corporate bonds: Bank of America, Merrill Lynch, U.S. corporate bond yields. A, BBB, BB, B, CCC, and lower-rated indexes are matched to similarly rated bonds.

Nonagency commercial mortgage-backed securities (CMBSs): Markit, CMBX index.

Nonagency residential mortgage-backed securities (RMBSs): Markit, ABX.HE index.

Asset-backed securities (ABSs): Bank of America, Merrill Lynch, U.S. bond yields, asset-backed securities fixed-rate index.

Agency MBSs: Asset-weighted blend of Merrill Lynch mortgage-backed securities, Ginnie Mae and Fannie Mae indexes.

Treasury bonds: One-, three-, and six-month, and one-, two-, three-, five-, seven-, 10-, 20-, and 30-year Treasury yields for similar-maturity bonds.

Municipal bonds: Bank of America, Merrill Lynch, U.S. bond yields, municipals (tax-exempt) master index.

Equities: S&P 500 index for common stock, and S&P preferred stock index for preferred stock.

Index values were provided by Haver Analytics and Bloomberg. When necessary, we convert yields to prices assuming a par value of 100, coupon rate as a one-month lag of the yield, and a 10-year average maturity if no maturity is disclosed for the index. When multiple indexes are listed for a category, we weight by the share of each item on the aggregate life insurance industry balance sheet, except as noted.

In addition:

- We assume that the returns for corporate bonds and foreign bonds are similar, since we do not have a foreign bond index.
- We assume that standard deviations of returns for each ratings class of private corporate bonds are one percentage point higher than the corresponding returns for public corporate bonds, since we do not have a private corporate bond index.
- We assume that affiliated bonds have returns equal to the smallest daily return across the other categories of bonds.
- We assume that the returns for agricultural and commercial mortgage loans are similar to the returns for CMBSs.
- We assume that the returns for residential mortgage loans are similar to the returns for RMBSs.
- We assume that the returns for real estate are similar to the overall returns for mortgage loans.
- We assume that policy loans and cash retain 100 percent of their value at all times. Policy loans are loans originated to policyholders that are financed by cash that has accrued in their policies. They do not depreciate in value, because failure to repay a policy loan results in policy termination.
- We assume that derivatives and other investments have returns equal to the smallest daily return across the other categories of assets.

NOTES

1. The material presented in this chapter reflects the views of the authors and is not necessarily representative of the views of the Federal Reserve Bank of Chicago or the Federal Reserve System.
2. Due to the size and importance of this segment of the financial sector, researchers at the Chicago Fed Insurance Initiative are analyzing the role

the life insurance sector plays in the economy (more details are available at www.chicagofed.org/webpages/markets/insurance_initiative.cfm).

3. Based on data from the Board of Governors of the Federal Reserve System, *Flow of Funds Accounts of the United States*, Z.1 statistical release, June 6, 2013, available at www.federalreserve.gov/releases/z1/Current/z1.pdf. The banking sector is defined as all "private depository institutions," which include U.S.-chartered depository institutions, foreign banking offices, banks in U.S.-affiliated areas, and credit unions.

4. Ibid.

5. Based on data from the 2010 Survey of Consumer Finances, conducted by the Board of Governors of the Federal Reserve System.

6. Note that other researchers produce measures of systemic risk that suggest that insurers may be vulnerable from shocks that flow from banks but that they do not themselves pose risks to other financial firms (see, e.g., Chen et al. 2013).

7. See www.moodys.com/credit-ratings/General-American-Life-Insurance-Company-credit-rating-339600 (registration required) or Moody's Investors Service, "General American: A Case Study in Liquidity Risk," New York: Global Credit Research, August 1999.

8. Funding agreements are similar to bank certificates of deposit.

9. The ABX.HE index is a credit derivative that references 20 equally weighted subprime RMBS tranches. Gorton argues that the introduction of the ABX.HE index in 2006 created a new market that priced subprime risk, since subprime instruments do not trade in public markets.

10. This analysis builds on material presented in McMenamin, Mohey-Deen, Paulson, and Rosen. (2012) and McMenamin, Paulson, Plestis, and Rosen. (2013).

11. Ibid.

12. Not all gains and losses on separate-account assets are necessarily passed on to customers. Separate-account liabilities often include embedded guarantees. These guarantees are claims against the general account, and are therefore supported by general-account assets. These guarantees are more likely to be triggered when interest rates have declined sharply and when equity returns are very low. We do not address potential risks from embedded guarantees in this article.

13. The cash value is an amount of cash that has accumulated in a policy. It may be extracted by the policyholder subject to certain limitations and restrictions. It represents the savings element of a policy.

14. Delayed cash value growth is more typical of life insurance policies than of annuities.

15. Surrender charges are more commonly found in annuities than in life insurance policies.

16. In addition, withdrawals may be subject to tax penalties, and policy-holders may also be reluctant to surrender policies that might be difficult or expensive to replace, given changes in the policyholder's age or health status.

17. The buckets are adaptations of those in "Special Report: Moody's Global Liquidity Stress Test for Life Insurance Operating Companies" by Joel Levine (Report No. 121220, Moody's Investors Service, March 2010).

18. Replacing life insurance policies may be costly for policyholders due to: (1) potential acquisition costs associated with purchasing new policies, and (2) readjusted premiums in new policies due to changes in health since the previous policy was issued.

19. Both products are deposit-type contracts.

20. Specific assumptions are based on historical, company-level withdrawals data as well as the authors' research.

21. Reinsurance involves the transfer of risk between two insurance companies. Under a traditional reinsurance arrangement, one insurer cedes a block of policies to an unaffiliated insurer. Any liabilities that result from such arrangements are very liquid because either side will usually attempt to wind down the transaction when the other side faces financial stress.

22. Authors' calculations based on insurance statutory filings data from SNL Financial.

23. Recall that we focus our attention on general-account assets and liabilities because life insurers typically do not pass investment gains and losses on general-account assets to their customers, so they must manage the associated liquidity and valuation risks of these assets.

24. Based on data from the Board of Governors of the Federal Reserve System, *Flow of Funds Accounts of the United States*, Z.1 statistical release, June 6, 2013, available at www.federalreserve.gov/releases/z1/Current/z1.pdf. Financial firms exclude asset-backed securities issuers and real estate investment trusts.

25. Mortgage-backed securities include nonagency MBSs and agency MBSs, as reported in Table 6.5.

26. Based on data from the Board of Governors of the Federal Reserve System, *Financial Accounts of the United States*, Z.1 statistical release, June 6, 2013, available at www.federalreserve.gov/releases/z1/Current/z1.pdf.

27. In this analysis, assets are limited to include only those from U.S.-based life insurance operating companies. Assets from foreign and/or noninsurance companies are excluded.

28. However, note that stock prices are often influenced by noninsurance and/or foreign activities of the holding company, in addition to other

factors. Therefore, stock prices may not be a perfect representation of the equity of domestic operating insurance companies.

29. The one-month-in-60 loss for the SNL Life Insurance stock index is calculated using daily price data from 2002 to 2012.

REFERENCES

Acharya, Viral, Yakov Amihud, and Sreedhar Bharath. 2010. "Liquidity Risk of Corporate Bond Returns: A Conditional Approach." Revised October 2012. *Journal of Financial Economics*, forthcoming.

Acharya, Viral, Lasse Pedersen, Thomas Philippon, and Matthew Richardson. 2010. "Measuring Systemic Risk." Revised May 2010, AFA 2011 Denver Meetings Paper.

Acharya, Viral, Thomas Philippon, Matthew Richardson, and Nouriel Roubini. 2009. "The Financial Crisis: Causes and Remedies." *Financial Markets, Institutions, and Remedies* 18 (2): 89–137.

Berends, Kyal, Robert McMenamin, Thanases Plestis, and Richard Rosen. 2013. "The Sensitivity of Life Insurance Firms to Interest Rate Changes." Federal Reserve Bank of Chicago, *Economic Perspectives*, forthcoming.

Billio, Monica, Mila Getmansky, Andy Lo, and Loriana Pelizzon. 2012. "Econometric Measures of Connectedness and Systemic Risk in the Finance and Insurance Sectors." *Journal of Financial Economics* 104:535–559.

Board of Governors of the Federal Reserve System. 2013. *Flow of Funds Accounts of the United States.* Z.1 statistical release, June 6. Available at www.federalreserve.gov/releases/z1/.

Brunnermeier, Markus. 2009. "Deciphering the Liquidity and Credit Crunch 2007–08." *Journal of Economic Perspectives* 23 (1): 77–100.

Chen, Hua, J. David Cummins, Krupa S. Viswanathan, and Mary A. Weiss. 2013. "Systemic Risk and the Inter-Connectedness between Banks and Insurers: An Econometric Analysis." *Journal of Risk and Insurance*.

Covitz, Daniel, Nellie Liang, and Gustavo Suarez. 2012. "The Evolution of a Financial Crisis: Collapse of the Asset-Backed Commercial Paper Market." *Journal of Finance*, forthcoming.

Diamond, Douglas, and Philip Dybvig. 1983. "Bank Runs, Deposit Insurance, and Liquidity." *Journal of Political Economy* 91 (3): 401–419.

Dwyer, Gerald. 2009. "Stock Prices in the Financial Crisis." Federal Reserve Bank of Atlanta, *Notes from the Vault*. Available for electronic download at www.frbatlanta.org/filelegacydocs/cenfis_notes_0909.pdf.

Gorton, Gary. 2008. "The Subprime Panic." National Bureau of Economic Research, Working Paper 14398.

Harrington, Scott. 2009. "The Financial Crisis, Systemic Risk, and the Future of Insurance Regulation." *Journal of Risk and Insurance* 76 (4): 785–819.

Levine, Joel. 2010. "Special Report: Moody's Global Liquidity Stress Test for Life Insurance Operating Companies." Report No. 121220, Moody's Investors Service, March.

Lohse, Deborah. 1999. "How General American Got Fancy in Investing, Lost Its Independence." *Wall Street Journal.* Available for electronic download at http://online.wsj.com/article/SB936310659442544935 .html.

McMenamin, Robert, Anna Paulson, Thanases Plestis, and Richard Rosen. 2013. "What Do U.S. Life Insurers Invest In?" Federal Reserve Bank of Chicago, Chicago Fed Letter, No. 309.

McMenamin, Robert, Zain Mohey-Deen, Anna Paulson, and Richard Rosen. 2012. "How Liquid Are U.S. Life Insurance Liabilities?" Federal Reserve Bank of Chicago, Chicago Fed Letter, No. 302.

Moody's Investors Service. 1999. "General American: A Case Study in Liquidity Risk." New York: Global Credit Research, August.

U.S. Government Accountability Office. 1992. "Insurer Failures: Regulators Failed to Respond in Timely and Forceful Manner in Four Large Life Insurer Failures." Available for electronic download at www.gao.gov/ assets/110/104752.pdf.

CHAPTER 7

Systemic Risk and Regulation of the U.S. Insurance Industry

J. David Cummins and Mary A. Weiss

Temple University

This chapter analyzes the characteristics of U.S. insurers for purposes of determining whether they are systemically risky. More specifically, primary indicators (size, interconnectedness, and lack of substitutability) and contributing factors (leverage, liquidity risk and maturity mismatch, complexity, and government regulation) associated with systemic risk are assessed for the insurance sector. A distinction is made between the core activities of insurers (e.g., underwriting, reserving, claims settlement, etc.) and noncore activities (such as providing financial guarantees). Statistical analysis of insurer characteristics and their relationship with a well-known systemic risk measure, systemic expected shortfall (SES), is provided.

Consistent with other research, the core activities of property-casualty (P-C) insurers are found not to be systemically risky. However, we do find evidence that some core activities of life insurers, particularly separate accounts and group annuities, may be associated with systemic risk. The noncore activities of both property-casualty and life insurers can contribute to systemic risk. However, research findings indicate that generally insurers are victims rather than propagators of systemic risk events. The study also finds that insurers may be susceptible to intrasector crises such as reinsurance crises arising from counterparty credit risk. New and proposed state and federal regulations are reviewed in light of the potential for systemic risk for this sector.

INTRODUCTION

Systemic risk can be defined as the risk that an event will trigger a loss of economic value or confidence in a substantial segment of the financial system that is serious enough to have significant adverse effects on the real economy with a high probability.[1] Embedded in this definition of systemic risk are two important criteria: (1) Economic shocks become systemic because of the spillover effects whereby there is a contagious loss of value or confidence that spreads throughout the financial system. Thus, the failure of one financial institution, even a very large one, that does not spread to other institutions is not a systemic event. (2) Systemic financial events are sufficiently serious to have significant adverse effects on real economic activity. The financial crisis of 2007–2009 is a clear example of a systemic event that began in the housing market and spread to other parts of the financial system, resulting in significant declines in stock prices and real gross domestic product (GDP).

In response to the most recent systemic crisis, the Dodd-Frank Wall Street Reform and Consumer Protection Act of 2010 was passed into law. This law required the formation of an important new regulatory agency with potential authority over insurance holding companies, the Financial Stability Oversight Council (FSOC). One of the primary purposes of FSOC is to identify risks to the financial stability of the United States that could arise from the activities of large, interconnected bank holding companies or nonbank financial companies (FSOC 2012). Therefore, one of the activities of FSOC is the identification of nonbank financial companies that are systemically important financial institutions (SIFIs). Insurers are examples of nonbank financial companies that could potentially be designated as SIFIs. Organizations designated as SIFIs would come under the supervision of the Federal Reserve Board and be subject to enhanced capital requirements, liquidity requirements, short-term debt limits, and public disclosures, as mandated under the Dodd-Frank Act.

The purpose of this chapter is threefold: First, the activities of U.S. insurers are evaluated to determine whether U.S. insurers are systemically risky. An important distinction in this analysis is made between the *core activities* of insurers, such as insurance underwriting, reserving, claims settlement, and reinsurance, and the *noncore* or *banking activities* engaged in by some insurers, such as American International Group (AIG). Noncore activities include provision of financial guarantees, asset lending, issuing credit default swaps (CDSs), investing in complex structured securities, and excessive reliance on short-term sources of financing. Second, we conduct a statistical analysis that consists of a correlation analysis of insurer characteristics (such as the notional value of derivatives not used for hedging) and a well-known systemic risk measure, SRISK (see Acharya, Engle, and Richardson [2012] for a discussion of this measure). Robust ordinary least squares (OLS) analysis is performed also on a small set of insurers to determine firm characteristics associated with systemic risk. Finally, we discuss regulatory responses to the financial crisis as they relate to insurers. These include criteria that FSOC uses to designate nonbank financial companies as SIFIs.

Although prior studies have concluded that the insurance industry as a whole is not systemically risky, this research still contributes to the literature for a number of reasons. First, recent micro studies of insurers (i.e., studies of individual insurers) have suggested that linkages between banks, insurers, hedge funds, and other financial firms may be more significant than prior research indicates (Billio et al. 2011; Acharya et al. 2010). A second reason for conducting further analysis of the U.S. insurance industry is that most prior studies have been oriented toward the global insurance and reinsurance industries rather than conducting an in-depth analysis of the U.S. industry (e.g., Swiss Re 2003; Group of Thirty 2006; Bell and Keller 2009; Geneva Association 2010; Baluch, Mutenga, and Parsons 2011). A third rationale is that several of the prior studies on the topic have been published or sponsored by the insurance industry (e.g., Swiss Re 2003; Bell and Keller 2009; Geneva Association 2010). Therefore, it is important to provide an independent, third-party analysis. The fourth reason to conduct additional analysis of systemic risk in the U.S. insurance industry is that the reinsurance counterparty risk of U.S. licensed insurers has rarely been investigated systematically in any detail.[2]

This chapter contributes to the literature in other ways. A systemic risk measure developed by Acharya et al. (2010) is analyzed to determine which aspects of an insurer are associated with systemic risk. This analysis relies on data obtained from the 10-K reports filed with the Securities and Exchange Commission (SEC) by each individual insurer as well as data available from public databases such as the SNL Financial database, Compustat, and the National Association of Insurance Commissioners (NAIC). The sample period studied is 2001 to 2011, and the sample includes all major publicly traded life and property-casualty (P-C) insurance groups for which data are available.

The findings of this study provide a somewhat more nuanced view of systemic risk in the insurance industry than most prior research has provided. By way of preview, we find that the core activities of P-C insurers do not contribute to systemic risk. However, we find evidence suggesting that some activities of life insurers, particularly group annuities and separate accounts, do contribute to systemic risk. However, in general, insurers are victims rather than propagators of systemic risk. As was demonstrated by the AIG debacle, the noncore activities of insurers do constitute a potential source of systemic risk, and interconnectedness among financial firms has grown significantly in recent years. Therefore, on a worldwide scale, regulators need to improve significantly their capabilities in group supervision.

The remainder of this chapter proceeds as follows. First, a short literature review on systemic risk and the insurance industry is conducted. Following this, we discuss primary indicators and contributing factors to systemic risk. Then these criteria are evaluated with respect to the U.S. insurance industry. The next section analyzes the noncore activities of insurers in terms of their potential for causing systemic risk. In the succeeding section, data analysis based on insurers' systemic risk measures is conducted. Following this, we discuss potential forthcoming changes in insurance regulation to address systemic concerns, and the last section contains concluding comments.

LITERATURE REVIEW

There have been a few prior studies of systemic risk in the insurance industry. These can be broadly classified as industry-sponsored or academic. Both types of research are reviewed briefly.

Industry-Sponsored Research

Some prior research has focused on whether reinsurance creates systemic risk for the insurance industry. Swiss Re (2003) investigates whether reinsurers pose a major risk for their clients, the financial system, or the economy. The broad conclusion is that systemic risk does not exist in reinsurance, but the study concedes (presciently) that reinsurers are linked to the banking sector via credit derivatives, the same instruments that brought down AIG. A study by the Group of Thirty (2006) also investigates the degree to which the reinsurance sector may pose systemic risk. The study presents the results of a stress test projecting the results of reinsurer failures equivalent to 20 percent of the global reinsurance market. The conclusions are that even failures of this magnitude would be unlikely to trigger widespread insolvencies among primary insurers and that the effects on the real economy would be minimal.

Bell and Keller (2009) investigate the systemic risk of the insurance industry, concluding that insurers engaged in insurance (core) activities are not systemically risky. As a consequence, they are not "too big to fail" (TBTF) or "too interconnected to fail." However, they argue that insurers engaging in nontraditional activities such as credit derivatives can pose systemic risk, which can be controlled through more rigorous risk-based capital requirements. Similar to Bell and Keller (2009), the Geneva Association (2010) concludes that insurers did not play a major role in the financial crisis aside from monolines and insurers engaging in nontraditional activities such as credit default swaps. Two noncore activities are identified as potential sources of systemic risk: (1) derivatives trading on noninsurance balance sheets and (2) mismanagement of short-term funding from commercial paper or securities lending.

Academic Studies

Grace (2010) conducts a series of tests on insurer stock prices to help determine "whether insurers contribute to systemic risk or whether they are potential victims of systemic risk." The findings suggest that AIG was systemically important but that generally the insurance industry is not a significant source of systemic risk.

Acharya et al. (2010) use stock price data and find that several insurers ranked highly based on an econometric measure of systemic risk when compared to systemically important banks. Billio et al. (2011) also use stock price data and conclude that "a liquidity shock to one [financial] sector propagates to other sectors eventually culminating in losses, defaults, and a systemic event." The study also finds that financial firms have become more highly interrelated and less liquid during the past decade. A more recent micro-level analysis by Chen et al. (2014) constructs a systemic risk measure to examine the interconnectedness between banks and insurers. The results indicate that the impact of banks on insurers is stronger and of longer duration than the impact of insurers on banks. Stress tests confirmed that banks create economically significant systemic risk for insurers but not vice versa.

Baluch, Mutenga, and Parsons (2011) investigate the role of the insurance industry in the financial crisis with an emphasis on European markets. Their analysis reveals significant correlation between the banking and insurance sectors and finds that the correlation increased during the crisis period. They conclude that systemic risk is lower in insurance than in banking but has grown in recent years due to increasing linkages between banks and insurers and growing exposure to nontraditional insurance activities.

Cummins and Weiss (2014) perform an analysis of the overall U.S. insurance industry with respect to systemic risk and conclude that the core activities of U.S. insurers do not pose systemic risk. To provide further information on the noncore activities of insurance firms, an analysis was conducted on systemic and nonsystemic risk samples. The results indicated that the systemic firms had more business segments on average than nonsystemic insurers had and the difference was statistically significant. Based on their tests, systemic firms on average had higher derivatives holdings both for hedging and for nonhedging purposes than the nonsystemic firms had.[3] Also, systemic insurers had larger amounts of multiclass commercial mortgage-backed securities (MBSs) and total private asset-backed securities (ABSs).

Thus, the hallmarks of previous research are that, taken as a whole, insurers are not systemically risky, as long as they are engaged in insurance core activities (insurance underwriting, reserving, claims settlement, and reinsurance). Studies of individual insurers, based primarily on stock prices and/or credit default swap spreads, suggest that some individual insurers rank highly with respect to systemic risk measures. Of course, stock prices and credit default swap spreads reflect both core and noncore activities of insurers. This leaves open the question as to whether it is noncore activities that are causing high systemic risk measures in individual insurer studies.

PRIMARY INDICATORS AND CONTRIBUTING FACTORS FOR SYSTEMIC RISK

This analysis distinguishes between primary indicators of systemic risk and factors contributing to vulnerability to systemic risk (Financial Stability Board 2009). The primary indicators are criteria that are useful in identifying systemically risky markets and institutions, whereas the contributing factors are criteria that can be used to gauge financial vulnerabilities and the capacity of the institutional framework to deal with financial failures. That is, it is possible for an institution to be systemically important but not relatively vulnerable. This discussion provides conceptual background for the analysis of the systemic importance and vulnerability of the U.S. insurance industry.

It should be emphasized that instigating or causing a systemic crisis is not the same as being susceptible to a crisis. To instigate a systemic crisis, the shock or event must first emanate from the insurance sector due to specific activities conducted by insurers and then spread to other financial sectors and to the real economy. Thus evidence that the insurance industry did poorly in the financial crisis does not necessarily mean it is systemically important in the sense of being the cause of systemic events. Chen et al. (2014) provide empirical evidence that most insurers tend to be victims rather than propagators of systemic events.

Primary Indicators for Systemic Risk

The three primary indicators of systemic risk are: (1) size of exposures (volume of transactions or assets managed), (2) interconnectedness, and (3) lack of substitutability.[4] These factors have been identified as having a high potential for generating systemic risk; that is, they are not necessarily associated with systemic risk in every instance. This is especially true of size. For example, a large firm may not pose a systemic problem if it is not interconnected or if its products do not lack substitutes.[5] The remainder of this section discusses these indicators.

The size of an institution is frequently measured by its assets or equity, in absolute terms or relative to GDP. However, the financial crisis of 2007–2009 demonstrated that conventional balance sheet measures of size may not capture an institution's systemic importance. For example, the now-defunct Financial Products division of AIG wrote hundreds of billions of dollars of credit default swap coverage with relatively little capitalization, suggesting that notional value of derivatives exposure and potential loss to a firm's counterparties should also be considered when analyzing size. Gauges of size that may be more relevant than conventional measures are the value of off-balance-sheet (OBS) exposures of the institution and the volume of transactions it processes. Systemic risk associated with size can also arise from clusters of smaller institutions with similar business models and highly correlated assets or liabilities, such that the cluster has the systemic impact of a much larger firm.

Interconnectedness, the second primary risk factor, refers to the degree of correlation and the potential for contagion among financial institutions (i.e., the extent to which financial distress at one or a few institutions increases the probability of financial distress at other institutions because of the network of financial claims and other interrelationships). This network or chain effect operates on both sides of the balance sheet as well as through derivatives transactions, OBS commitments, and other types of relationships. The propagation of systemic problems through interconnectedness or contagion usually requires exposure to a common shock or precipitating event such as a depression in agriculture or real estate or an increase in oil prices (Kaufman and Scott 2003). In the crisis of 2007–2009, the common shock was the bursting of the housing price bubble. The housing shock triggered losses on MBSs and generated a run on the shadow banking system involving interbank lending, commercial paper, and the market for short-term repurchase agreements (repos).[6]

The third primary indicator of systemic risk is lack of substitutability, where substitutability is defined as the extent to which other institutions or segments of the financial system can provide the same services that were provided by the failed institution or institutions. In order for lack of substitutability to pose a systemic problem, the services in question must be of critical importance to the functioning of other institutions or the financial system; that is, other institutions must rely on the services to function effectively (e.g., payment and settlement systems). So, in analyzing the systemic risk of the insurance industry, it is important to determine not only whether there are adequate substitutes for insurance, but also whether insurance is actually critical for the functioning of economic markets to the same degree as the payment and settlement systems, liquidity, and short-term credit.

One quantitative indicator that captures aspects of substitutability is market concentration, measured by market shares of the leading firms or the Herfindahl index. Ease of market entry is also important, including technological, informational, and regulatory barriers that prevent new entrants from replacing the services of financially troubled firms. Qualitative evaluations of the degree to which key financial sector participants depend on specified services also are important in determining substitutability.

Contributing Factors to Systemic Risk

Although the number of factors contributing to systemic risk is potentially larger, four factors are emphasized in this discussion: (1) leverage, (2) liquidity risks and maturity mismatches, (3) complexity, and (4) government policy and regulation. These measures can be considered indicators of the vulnerability of systemically important institutions to financial distress resulting from idiosyncratic or systemwide shocks.

Leverage is an indicator of vulnerability to financial shocks and also of interconnectedness (i.e., the likelihood that an institution will propagate distress in the financial system by magnifying financial shocks). Highly levered firms are vulnerable to loss spirals, because declines in asset values erode the institution's net worth much more rapidly than its gross worth (total assets) (Brunnermeier 2009). For example, a firm with a 10-to-1 assets-to-equity ratio that loses half of its equity due to a loss of asset value would have to sell nearly half of its assets to restore its leverage ratio after the shock.[7] But selling assets after a price decline exacerbates the firm's losses. If many institutions are affected at the same time, the quest to sell assets puts additional downward pressure on prices, generating the loss spiral. Leverage can be measured in various ways, including the ratio of assets to equity or debt to equity. Ideally, a measure of leverage would include both on- and off-balance-sheet positions. Leverage can also be created through options, through buying securities on margin, or through some financial instruments.

Liquidity risk and asset-liability maturity mismatches also increase financial firm vulnerability to idiosyncratic and systemic shocks. Liquidity can be broken down into two categories: market liquidity (the tradability of an asset) and funding liquidity (the ability of the trader to fund its trades) (Brunnermeier and Pedersen 2009). Market liquidity risk arises if an institution holds large amounts of illiquid assets. Such positions are vulnerable if the institution encounters difficulties obtaining financing (funding liquidity risk), triggering the need to liquidate all or part of its asset holdings. Liquidity risk is exacerbated by the extent of an institution's asset-liability mismatch. For example, in the recent crisis, the use of short-term financing vehicles exposed the shadow banks to funding liquidity risk (i.e., the risk that investors will stop investing in commercial paper and other short-term investments), requiring the banks to liquidate positions in longer-term assets under unfavorable market conditions.

Related to liquidity is optionability or marginability of a firm's assets, liabilities, or derivatives positions. Optionability refers to the ease with which an institution's counterparties can reverse their positions and/or require the institution to post additional margin or collateral to such positions. Optionability is a function of the contractual relationships between counterparties. Some types of financial contracts (e.g., bank demand deposits) are optionable, while other types are not (e.g., P-C insurance policies). In the former case, depositors can demand their deposits at any time, whereas in the latter, the policyholder must have a legitimate claim, which is subject to an orderly settlement process.

The complexity of a financial institution and/or its asset and liability positions also can exacerbate vulnerability to financial shocks. Complexity has three important dimensions:

1. *Complexity of the organization*, including its group structure and subsidiaries. For example, diversified financial services firms offering banking, insurance, and investment products are more complex than single-industry firms.
2. *Geographical complexity.* That is, firms operating internationally are more complex than those focusing on only one or a few national markets. Multinational firms are exposed to a wider variety of local and regional risk factors as well as multijurisdiction regulatory risk.
3. *Product complexity.* Firms that are highly exposed to new and complex financial products are more vulnerable to shocks. Such products expose firms to risks that may not be completely understood.

Complexity played a major role in the AIG debacle during the financial crisis. AIG was a large and complex organization, and its Financial Products division was heavily involved in complex CDS operations without fully understanding the risks. The complexity and opacity of the organization, its geographical diversity, and its complex products impeded monitoring by both management and regulators, contributing to the crisis.

Government policy and regulation also can contribute to financial system fragility. For example, deposit insurance and insurance guaranty fund protection reduce the probability of bank or insurance runs but also create moral hazard for banks and insurers, increasing the risk of financial distress (Acharya et al. 2009). Regulation can also create other types of adverse incentives. AIG sold large quantities of CDSs to European banks that were using the contracts to reduce their required capital through regulatory arbitrage. The complexity and opacity of AIG Financial Products contributed to creating a regulatory blind spot that permitted the subsidiary to operate with excessive leverage. Further, regulation intended to enhance the solvency of the regulated financial institution actually can exacerbate a crisis. For example, an increase in capital requirements can occur in times of financial distress, resulting in asset sales or further restrictions on the ability to create credit. Thus, capital requirements can be procyclical.

PRIMARY INDICATORS AND CONTRIBUTING FACTORS FOR U.S. INSURERS: CORE ACTIVITIES

This section discusses the systemic importance of the United States insurance industry in terms of the primary indicators and contributing factors discussed in the preceding section. The focus of the section is on the core activities of insurers, that is, the functions performed in providing insurance policies and annuities, investing funds, and settling claims. We provide empirical information on whether the insurance industry poses a systemic risk in terms of its size, interconnectedness, or critical importance to the functioning of the financial system (lack of substitutability). We also consider the insolvency risk of the industry and the resolution of insurer insolvencies. Empirical information is also provided on contributing factors to systemic risk to determine the vulnerability of insurers to financial shocks. We conclude that the solvency record of the insurance industry has been excellent and that the core activities of insurers do not pose a systemic risk.

Size and Core Activities

The first primary indicator of systemic risk is size. In terms of balance sheet aggregates, insurers are smaller than banks. U.S. insurers (including life and P-C) had $7.1 trillion of assets in 2011 including separate accounts and $5.3 trillion excluding separate accounts, compared to $12.6 trillion in the banking sector. The largest U.S. insurance group, MetLife, had $612.8 billion in assets in 2011, compared with more than $2.3 trillion for the top bank, JPMorgan Chase.[8] Insurance contributes about 3.0 percent to total GDP, and insurers hold 7.8 percent of U.S. credit market debt outstanding. To see more details of the role of insurers in the securities markets, refer to Table 7.1, which shows the percentage share of banks and insurers in the markets for various types of assets. P-C insurers are not a very important source of funds in any of the asset categories shown, with the exception of municipal securities, where they account for 8.8 percent of outstanding asset holdings in 2011. Life insurers are more important, accounting for

TABLE 7.1 Holdings of Financial Assets by Insurers and Commercial Banks

Asset/Holdings	2007	2008	2009	2010	2011
Treasury securities	$5,099,199	$6,338,184	$7,781,929	$9,361,488	$10,428,308
Banks*	2.2%	1.5%	2.3%	3.0%	2.3%
Property-casualty insurers	1.4%	1.0%	1.1%	1.0%	0.9%
Life insurers	1.4%	1.7%	1.7%	1.7%	1.6%
Agency and GSE† securities	$7,397,749	$8,166,697	$8,106,793	$7,598,157	$7,577,392
Banks*	16.1%	16.1%	18.1%	20.6%	22.0%
Property-casualty insurers	1.7%	1.4%	1.4%	1.5%	1.6%
Life insurers	5.2%	4.5%	4.6%	4.9%	5.1%
Municipal securities	$3,448,076	$3,543,420	$3,697,882	$3,795,591	$3,743,366
Banks*	5.9%	6.3%	6.2%	6.8%	8.0%
Property-casualty insurers	10.8%	10.8%	10.0%	9.2%	8.8%
Life insurers	1.2%	1.3%	2.0%	3.0%	3.3%
Corporate and foreign bonds	$11,543,006	$11,118,323	$11,576,850	$11,538,517	$11,586,995
Banks*	9.4%	9.5%	7.9%	6.8%	6.8%
Property-casualty insurers	2.5%	2.4%	2.6%	2.8%	3.1%
Life insurers	16.1%	16.3%	16.6%	17.6%	18.4%
Corporate equities	$25,580,900	$15,640,457	$20,123,185	$23,249,520	$22,522,227
Banks*	0.3%	0.2%	0.3%	0.3%	0.3%
Property-casualty insurers	0.9%	1.2%	1.1%	0.9%	1.0%
Life insurers	5.7%	6.4%	6.0%	6.0%	6.4%

(continued)

TABLE 7.1 *(Continued)*

Asset/Holdings	2007	2008	2009	2010	2011
Multifamily residential mortgages	$784,628	$837,675	$846,965	$837,772	$844,214
Banks*	33.3%	33.5%	32.0%	30.8%	29.8%
Property-casualty insurers	0.0%	0.0%	0.0%	0.0%	0.0%
Life insurers	6.6%	6.2%	5.7%	5.6%	5.9%
Commercial mortgages	$2,447,855	$2,566,445	$2,478,077	$2,314,001	$2,232,357
Banks*	54.9%	56.8%	57.3%	57.0%	56.2%
Property-casualty insurers	0.2%	0.2%	0.2%	0.2%	0.2%
Life insurers	10.3%	10.4%	10.4%	10.9%	11.8%

*Includes U.S.-chartered depository institutions, foreign banking offices in the United States, and banks in U.S.-affiliated areas. Credit unions are excluded.
†GSE = government-sponsored enterprise.
Note: Asset holdings are in millions of dollars.
Source: Federal Reserve Flow of Funds Accounts (Washington, DC: Board of Governors of the Federal Reserve System).

18.4 percent of corporate and foreign bonds, 11.8 percent of commercial mortgages, and 6.4 percent of equities in 2011.

However, because insurer insolvency resolutions are orderly and take place over lengthy periods of time, the amount of assets that would be liquidated in even the largest insurer insolvency would be small relative to securities markets. The failure rates of U.S. insurers and commercial banks are shown in Figure 7.1. This table confirms that life insurers and banks were much more strongly affected by the financial crisis than were P-C insurers.[9] The bank failure rate increased by a factor of 10, from 0.2 percent in 2007 to 1.9 percent in 2009–2010 and recovered somewhat to 1.6 percent in 2011. The life insurer failure rate rose by a factor of five from 0.19 percent in 2006 to 0.94 percent in 2009 but declined to 0.14 percent by 2011. By contrast, the P-C failure rate in 2009–2010 was about the same as the failure rate in 2005–2006. During the crisis, the P-C failure rate remained significantly below earlier peaks in 1989 to 1993 and from 2000 to 2003, which were driven by catastrophic events such as Hurricane Andrew and the 2001 terrorist attacks. Thus, historically, underwriting events have created more insolvency risk for P-C insurers than financial crises have, whereas banks and life insurers are more susceptible to financial market shocks. The bivariate correlations of the failure rates for the three types of institutions are statistically significant, providing evidence of susceptibility to common shocks (see Figure 7.1). Failure rates of the two types of insurers are more highly correlated with each other than with bank failure rates.

Insurers that are seriously financially impaired are handled in one of two ways in the United States. The insurer may be placed into receivership while the liabilities are "run off."[10] Note that loss payments under policies do not actually become due until some point in the future (often years), so the receiver operates the insurer to pay off (or run off) losses as they actually come due. This spreads the effect of the insolvency over several future years. Alternatively, especially for life insurers, the business of the insolvent insurer may be sold to another insurer, with the policies continued under the new insurer.[11] For a life insurer insolvency resolved by selling the insolvent insurer's business to another insurer, the guaranty fund (described shortly) assesses an amount sufficient to make the sale attractive to the acquirer.

In P-C insurance, it is necessary to have a valid claim, which is processed through an orderly settlement process, in order to obtain payment from the insurer. Some claims on life insurers do represent withdrawable assets, and there is some risk that many policyholders would surrender their policies as an insurer becomes financially distressed, causing a liquidity problem. However, insolvent insurers typically have substantial assets on hand to cover liabilities when they fail, because losses are prepaid through premiums. Thus liquidation of assets at distressed prices usually does not

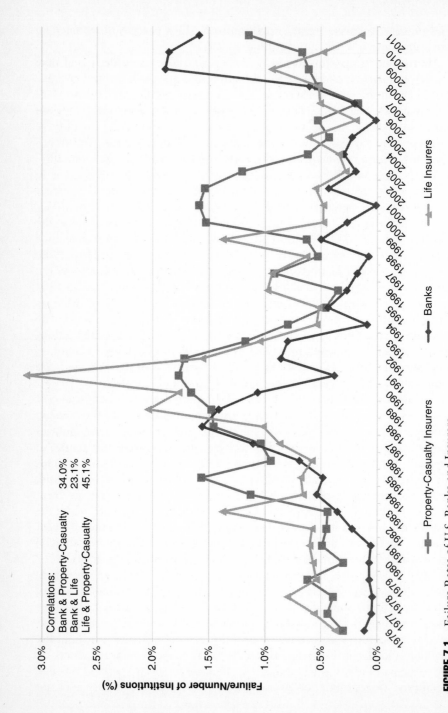

FIGURE 7.1 Failure Rates of U.S. Banks and Insurers

Sources: A.M. Best Company (2012a, 2012b), Federal Deposit Insurance Corporation.

occur, nor are immediate settlements to all policyholders made at the time of bankruptcy.[12]

In many countries, a safety net exists to provide protection for policy-holders of insolvent insurers in the form of guaranty funds. Each state in the United States operates a life insurance guaranty fund and at least one P-C guaranty fund. The typical funding approach in the United States is *ex post* assessment[13]—solvent insurers are assessed each year to cover shortfalls in loss payments for insolvent insurers subject to annual maxima. There are restrictions on guaranty fund coverage (e.g., on maximum loss payable), and coverage generally does not apply to all lines of business.[14]

U.S. guaranty fund coverage and the state regulatory solvency resolution system in general apply to insurance companies that are U.S. licensed and regulated. Hence the creditors of AIG Financial Products were not covered by U.S. guaranty funds. If any of AIG's U.S.-licensed insurance subsidiaries had become insolvent as the result of their asset lending operations, the policyholders of the insurers but not the asset lending counterparties would have been covered by guaranty funds.

The assessment system is designed to place minimal stress on solvent insurers while protecting the policyholders of insolvent insurers. Guaranty funds in the United States have the ability to borrow against future assess-ments if losses covered by the guaranty fund in any one year would place a financial strain on solvent insurers. U.S. guaranty funds have successfully paid claims of several large insolvent insurers, including Reliance, Executive Life, and Mutual Benefit Life. In 2010, the maximum annual assessment capacity of life insurers was $10.3 billion, and the assessment capacity of P-C guaranty funds was $6.7 billion.[15] Insolvencies larger than the annual assessment capacity could be financed because insurer insolvencies tend to be resolved over several years and because the shortfall between liabilities and assets typically is not very large.[16] Thus, assessments would be likely to continue until all claims are paid (Gallanis 2009).

Table 7.2 provides statistics regarding guaranty fund assessments for the period 1988 to 2010. Because of the orderly resolution of insurer insolvencies, guaranty funds assessments in both life and P-C insurance historically have been quite small. The total amounts of assessments from life-health and P-C guar-anty funds from 1988 to 2010 were $6.3 billion and $12.5 billion, respectively; and the average annual assessments were $276 million for life insurers and $544 million for P-C insurers. Annual assessments never exceeded 0.35 percent of total premiums for either life-health or P-C insurers. Thus, historically, the guaranty fund system has stood up very well; but the system has never been required to deal with a widespread solvency crisis in insurance markets.

In summary, with respect to size, insolvency resolutions are orderly and take place over lengthy periods of time; hence, the amount of assets that

TABLE 7.2 Solvency Record and Guaranty Fund Assessments, 1988–2010

Year	Life-Health				Property-Casualty			
	No. of Failures	Failure Rate	Assessments ($ Millions)	Assessments % of Premiums	No. of Failures	Failure Rate	Assessments ($ Millions)	Assessments % of Premiums
1988	27	1.02%	80	0.0351	48	1.46%	465	0.2298
1989	55	2.04%	103	0.0421	49	1.48%	714	0.3418
1990	47	1.77%	198	0.0748	55	1.66%	434	0.1988
1991	82	3.14%	529	0.2006	60	1.77%	435	0.1948
1992	39	1.56%	735	0.2607	59	1.72%	384	0.1685
1993	25	1.05%	632	0.1977	41	1.18%	520	0.2152
1994	12	0.54%	843	0.2493	28	0.80%	498	0.1985
1995	11	0.52%	876	0.2493	16	0.46%	67	0.0256
1996	20	0.98%	574	0.1519	12	0.35%	95	0.0355
1997	18	0.94%	448	0.1104	32	0.92%	236	0.0854
1998	12	0.63%	275	0.0620	17	0.53%	239	0.0843
1999	26	1.38%	167	0.0341	20	0.63%	179	0.0620
2000	9	0.48%	149	0.0275	48	1.53%	306	0.1012

Year									
2001	9	0.48%	129	0.0268	49	1.59%	713	0.2168
2002	10	0.55%	71	0.0138	47	1.54%	1,184	0.3125
2003	5	0.28%	33	0.0064	37	1.21%	874	0.2106
2004	6	0.34%	90	0.0166	19	0.62%	953	0.2182
2005	10	0.61%	78	0.0145	13	0.43%	836	0.1910
2006	3	0.19%	25	0.0043	16	0.53%	1,344	0.2966
2007	8	0.51%	80	0.0132	5	0.17%	943	0.2085
2008	9	0.52%	58	0.0090	16	0.53%	385	0.0867
2009	13	0.94%	125	0.0240	19	0.61%	478	0.1122
2010	7	0.48%	42	0.0073	21	0.67%	219	0.0510
Totals	463		6,340		727		12,503	
Average	20.1	0.91%	276	0.0796	31.6	0.97%	544	0.1672

Note: The failure rate is the number of insolvencies divided by the total number of insurers. Assessments % of premiums is guaranty fund assessments divided by total insurance premiums for life-health and property-casualty insurers, respectively. Life-health assessments are "called" minus "refunded."

Sources: A.M. Best Company (2012a, 2012b); National Conference of Insurance Guaranty Funds; National Organization of Life & Health Insurance Guaranty Associations; American Council of Life Insurers, *Life Insurers Fact Book 2011.*

would be liquidated in even the largest insurer insolvency would be small relative to securities markets. Therefore, in terms of their core activities, insurers are not large enough to be systemically important, although the failure of a large insurer, such as a large subsidiary of MetLife, could cause significant dislocations in *insurance* markets and possibly strain the liquidity of insurance guaranty funds.

Interconnectedness and Core Activities

Insurance core activities do not seem to be systemically important in terms of the second primary indicator, interconnectedness. Unlike in many European countries, the cross-holdings of stocks and bonds between the U.S. insurance and U.S. banking industries are small, and neither industry provides a significant source of financing for the other. Thus, a commercial paper–like credit crunch arising from the U.S. insurance industry is highly unlikely.

That is, in 2010, bank bonds represented only 5.4 percent of the bond portfolios of P-C insurers, and bonds of other financial firms represented only 1.2 percent of P-C bonds.[17] Banking and financial firm bonds represent 11.4 percent of equity for P-C insurers. Thus, defaults by financial firms do not pose a serious threat to P-C insurers. Life insurers have 8 percent of their bond portfolios invested in bank bonds and 1.7 percent invested in the bonds of other financial firms. Bank and finance bonds represent 62.1 percent of equity for life insurers. Hence, life insurers do face a potential threat from bond defaults by financial firms, although massive defaults would have to occur in order to pose an industry-wide threat to solvency. In 2008, less than 1 percent of stocks held by U.S. insurers were invested in bank stocks and a negligible proportion in stocks of securities firms.

Regarding the importance of insurers as sources of funds for other financial institutions, U.S. insurers held approximately 9.4 percent of banks' "other borrowed money" in 2008. However, borrowed money is not the primary source of financing to banks, amounting to less than 10 percent of liabilities. U.S. insurers held 14.1 percent of securities firms' outstanding corporate bond debt in 2008, but bonds represent only 11.2 percent of securities firms' financings (liabilities). U.S. insurers hold only negligible portions of securities firms' and banks' stock outstanding. Hence, interconnectedness risk from security holdings in other types of financial firms does not seem to be a significant problem for U.S. insurers.[18]

Also with respect to interconnectedness, the bank failure rate has a bivariate correlation of 34 percent with the P-C insurer failure rate and 23 percent with life insurers, suggesting that banks and insurers are somewhat interconnected with respect to susceptibility to common economic and financial shocks. Chen et al. (2014) find that banks create significant systemic risk for insurers but not vice versa (i.e., suggesting that insurers are victims rather than propagators of systemic risk).

To provide further information on interconnectedness in the U.S. insurance industry, the principal triggering events for life and P-C insurer insolvencies are shown in Table 7.3 for the period 1969 to 2011. Table 7.3 shows that life insurers have been vulnerable to interconnectedness with affiliates—affiliate problems are associated with 18.1 percent of life insurer failures. Life insurers are also susceptible to asset quality issues—investment problems trigger 15 percent of insolvencies. The primary triggers of life insurance insolvencies arise from bad management decisions such as underpricing (29.1 percent of insolvencies), excessive growth (14.1 percent of insolvencies), and alleged fraud (8.8 percent of insolvencies). Likewise, for P-C insurers, underpricing, excessive growth, and fraud together account for 62.5 percent of insolvencies. Interconnectedness with reinsurers and affiliates together are the triggering events for 11.5 percent of P-C insurer insolvencies.[19] Unlike life insurers, P-C insurers are vulnerable to natural catastrophes, which account for 7.1 percent of failures. Therefore, except perhaps for life insurer affiliate problems, interconnectedness has not been a major cause of insurer insolvencies.

As a final comment on relationships with noninsurance corporations, life insurer participation in markets for products such as group annuities

TABLE 7.3 Insurer Insolvencies: Primary Triggering Events, Life-Health Insurers and Property-Casualty Insurers, 1969–2011

	Life-Health	Property-Casualty
Inadequate pricing/deficient loss reserves	29.1%	41.9%
Affiliate problems	18.1%	8.3%
Investment problems (overstated assets)	15.0%	7.0%
Excessive growth	14.1%	13.1%
Alleged fraud	8.8%	7.5%
Miscellaneous	8.1 %	8.3%
Catastrophe losses	NA	7.1%
Significant business change	4.5%	3.6%
Reinsurance failure	2.1 %	3.2%
Average number of failures per year	16.9	25.8

Note: Data are only on companies where the cause of impairment was identified.
Source: A.M. Best Company (2012c, 2012d).

and separate accounts may create interconnectedness risk. In terms of these products, life insurers are often dealing with large corporate clients that control large blocks of assets, and such products are susceptible to withdrawals and other interruptions of cash flows during a crisis. Further research is needed to determine the relationship between various life insurance products and systemic risk.

Interconnection risk for core activities *within* the insurance industry is considerably higher than between insurance and banking, although risk confined within a specific sector is not systemic by definition. In particular, reinsurance is the primary source of interconnectedness within the insurance industry. Although past research indicates that reinsurance has not been an overriding cause of insolvencies in the past (see Table 7.3 and the literature review section of this paper), the reinsurance market has become increasingly concentrated over time, through mergers and acquisitions and organic growth (Cummins and Weiss 2000; Cummins 2007).

In addition, interlocking relationships permeate the industry, such that reinsurers retrocede (or resell) reinsurance to other reinsurers, who then retrocede business to still other reinsurers in a pattern reminiscent of the counterparty interrelationships that brought down the shadow banking system.[20] Thus, the reinsurance market is vulnerable to a retrocession spiral whereby the failure of major reinsurers triggers the failure of their reinsurance counterparties, who in turn default on their obligations to primary insurers, resulting in a crisis permeating the insurance industry on a worldwide scale. An example of a reinsurance spiral is the London Market Excess (LMX) spiral that unfolded in the late 1980s and early 1990s (Neyer 1990). Baluch, Mutenga, and Parsons (2011) argue that if Lloyds had failed, the lack of cover for the types of risks typically underwritten by Lloyds would have caused "significant economic disruption." Thus analysis of reinsurance counterparty relationships is important in understanding systemic risk in insurance.

Insurers conduct reinsurance transactions with both affiliates and nonaffiliates. Although nonaffiliate reinsurance is generally considered to pose more counterparty risk than affiliate reinsurance, the analysis of insurer insolvency history shows that affiliate problems also can pose an insolvency threat to insurers. Therefore, this analysis considers reinsurance with both affiliates and nonaffiliates. The analysis also focuses on primary insurer cessions into the reinsurance market rather than reinsurance assumed.[21] Ceding reinsurance creates more counterparty risk than assuming reinsurance because the ceding insurer is dependent upon the reinsurer to pay claims. Additionally, the reinsurance counterparty usually holds the funds, unlike reinsurance assumed, where the assuming insurer usually holds the funds.

Several important financial statement variables measure an insurer's exposure to reinsurance counterparty risk. One measure that is important in both life and P-C insurance is reinsurance premiums ceded. Reinsurance receivables, which represent funds currently owed to the insurer under reinsurance transactions, are also an important measure of exposure.[22] One of the benefits of buying reinsurance is that the buyer is generally permitted to reduce its reserve liabilities to the extent of the reinsurer's liability, improving its leverage ratio and expanding its capacity to write insurance.[23] For life insurers, the result of the write-down is called the *reserve credit taken*, which represents estimated liabilities of the primary insurer that have been assumed by the reinsurer; and for P-C insurers the account is called *net amount recoverable* from reinsurers.[24] Because policyholder claims on an insurer are not affected by reinsurance, the insurer remains liable for the policyholder obligations if the reinsurer defaults even though the balance sheet credit for reinsurance can be substantial.

Life insurers ceded $60.4 billion in premiums to nonaffiliates and $78.1 billion to affiliates in 2011, representing in total 20.2 percent of direct premiums written and 43.4 percent of surplus. P-C insurers ceded $69.6 billion of premiums to nonaffiliates and $38.8 billion to affiliates, representing in total 21.6 percent of direct premiums and 18.9 percent of surplus. Hence, life insurers' surplus exposure to reinsurance counterparty risk is higher than for P-C insurers, but counterparty risk from premiums ceded does not seem excessive for either type of insurer.

Reinsurance receivables represent about 12 percent of equity capital for life insurers and 7.5 percent of equity for P-C insurers. Hence, purely in terms of current receivables, insurer equity is not seriously exposed to counterparty risk. However, when the reinsurance counterparty exposure for estimated future losses and benefits is included, the total is much higher. For life insurers, the reserve credit taken due to transactions with nonaffiliated reinsurers is 65.7 percent of surplus, and the credit taken for affiliate reinsurance is 97 percent of surplus. P-C insurers are less exposed to nonaffiliated reinsurers in terms of the net reinsurance recoverable than life insurers (25.3 percent of surplus) and have even less net exposure to affiliated reinsurers (14.9 percent of surplus).[25] Thus, the degree of interconnectedness within the insurance industry due to reinsurance is significant, particularly for life insurance. However, this risk likely is not systemic in the sense of spilling over into other financial sectors. Cummins and Weiss (2014) provide more detailed concentration information for reinsurance from 2008. According to their results, at the median, P-C insurers cede 9.1 percent of direct and assumed premiums to the top four nonaffiliated reinsurers. Concentration of recoverables in the top counterparties is high. The proportion of the total recoverables owed by the top one, four, and 10 counterparties at the median is 47.4 percent.

90.5 percent, and 100 percent, respectively. The Herfindahl index for recoverables at the median is 3,248, approximately equivalent to having recoverables equally divided among three counterparties.

Exposure of surplus to reinsurance recoverable from nonaffiliates varies widely across the P-C industry according to Cummins and Weiss (2014). At the median, exposure does not seem excessive; the ratio of reinsurance recoverable to surplus for all counterparties is 21 percent. At the 75th percentile, reinsurance recoverable to surplus from all counterparties is 52.2 percent. Therefore, it appears from these statistics that at least one-fourth of P-C insurers could be seriously at risk if several large reinsurers were to fail.

Park and Xie (2011) conducted the first detailed examination on the likely impact of a major global reinsurer insolvency on the U.S. P-C insurance industry by running scenario analyses, in which one of the top three reinsurers (Swiss Re, Munich Re, and Berkshire Hathaway) is allowed to become insolvent. They traced the effects of the reinsurer defaults as they flow through the industry, using financial statement data on reinsurance counterparty relationships. Even under an extreme assumption of a 100 percent reinsurance recoverable default by one of the top three global P-C reinsurers, only about 2 percent of U.S. P-C primary insurers would suffer financial ratings downgrades and only 1 percent of insurers would become insolvent. Hence, the potential for reinsurance problems in the P-C industry does not seem high.

The exposure to nonaffiliated reinsurance counterparties in the life insurance industry is discussed in Cummins and Weiss (2014), also. Life insurance premium cessions are even more concentrated in the top counterparties than for P-C insurers. At the median, 53.0 percent of premiums are ceded to the top reinsurer, 93.5 percent to the top four reinsurers, and 100.0 percent to the top 10. The ratios of reserve credit taken to surplus at the median are not very high (e.g., 20.9 percent for the top four reinsurers and 24.5 percent for all reinsurers). However, a substantial proportion of companies in the industry have very high ratios of reserve credit taken to surplus; at the 75th percentile, the ratio is 58.2 percent for the top reinsurer and 100.3 percent for the top four reinsurers. Thus, at least 25 percent of life insurers would find their surplus severely eroded if an intrasector crisis developed in the reinsurance industry.

In conclusion, an insolvency crisis in the reinsurance market could potentially cause intrasector problems in the insurance industry. Nevertheless, purely from their core activities, insurers are not sufficiently interconnected with noninsurance institutions such that the reinsurance problems would spill over into the banking and securities industries. However, a reinsurance crisis could potentially cause spillover risk due to interconnectedness of insurers and other institutions through insurers' noncore activities (and this is discussed later).

Lack of Substitutability and Core Activities

For an activity to pose a systemic threat to lack of substitutability, it is necessary not only that the activity not have substitutes but also that it is critical to the functioning of the economy. Banks pose substitutability problems because of their role in the payment and settlement systems, in transmitting central bank monetary policy, and in providing a critical source of liquidity and financing for consumers and businesses. Although insurance plays an important role in the economy, it does not suffer from lack of substitutability to the same extent as banking.

The bulk of financial transactions in life insurance relate to asset accumulation products rather than mortality/longevity risk bearing, and there are many substitutes for investing through life insurance, and annuities. For mortality/longevity risks, which are unique to insurance, many insurers are available to fill coverage gaps created by the failure of one or a few firms, and hedging mortality risk is not central to the economy as are payments settlement or monetary policy. Thus, life insurance has substitutes and is not critical to the functioning of other firms.

Unlike life insurance, P-C insurance exists primarily to provide risk management and risk-bearing services rather than serving an asset accumulation function. Certainly for individual insurance customers, there is no substitute for products such as automobile and homeowners insurance. However, even if the supply of individual P-C products was dramatically reduced, it is unlikely that real economic activity would be affected significantly. Even if several major insurers were to encounter severe financial difficulties, many other insurers are available to fill the coverage gap. The same would be true for small and medium-sized commercial buyers. Large corporate buyers have many effective substitutes for P-C insurance, including self-insurance, captive insurance companies, and securitization of insurance-type risks. There has been considerable debate in the finance literature about whether widely held corporations should even buy insurance, other than to access the risk management and claims-settlement expertise of insurers and perform other corporate risk management functions (MacMinn and Garven 2000). Thus, lack of substitutability does not seem to create a systemic risk as it relates to insurance. Because of the dominance of large insurers in the (non-UK) European market, substitutability may be more of a problem for P-C insurance there.

Nonetheless, some P-C insurance lines were harder hit by the financial crisis than other lines. These harder-hit lines include errors and omissions (E&O) insurance and directors and officers (D&O) liability. AIG, Chubb, XL, and Lloyds of London are large writers of these coverages. Estimating the cost of such claims is very difficult because claims are hard to prove. However, there appears to be no shortage of supply in these lines at the present time, although prices for these products have risen. Credit insurance is another type of coverage hit hard by the crisis. According to Baluch, Mutenga, and Parsons (2011), the economic downturn was reinforced by a decline in the supply of credit insurance. In fact, several governments, concerned about the availability of credit insurance, have taken actions to safeguard credit insurance and trading activity.

Of course, even for those functions that are unique to insurance, ease of entry into the insurance industry means that supply is unlikely to be disrupted for a significant period of time. Berry-Stölzle, Nini, and Wende (2011) show that substantial new capital flowed into the life insurance industry in response to the financial crisis, and Cummins (2008) shows that there has been substantial entry into the P-C insurance market, particularly in Bermuda.

Contributing Factors and Core Activities

Except for some of the core activities of life insurers, most of the core activities of insurers generally do not lead to the identification of insurers as systemically important according to the primary indicators. Accordingly, the discussion of the contributing factors mainly relates to their role in creating financial vulnerabilities within the insurance industry. In this respect, we consider life and P-C insurers separately, except for regulation, where we discuss the regulatory framework more generally.

Leverage   Defining leverage as the ratio of capital to assets, P-C insurers are much more highly capitalized than life insurers or banks, and their capital-to-assets ratios have been increasing over time. The capital-to-assets ratio for P-C insurers was 27.8 percent in 1985, increasing to 39.6 percent by 2011. Of course, one reason P-C insurers hold more capital than life insurers or banks is that they are subject to catastrophe risk from events such as hurricanes and earthquakes. Life insurer capital-to-assets ratios are comparable to those of banks, both of which have been running at about 10 percent. Berry-Stölzle, Nini, and Wende (2011) found that life insurers were able to recover quickly from losses sustained during the financial crisis by raising new capital, and insurer failure rates and guaranty fund assessments remain very low. Life insurers' reserve credit taken (162.7 percent of surplus on average) represents additional leverage that would come back onto life insurer balance sheets in the event of reinsurance failures. Thus, life insurers have the potential for significantly higher leverage due to reinsurer defaults. However, reinsurer defaults have not played a significant role historically in causing insurer insolvencies, and no such defaults occurred during the financial crisis.

Liquidity Risk   Life insurers have high liquidity risk due to their heavy investment in privately placed bonds. Total holdings of private placements represent 25.6 percent of life insurer bond portfolios and 209.5 percent of equity capital as of 2011. In addition, life insurers hold 26.5 percent of their bonds (19 percent of assets) in MBSs and other ABSs, including pass-through collateralized mortgage obligations (CMOs) and real estate mortgage investment conduits (REMICs). The amounts invested in MBSs and ABSs represent 216.6 percent of life insurer equity capital (policyholders surplus). Thus, MBSs, ABSs, and single-issuer private placements represent 378.5 percent of life insurer surplus. These numbers are relevant because ABSs and MBSs were especially problematical during the financial crisis, and private placements are relatively illiquid.

Somewhat offsetting their asset liquidity risk, life insurers receive a significant amount of net cash from operations, defined as premiums plus investment income net of benefit payments, expenses, and taxes. Life insurers' net cash from operations represents 30.6 percent of benefit payments and 49.5 percent of equity capital as of 2011. Thus, life insurers could withstand significant increases in benefit payments without liquidating assets, partially explaining their heavy concentration of investments in privately placed bonds. However, it is not clear whether the coverage of cash flow to surplus is sufficient to completely offset their asset liquidity risk.

P-C insurers are much less exposed to mortgage-backed securities and privately placed bonds. For P-C insurers, MBS and ABS securities represent only 30.6 percent of surplus, and private placements represent only 12.9 percent of surplus in 2011. Hence, life insurers face higher exposure to housing markets and significant asset liquidity risk, in comparison with P-C insurers.

Complexity and Asset-Liability Mismatches   Life insurers also suffer from complexity, especially in terms of offering life insurance and annuity products with embedded options such as minimum interest rate guarantees. Life insurers are at least moderately exposed to optionability risk, due to the ability of policyholders to cash out their life insurance annuity policies. As mentioned, group annuities and separate accounts may be particularly susceptible to optionability risk, which may help to explain their association with systemic risk. The only contributing factor that does not seem to be a problem for life insurers is maturity risk, in that their asset and liability maturities seem to be well matched (see Cummins and Weiss 2014).

P-C insurers' core activities have low to moderate complexity, in comparison with complex banking products and life insurance products with

embedded options. P-C insurers are vulnerable to catastrophe risk but
have been able to withstand large catastrophes such as Hurricanes Andrew
and Katrina. P-C insurers' vulnerability to intrasector crises appears low,
although some insurers do have high exposure to nonaffiliated reinsurance.

Government Regulation   U.S. insurance regulation prevented insurers from
engaging in the dramatic increases in leverage that occurred for the shadow
banks during the period preceding the crisis. The effectiveness of regulation is demonstrated by the low insurance insolvency rates in the United
States. Although U.S. regulation is balkanized and the cumbersome regulatory structure often impedes necessary reforms, federal bank regulators did
not perform well in the period leading up to the financial crisis, and it is not
clear that federal regulators would be more effective than state regulators.
Although the lack of a single overseer does create problems in managing
multistate insolvency risk (Acharya et al. 2009), nationally significant insurers are reviewed every quarter by the NAIC, and those that appear to be
performing poorly are prioritized for further analysis by experienced regulators (the Financial Analysis Working Group).

Moral hazard could be created by the existence of insurance guaranty
funds because guaranty fund premiums are not risk-based (Acharya et al.
2009). This feature of guaranty funds can lead to excessive risk taking by
insurers. However, moral hazard is mitigated somewhat by the fact that
insurance guaranty funds have claim payment limits, giving policyholders
an incentive to monitor insurers. Hence, more market discipline is present
for insurers than for other financial institutions such as banks (Harrington
2009). Moreover, the NAIC's risk-based capital system penalizes insurers
that take excessive risk, further reducing incentives for risk taking.

SYSTEMIC RISK AND NONCORE ACTIVITIES

The core activities of P-C insurance companies involve providing various
types of insurance coverage. The core activities of life insurers include providing asset-accumulation products to consumers and businesses as well
as insurance against mortality and longevity risk. In addition to their core
products, insurers also have undertaken a variety of noncore activities. Some
of these activities have the potential to create interconnectedness with other
financial institutions and nonfinancial sectors of the economy and thereby
foster systemic risk.

Although insurer involvement in noncore activities is usually associated
with the passage of the Gramm-Leach-Bliley Act in 1999, insurers expanded
their operations beyond traditional core insurance products decades earlier.[26]

Insurers have invested in privately placed bonds at least since the 1970s, in direct competition with the bond underwriting functions of investment banks, and also in competition with banks in commercial mortgages. Life insurers introduced guaranteed investment contracts (GICs) and single-premium deferred annuities in the 1970s, competing directly with bank certificates of deposit. Beginning in the 1970s, many insurers also introduced proprietary mutual fund families to compete with banks and securities firms. Insurers also engage in investment management for consumer and business clients. Following passage of the Gramm-Leach-Bliley Act, a few insurers also acquired or established thrift institutions to offer banking services. Insurers have expanded into the provision of financial guarantees, asset lending, and credit default swaps (CDSs), as well as investing in ABSs, MBSs, and other complex structured securities. Insurers are active in trading derivatives such as foreign exchange and interest rate options. Insurers have entered the market for securitization, most prominently for catastrophe-linked securities, but also for other types of risks.[27] Some of these activities, such as writing CDSs and providing financial guarantees, contribute to systemic risk, while others such as investing in MBSs and ABSs mainly increase the susceptibility of insurers to crises.

Detailed quantitative information on insurer noncore activities is not readily available. However, aggregate data on outstanding CDSs by counterparty type are available from the Bank for International Settlements (BIS). The BIS data reveal that total CDSs outstanding were $58.2 trillion in the second half of 2007, declining to $29.9 trillion by 2010 as a result of the financial crisis. The majority of CDSs were held by reporting dealers, mainly large commercial and investment banks that have an active business with large customers (BIS 2007). Insurers held $492 billion in CDSs outstanding in 2007 and $270 billion in 2010. Thus, insurers have remained active in the CDS market even after the AIG debacle. Although insurers represent a small part of the CDS market, $270 billion is a large exposure relative to industry capitalization.

Insurers can be at risk from selling CDSs, but insurers also purchase protection products to hedge risk from their own investment holdings (bonds and stocks), exposing insurers to counterparty credit risk. CDSs are frequently sold in the secondary market, so that a CDS may change hands many times (Baluch, Mutenga, and Parsons 2011). It can turn out to be difficult to identify the counterparty to the trade in case of default so that unwinding the trade becomes difficult. Thus, insurers can experience significant credit risk, especially if the asset has a high notional value relative to assets.

Recent research on the stock prices of financial institutions provides evidence on the degree of interconnectedness within the financial industry. Billio et al. (2012) develop econometric measures of systemic risk and analyze stock price data on hedge funds, banks, brokers, and insurers for the period 1994–2008. They examine index returns on the four groups of financial institutions as well as the returns of the 25 largest entities in each group. They utilize principal components analysis to study the correlations among the four groups of institutions and Granger causality tests to analyze the direction of the relationships among the sample firms. They do not observe significant causal relationships between financial institutions in the first part of the sample period (1994–2000) but find that financial institutions have become significantly linked during the second part of the sample period (2001–2008). They find that the relationships are asymmetrical—the returns of banks and insurers have a more significant impact on hedge funds and brokers than vice versa. Insurers identified as systemically important include ACE Group, AIG, Progressive, and XL Capital. Billio et al. attribute the growing interrelationships among institutions to the existence of frictions in the financial system, including "value-at-risk constraints, transactions costs, borrowing constraints, costs of gathering and processing information, and institutional restrictions on short sales" (Billio et al. 2012, 10).

Acharya et al. (2010) developed an alternative measure of systemic risk, the *systemic expected shortfall* (SES), which gauges the propensity of a financial institution to be undercapitalized when the system as a whole is undercapitalized. Specifically, SES measures the amount by which a financial institution's capital drops below its target level conditional on the occurrence of a financial crisis. "SES is therefore the probability of an aggregate crisis times the conditional loss . . . in such a crisis. The important point is that the expectation is conditional on a macroeconomic shortfall" (Acharya et al. 2010, 14).

They analyze the stocks of the 102 financial institutions that had market capitalization exceeding $5 billion as of June 2007, including four financial industry segments: depository institutions (29 firms), securities dealers and commodities brokers (10 firms), insurance companies (36 firms), and other financial institutions (27 firms). The period of analysis is 2006–2008. Their results indicated that "insurance firms are overall the least systemically risky, next were depository institutions and most systemically risky are the securities dealers and brokers" (Acharya et al. 2010, 21). In terms of specific insurers, AIG appears "more systemic" than Berkshire Hathaway. They also point out that the top three insurance companies in terms of systemic risk (Genworth, Ambac, and MBIA) were heavily involved in providing financial guarantees for structured products in the credit derivatives market.

Billio et al. (2012) and Acharya et al. (2010) reveal that financial firms are highly interconnected and that insurance firms can be a source of systemic risk.

These studies strongly suggest that the interconnectedness among institutions extends beyond exposure to common shocks. The analysis presented in our chapter suggests that any systemic risk originating from the insurance sector is not attributable to the core activities of insurers, with the exception of certain life insurance products. Rather, the interconnectedness between insurers and other financial firms is more likely attributable to the noncore or banklike activities of insurers, particularly large, publicly traded firms. Also playing a role are the financial market frictions identified by Billio et al. (2012).

In the next section, the measure of systemic risk discussed in Acharya, Engle, and Richardson (2012), SRISK, is analyzed for a sample of insurer groups. Factors associated with SRISK are identified for purposes of understanding what may make insurers prone to systemic risk.

STATISTICAL ANALYSIS OF INSURER CHARACTERISTICS AND A MEASURE OF SYSTEMIC RISK

In this section, correlation analysis and regression analysis are conducted to determine the relationship between characteristics of an insurer sample and a measure of systemic risk, SRISK (Acharya, Engle, and Richardson 2012). SRISK is defined as the expected capital shortfall of the firm in a financial crisis. It is related to SES but extracts the probability of a crisis occurring and focuses only on the expected capital shortfall (Acharya, Engle, and Richardson 2012, 60). SRISK is estimated using data on daily equity returns on the stocks of financial firms and on a broad market index. Bivariate time series models are estimated using the daily stock return series. Simulations are then conducted to estimate the losses of equity capital in the event of future crises. A crisis is defined as a situation where the broad market index declines by 40 percent over the next six months (Acharya, Engle, and Richardson, 2012, 60–61).

Although the SRISK is commonly referred to as a measure of systemic risk, it cannot be used to distinguish between whether insurers are instigators of crises or merely victims of crises. That is, it only measures the extent to which a firm is undercapitalized when the market as a whole is undercapitalized. To determine whether insurers cause crises, a different type of analysis is necessary such as Granger causality.[28] Nevertheless, it is important for investors and regulators to understand how a firm will respond in a crisis (e.g., its tendency to be undercapitalized) regardless of who or what instigated the crisis. SRISK provides such a measure.

The data used in the analysis are described in the next subsection. The results of the statistical analysis are provided in the following subsections beginning with correlation analysis.

Data

Data for the analysis are obtained from various sources. Data on derivatives activity are hand collected from the 10-K reports of insurers analyzed by Acharya et al. (2010). This includes the total fair value of derivatives, the notional amount of derivatives not used for hedging, the total notional amount of derivatives, and the capital-to-assets ratio. NAIC data from insurers' annual statements are also obtained, particularly information on premiums by lines of business and investment allocations (e.g., amount of MBS) and whether the insurer is a life insurer or a P-C insurer, or conducts both types of business. These data are combined with data from Compustat that contain information on liabilities of the traded company. Finally, the measure of systemic risk (SRISK) and the beta for the traded company are obtained from New York University.[29]

Correlation Analysis

We conducted correlation analysis between the SRISK systemic risk measure and insurer characteristics. Because SRISK is the conditional capital shortfall, it is dollar denominated and scaled to millions. As a robustness check, we also conducted the analysis with SRISK expressed as a ratio to equity capital. The results are similar, so only the correlations with SRISK itself are shown in the tables.

The results of the correlation analysis are presented in Table 7.4. This table contains correlations between SRISK and different company characteristics, between SRISK and specific lines of business, and between SRISK and off-balance-sheet activities. Most of the variables discussed are expressed as ratios to equity capital. This is because it is the capital or equity of the insurer that is available to absorb adverse fluctuations from activities related to the variables included in the table and discussed in the following paragraphs. To help determine whether some lines of business are related to the systemic risk measure, the correlation between the proportion of premiums written in a line of business and the systemic risk measure is provided.

The size of an entity is typically associated with systemic risk. In the correlation analysis, a measure of firm size, the Ln(Assets), is positively and significantly related to the SRISK. Recall earlier that firm size was considered to be a primary indicator associated with systemic risk for insurers, although it was also argued that insurer insolvencies are resolved in an orderly fashion with payouts continuing for years after the insolvency. Thus, overall, Table 7.4 indicates that larger insurers are more sensitive to systemic risk. It should be kept in mind, however, that included in these assets amounts are all of the assets for all of the businesses that the insurer is involved in,

TABLE 7.4   Correlations of the Systemic Risk Measure SRISK with Selected Variables

Variable	Correlation	*p*-Value
Company Characteristics		
Ln (Assets)	0.5988	0.0000***
Capital/Assets	−0.0331	0.5676
Beta	0.4015	0.0000***
MBS/Capital	−0.1229	0.1263
Total premiums ceded/Capital	0.0205	0.7638
Total reinsurance liabilities/Capital	0.1839	0.0043***
Separate accounts assets/Total assets	0.2081	0.0007***
Total customer deposits (bank)/Capital	0.4769	0.0000***
Commercial paper/Capital	0.3477	0.0000***
Life insurer dummy (= 1 if life insurer)	−0.0327	0.5659
Life and P-C insurer business dummy (= 1 if operations in both lines)	0.1191	0.0360**
Lines of Business		
Workers' compensation premiums/Capital	−0.1407	0.0522*
Homeowners multiple peril premiums/Capital	−0.2144	0.0029***
Total other liability premiums/Capital	−0.2477	0.0005***
Private passenger automobile liability premiums/Capital	−0.1929	0.0075***
Individual life insurance premiums/Capital	0.0125	0.8378
Ordinary individual annuity premiums/Capital	−0.0019	0.9751
Group life premiums/Capital	−0.0234	0.7018
Group annuity premiums/Capital	0.1259	0.0384**
Workers' compensation premiums/Total premiums	−0.2867	0.0022***
Homeowners multiple peril premiums/Total premiums	−0.2878	0.0023***
Total other liability premiums/Total premiums	−0.2848	0.0021***
Private passenger automobile liability premiums/Total premiums	−0.3068	0.0010***
Individual life insurance premiums/Total premiums	0.0400	0.6758
Ordinary individual annuity premiums/Total premiums	0.5178	0.0000***
Group life premiums/Total premiums	0.4189	0.0000***
Group annuity premiums/Total premiums	0.6675	0.0000***

(*continued*)

TABLE 7.4   (*Continued*)

Variable	Correlation	*p*-Value
Off-Balance-Sheet Activities		
Long-term debt due in one year/Total liabilities	0.3654	0.0000***
Total fair value of derivatives/Capital	0.5123	0.0000***
Total notional amount of nonhedge derivatives/Capital	0.5427	0.0000***
Total notional amount of all derivatives/Capital	0.5226	0.0000***

Note: ***, **, and * signify significance at the 1, 5, and 10 percent levels, respectively.

including businesses such as banking. Therefore, the significant relationship between SRISK and asset size may not mean that large insurers are actually systemically risky.

The systematic risk of the firm as proxied by the market equity beta of the firm is positively and significantly related to SRISK according to the table. A leverage measure (the ratio of capital to assets) is included in the correlation analysis, but this variable is not significant. Recall that leverage was considered to be a secondary or contributing factor to systemic risk rather than a primary factor. Two reinsurance variables are included in the correlation analysis: total reinsurance premiums ceded/equity capital and total reinsurance liabilities/equity capital. The premiums ceded variable is not significantly correlated with SRISK, but the ratio of reinsurance liabilities to capital is positively correlated with SRISK and significant at better than the 1 percent level. Thus, reinsurance exposure is associated with systemic risk for insurers.

Life insurers conduct many of their activities through the operation of separate accounts. The total amount of separate account assets relative to total insurer assets is positively and significantly related to SRISK. In separate accounts, insurers may provide annuity products embedded with options, guaranteed investment contracts (GICs), and other banking-type contracts. Therefore, it is not surprising that this characteristic of an insurer is significantly related to the systemic risk measure.

Some of the large insurers in the sample also include banks within their holding company structures. The correlation analysis indicates that the ratio of banking customer deposits to equity capital is significantly and positively related to SRISK. Recall that Geneva Association (2010) argued that reliance on short-term financing (such as commercial paper) could make an insurer systemically risky. Supporting this argument, the ratio of insurer commercial paper borrowings to equity capital is positively and significantly related to the SRISK. Finally, with respect to company characteristics, a significant and positive correlation between insurers operating in both life and P-C lines of business and SRISK exists. Perhaps this is because such insurers are more complex than insurers specializing in life or P-C insurance. The life insurer dummy variable is not significantly related to the systemic risk measure in the correlation analysis.

Table 7.4 also provides information about the relationship between lines of business and the systemic expected shortfall. Two measures of business line mix are included: line of business premiums divided by total equity and the proportion of premiums written in various business lines divided by total premiums. We first discuss the results with respect to the ratios of premiums to equity and then discuss the percentage business mix variables.

In terms of ratios of premiums written to equity capital, all four P-C line of business variables are statistically significant and negatively related to the SRISK. The negative relationships provide evidence to suggest that writing P-C lines may act as a stabilizing factor during systemic crises and reinforce the argument made by insurance industry representatives that P-C insurance is not systemic. The ratios of life insurance premiums to equity capital are statistically insignificant except for the group annuities variable, which is significant and positive. Thus, there is some evidence that writing group annuities is associated with systemic risk.

In terms of the variables measuring the percentages of premium volume by line, the P-C variables are negative and statistically significant, providing further evidence that P-C insurance is not systemically risky. Three of four life insurance premium percentage variables are statistically significant and positive, providing further evidence that life insurance is associated with systemic risk. This is not surprising, considering that banks and life insurers both offer asset accumulation products and compete in many markets including pension plans and asset management.

Three variables are included in the analysis to measure noncore activities undertaken by insurers. These include the ratio of the notional amount of nonhedging derivatives, the total notional amount of derivatives, and the total fair value of derivatives. All three variables are measured as ratios to equity capital. All three variables have significant positive correlations with SRISK. This reinforces the inference that noncore activities of insurers can create systemic risk.

Noncore risk also can be created when insurers rely on short-term sources of financing. As a measure of exposure to short-term financing risk, we include in the analysis the ratio of long-term debt due in one year to total liabilities. This measure has a significant positive correlation with SRISK, providing evidence that relatively short-term financing is associated with systemic risk.

In summary, several important insurer characteristics are significantly related to SRISK, including insurer size, the market equity beta, and separate accounts relative to assets. The ratio of group annuities to equity and three of four life insurance line of business percentage variables are positively correlated with systemic risk. Also notably, the P-C line of business variables are all negatively correlated with systemic risk. This suggests that life insurance products are associated with systemic risk but that P-C insurance products are not.

The correlation analysis in this section measures bivariate relationships. In the next section, several of these variables are included in multivariate regressions to see whether these variables are significantly related to systemic risk while controlling for other variables.

Regression Analysis

Ordinary least squares analysis was conducted based on our sample of insurers. Summary statistics for the variables in the regressions are shown in Table 7.5, and the regression results are presented in Table 7.6.[30] Table 7.6

TABLE 7.5 Summary Statistics for Regression

Variable	Coefficient	Std Dev
SRISK (millions of dollars)	1.9682	3.8830
Ln(Asset)	11.4138	1.7915
Capital/Assets	0.8793	12.1966
Beta	1.0769	0.5171
MBS/Capital	0.5712	0.6790
Separate account assets/Assets	0.1441	0.1847
Life insurance dummy (= 1 if life insurer)	0.9188	0.2735
Life and P-C insurer business dummy (= 1 if operations in both lines)	0.1188	0.3241
Total other liability/Capital	0.0361	0.0637
Group annuity premiums/Capital	0.0698	0.1506
Total other liability premiums/Total premiums	0.0630	0.0892
Group annuity premiums/Total premiums	0.0882	0.1360
Total reinsurance liabilities/Capital	0.0250	0.1129
Total premiums ceded/Capital	0.0890	0.1275

TABLE 7.6 Robust Ordinary Least Squares Regression Results, Dependent Variable: SRISK

Variable	Coefficient	t-statistic	Coefficient	t-statistic
Ln(Asset)	0.3584	2.61**	0.3649	3.31***
Capital/Asset	−1.0322	−0.68	0.2751	0.22
Beta	0.6538	1.28	0.6643	1.30
MBS/Capital	0.5990	1.79*	0.5493	2.74**
Separate account assets/Assets	2.2916	2.29***	2.7700	3.12***
Life insurance dummy (= 1 if life insurer)	1.6844	2.40**	0.8668	0.98
Life and P-C insurer dummy (= 1 if both lines)	0.4182	1.01	0.4008	1.01
Total other liability/Capital	−2.0791	−0.84		
Group annuity premiums/Capital	2.4306	1.54		
Total other liability premiums/Total premiums			−0.3186	−0.25
Group annuity premiums/Total premiums			5.4150	2.70***
Total reinsurance liabilities/Capital	1.8765	4.46**	1.1456	2.07**
Total premiums ceded/Capital	−0.1349	−0.22	0.6390	1.14
Constant	−6.0470	−2.57**	−5.9180	−2.77***
F-statistic	43.17		26.99	
Adjusted R-squared	0.6042		0.6345	
No. of observations	112		112	

Note: *, **, and *** signify significance at the 10 percent, 5 percent, and 1 percent levels, respectively.

indicates that size is significantly related to the systemic risk measure (SRISK) in the multivariate context, reinforcing the correlation analysis.[31]

However, after controlling for the other variables in the equation, the market equity beta is not statistically significant. The capital-to-assets variable was insignificant in the correlation analysis, and it is also insignificant in the regression results.

The ratio of MBS holdings to equity capital and the ratio of separate account assets to total assets are both positively and significantly related to the SRISK. The separate accounts result is consistent with the correlation analysis. Hence, being active in separate accounts and investing in MBSs are positively associated with systemic risk.

To test for differences in systemic risk between life and P-C insurance, a dummy variable is included in the regressions set equal to one if the firm conducts life insurance business and to zero otherwise. This variable is positive and significant in one of the two regression models shown in Table 7.6, providing some evidence that offering life insurance is associated with systemic risk but that writing P-C insurance is not.[32] Perhaps the life insurance dummy is insignificant in the second regression due to the presence of the group annuity proportion variable in this model. The dummy variable for offering both life and P-C insurance is not statistically significant. This provides some evidence that writing both types of insurance does not increase complexity to the extent of creating significant systemic risk.

The ratios of group annuity premiums and other liability premiums to equity capital are not statistically significant in the first regression.[33] However, in the second regression, the ratio of group annuity premiums to total premiums is positive and significant at the 1 percent level. The ratio of other liability premiums to total premiums is not statistically significant in the second regression. Hence, the regressions provide further evidence that writing group annuities is positively associated with systemic risk but that writing P-C insurance does not seem to create significant systemic risk. Thus, the core activities of P-C insurers do not seem to be systemically risky but both separate account and group annuity business for life insurers are associated with systemic risk.

Two reinsurance-related variables are included in the regressions. The ratio of reinsurance premiums ceded to equity capital is insignificant in both regressions, consistent with the argument that reinsurance ceded is not systemically risky. However, the ratio of total reinsurance liabilities to equity capital is positive and highly significant in both regressions. This suggests that taking on significant reinsurance liabilities is positively associated with systemic risk. This could be because reinsurance exacerbates interconnectedness risk and/or because reinsurance is a relatively risky line of business. Future research on the nature of reinsurance assumed by insurers vis-à-vis systemic risk thus may be fruitful.

In summary, the regression results in Table 7.6 show that insurer size, the amount of MBS activity, and total reinsurance liabilities are all positively and significantly related to SRISK. The liability line of business variable for P-C insurers is not statistically significant. This is important because this line contains directors and officers (D&O) liability and errors and omissions (E&O) business, which one might expect to be positively related to crises. However, the group annuity variable is significant in one of the regressions, reinforcing the inference that writing group annuities may be associated with systemic risk.

SYSTEMIC RISK AND U.S. INSURANCE REGULATION

The preceding analysis indicates that some characteristics of insurance groups are associated with the systemic risk measure. Therefore, regulators need to improve the effectiveness of group supervision. This is especially true for global insurance-led financial groups (Geneva Association 2012). Large, global insurance groups have insurance subsidiaries that are regulated in the United States but also have financial subsidiaries located in other countries. Its London-based Financial Products division brought down AIG due to a failure of regulation, such that U.S. insurance regulators did not have jurisdiction and U.S. banking regulators failed to require adequate capitalization.[34] The NAIC, International Association of Insurance Supervisors (IAIS), and other regulatory bodies are currently working on improvements in group supervision. Because of the importance of noncore activities in potentially creating systemic risk, it is useful to review the present and proposed future status of insurance group regulation. We focus primarily on the United States and briefly mention international efforts. The following section considers proposed or actual changes in state regulation and federal regulation, and concludes by providing a few recommendations for future regulation.

State Insurance Regulation

Historically, U.S. insurance regulation has focused on the operations and financial results of insurers on a legal entity basis; that is, most regulatory efforts have targeted individual insurers that are members of groups and unaffiliated single insurers rather than insurance groups. However, two NAIC model laws specifically relate to insurance holding companies. They are Model Law (ML) 440, Insurance Holding Company System Regulatory Act, and ML 450, Insurance Holding Company System Model Regulation with Reporting Forms and Instructions. In light of the financial crisis, modifications to these laws have been proposed, and holding company analysis became an accreditation requirement effective January 1, 2012. A new proposed model law with implications for group supervision, the Risk Management and Own Risk and Solvency Assessment (RMORSA) Model Act, is also under consideration. We first consider the present regulatory rules under MLs 440 and 450 and then consider the proposed revisions to those laws and the key provisions of RMORSA as they relate to insurance groups.

An important objective of MLs 440 and 450 is to regulate transactions within the insurance group. Under ML 440, every insurer that is a member of an insurance holding company is required to register with the insurance commissioner. Transactions within an insurance holding company system to which a registered insurer is a party must satisfy legally specified requirements. Among other things, the terms of transactions within the holding company must be reasonable and fair. Prenotification to the state commissioner and commissioner approval are required for specified transactions involving a registered insurer and any person in its holding company system. Such specified transactions include large sales, purchases, exchanges, loans, or investments; significant modification of reinsurance agreements; and any material transactions that the commissioner believes may adversely affect the interests of the insurer's policyholders. In addition, registered insurers must provide annual information in a prescribed format, including capital structure, financial condition, and the identity and relationship of every member of the insurance holding company, as well as outstanding transactions and agreements between the insurer and its affiliates.

ML 450 is primarily directed toward providing rules and procedures necessary to carry out ML 440. Among other provisions, ML 450 requires insurance groups to file an annual Insurance Holding Company Registration Statement. In the Registration Statement, the holding company is required to report a variety of information, including disclosures regarding purchases, sales, or exchanges of assets; litigation or administrative proceedings pending or concluded within the past year; and financial statements and exhibits. In conclusion, currently existing model laws require the commissioner to be informed of material actions and transactions that affect domestically authorized insurers within insurance holding companies, including transactions with noninsurance affiliates, but commissioners do not have the authority to order an insurance subsidiary to provide other information on noninsurance affiliates.

State commissioners can take no direct action against noninsurance affiliates within an insurance holding company. However, state commissioners can place pressure on regulated insurance subsidiaries concerning holding company activities and the activities of noninsurance affiliates; for example, state commissioners can place pressure so that the books and records of affiliates are provided to the commissioner. In particular, state insurance commissioners could have inquired about the activities of AIG Financial Products even though the Financial Products unit was not regulated by the state commissioners. If any resulting disclosures had raised questions about threats to the financial condition of AIG's regulated U.S. insurance subsidiaries, U.S. regulators could have tightened regulatory requirements on the U.S. subsidiaries, including requiring the subsidiaries to operate with increased capital.

Revisions to MLs 440 and 450 have been proposed and have already been adopted by nine states.[35] The overall focus of the proposed revisions is on enterprise risk management (ERM), corporate governance, and increasing regulatory authority to obtain information and regulate the activities of insurance holding companies. The most important change is the introduction of new guidelines for reporting enterprise risk (a required annual Enterprise Risk Report [ERR]). The ERR must indicate (among other things) any material developments regarding strategy, internal audit findings, compliance, or risk management that, in the opinion of senior management, could adversely affect the insurance holding company system. Under the revised model laws, the commissioner may order any registered insurer to produce records, books, or other information that are deemed reasonably necessary to determine the financial condition of the insurer, including information on noninsurance affiliates.

The Risk Management and Own Risk and Solvency Assessment (RMORSA) Model Act is a new model law, tentatively scheduled for implementation in 2015. The purpose of the model law is to provide the requirements for maintaining a risk management framework and to provide instructions for filing an annual ORSA Summary Report with the insurance commissioner. The ORSA requirement applies to the insurer or the insurance group of which the insurer is a member. At a minimum, the ORSA Summary Report should describe the risk management framework and provide an assessment of risk exposure, group risk capital adequacy, and prospective solvency assessment. The report is to be supported by internal risk management materials and more detailed documentation. The goals of ORSA are to foster an effective level of ERM for all insurers and to provide a group-level perspective on risk management and capital.

The revisions to MLs 440 and 450 along with the RMORSA Model Act should provide insurance commissioners with more complete information on the risks facing insurance holding companies. The Enterprise Risk Report and the ORSA Summary Report, especially, should be instrumental in achieving this goal. The revisions to ML 440 clarify and strengthen regulatory authority to require information about noninsurance affiliates within an insurance holding company. The state insurance commissioner still would not have any direct control over noninsurance affiliates or affiliates outside of its geographic jurisdiction, but pressure can be brought to bear on the regulated affiliate if the state commissioner believes problems exist elsewhere in the group.

The revisions of MLs 440 and 450 strengthen regulatory authority over insurance holding companies and facilitate bringing pressures on regulated insurance subsidiaries to prevent spillovers of financial problems from noninsurance affiliates. However, because insurance in the United States is regulated by 50 states and the District of Columbia, regulators need to monitor carefully the noninsurance subsidiaries of insurance-led groups and coordinate efforts to communicate any danger signals across regulatory jurisdictions. In addition, regulators need to develop stronger groupwide supervision to monitor primary indicators and contributing factors such as interconnectedness, leverage, and liquidity risk to prevent future systemic events.

Federal Regulation

An important new regulatory agency with potential authority over insurance holding companies is the Financial Stability Oversight Council (FSOC), established by the Dodd-Frank Wall Street Reform and Consumer Protection Act of 2010. The FSOC has three primary purposes (FSOC 2012): (1) to identify risks to the financial stability of the United States that could arise from the activities of large, interconnected bank holding companies or nonbank financial companies; (2) to promote market discipline by eliminating expectations on the part of shareholders, creditors, and counterparties of such firms that the U.S. government will shield them from losses in the event of failure; and (3) to respond to emerging threats to the stability of the U.S. financial system.

The FSOC has established a three-stage process for designating a nonbank financial institution as a systemically important financial institution (SIFI). Stage 1 stipulates that the institution will be subject to further analysis if it has at least $50 billion of consolidated financial assets and meets or exceeds any one of several additional quantitative thresholds, including $30 billion in gross notional credit default swaps for which the nonbank financial company is the reference entity, $3.5 billion in derivative liabilities, or $20 billion of total debt outstanding. In Stage 2, the FSOC will further analyze those companies triggering the Stage 1 thresholds using a broad range of information from existing public and regulatory sources. The final step, Stage 3, involves direct contact by the FSOC with each nonbank financial institution that has passed through Stages 1 and 2 of the SIFI process to request additional information from the company. At the end of Stage 3, the FSOC makes a final determination about designating the company as a SIFI.

Institutions designated as SIFIs come under the regulatory authority of the Federal Reserve, which can impose "enhanced supervision and prudential standards, *whether they are banks or nonbanks*, and the ability to subject key market infrastructure firms to heightened risk-management standards" (U.S. Department of the Treasury 2012; emphasis added).

As of September 2013, the FSOC had designated three nonbank financial companies—American International Group, General Electric Capital, and Prudential Financial—as SIFIs; Met Life is in Stage 3 of the SIFI Process. The FSOC also had designated eight financial market utilities (FMUs) as systemically important, including the Clearinghouse Payments Company and ICE Clear Credit.[36] Financial firms designated as SIFIs will be subject to consolidated supervision by the Federal Reserve and enhanced prudential standards. As of the end of 2011, the top 26 U.S. life insurance groups all exceeded the $50 billion asset threshold under the SIFI Stage 1 criterion, but only five predominantly P-C groups exceeded the threshold (A.M. Best Company 2012a, 2012b).[37]

Issues to Consider for Future Regulation

In summary, the key to effective insurance regulation is to design a regulatory system that effectively encompasses both the core and noncore enterprises of the insurance sector and coordinates regulation across national boundaries. Given the limited information currently available on derivatives, asset lending, and other noncore activities of insurers, regulators should require more disclosure of these types of transactions. Disclosure enhances transparency and hence reduces the probability of the development of systemic crises. Regulators should also have the authority to regulate leverage by noncore subsidiaries of insurance firms.

In addition, large companies need a consolidated federal or state supervisor; for example, before the crisis, there was no single supervisor examining and regulating all aspects of AIG. But the supervision provided should focus on only those areas that relate to systemic risk. This will allow for the operation of a competitive market for insurers (and other financial institutions) with respect to nonsystemic activities.

In tandem with the appointment of a consolidated supervisor, resolution of large insurance groups should be considered. Under the present system, the state insurance regulator regulates insurance and the guaranty fund system is state-based. If an additional layer of regulation is added with a consolidated supervisor, should a consolidated guaranty structure be added for the activities regulated by the consolidated supervisor? The issue of who would bear the responsibility for the insolvency of a large national group that is regulated by both the state and a consolidated (federal) regulator arises.

New regulation should also be focused; a blanket approach should not be used. For example, blanket increases in the amount of capital that systemically important financial institutions need to hold will not necessarily make financial institutions safer or the economy stronger. That is, financial institutions designated as systemically risky can increase the riskiness of their activities in response to capital requirements, or other financial institutions not designated as systemically risky can begin to undertake systemically risky activity. Market disruptions for some products might also occur if capital requirements for the largest insurers are increased in an across-the-board, ad hoc fashion. Finally, it should be mentioned that the AIG group's problems were mostly liquidity-related rather than capital-induced.

Any new requirements (especially capital requirements for systemically important institutions) should specifically complement existing state regulatory requirements. It is worth keeping in mind that under the existing U.S. state regulatory framework, insurers fared well through the crisis. New regulation should not fix what is not broken.

New regulation should also be consistent with new global regulation likely to emanate from the IAIS. That is, U.S. insurers should not be placed at a global disadvantage. Further, if an international consolidated group supervisor is chosen for large groups, new issues would be created. For example, the questions of who would bear the responsibility for failed insurance groups and how assets of an insolvent group would be distributed among countries in which the global group operated would need to be considered.

One issue that would need to be resolved globally is the accounting system that insurers use. There is increasing pressure by federal regulators for insurers to use U.S. generally accepted accounting principles (GAAP) accounting in addition to (or in replacement of) statutory accounting. This requirement for U.S. insurers would be costly. Nevertheless, what is needed is a reporting system that allows all operations of the group to be consolidated together so that insurers' and groups' financial results can be compared internationally.

CONCLUSION

The primary conclusion of the chapter is that most of the core activities of the U.S. insurers are not associated with systemic risk. This is particularly true for P-C insurance because there is evidence that writing P-C insurance is inversely related to SRISK, an important measure of systemic risk. Although there are no substitutes for personal lines and small business P-C insurance, even the failure of several large P-C insurers would not significantly disrupt the market, because many other insurers would be able to step in to fill coverage gaps. P-C insurers for the most part are not sufficiently large enough or interconnected with other parts of the financial sector to create systemic risk through their core activities.

We do find some evidence that some core activities of life insurers, particularly separate accounts and group annuities, are positively associated with systemic risk. This is consistent with the observation that life insurance products are similar to banking products in many respects and that life insurers compete with banks in many categories of products. There is also some evidence that insurer investments in mortgage-backed securities (MBSs) are associated with systemic risk. The use of MBSs is more prevalent among life insurers than among P-C insurers.

We emphasize, however, that susceptibility to systemic risk is not equivalent to the propagation of systemic risk. Chen et al. (2014) provide evidence that banks create economically significant systemic risk for insurers but not vice versa. Hence, insurers tend to be the victims rather than the propagators of systemic risk. This is an important distinction that should be kept clearly in mind in developing any new insurance regulations.

Based on our analysis of susceptibility to intrasector crises, we find that life insurers are more vulnerable to crises than are P-C insurers. Life insurers are more highly levered than P-C insurers and are exposed to credit and liquidity risk due to their heavy investment in MBSs and privately placed bonds. They also offer complex financial products with embedded derivatives. Nevertheless, insolvency rates in the life insurance industry remain low, and life insurers weathered the financial crisis successfully in spite of their exposure to ABSs and MBSs. Life insurers also demonstrated the ability to recapitalize quickly following the worst of the financial crisis.

Both life and P-C insurers are potentially vulnerable to reinsurance crises and spirals because of their exposure to reinsurance counterparty credit risk, the main source of interconnectedness for insurers. Because reinsurance counterparty credit risk is highly concentrated, a reinsurance spiral potentially could be triggered by the failure of one or more leading reinsurers, triggering an insolvency crisis in the insurance industry. Nevertheless, recent research provides evidence that the failure of a large reinsurer would be minimally disruptive to the U.S. P-C insurance market, and reinsurance failures historically have not been an important causal factor in insurance insolvencies. We find that regulation is not an important source of sectoral risk with respect to insurer core activities.

As was demonstrated by the AIG debacle, the noncore activities of insurers can constitute a potential source of systemic risk, and interconnectedness among financial firms has grown significantly in recent years. Noncore activities include trading in derivatives (such as credit default swaps), asset lending, asset management, and providing financial guarantees. Statistical analysis indicates that factors such as derivatives trading, investing in ABSs, and life insurer separate account activity are associated with a measure of systemic risk—SRISK.

Most of the noncore activities conducted by insurers are beyond the traditional purview of insurance regulators and have not been rigorously regulated by banking authorities. Therefore, on a worldwide scale, regulators need to significantly improve their capabilities in group supervision. In the United States, regulators have some authority to tighten capital requirements and other regulations for regulated insurers deemed vulnerable due to the activities of noninsurance affiliates. Under proposed revisions to regulatory laws, regulators would have broad authority to require disclosures of information on the activities of noninsurance subsidiaries of insurance holding companies. Consequently, if the revisions are adopted, U.S. regulators will have the information to prevent another AIG-type crisis, although they still will not have direct authority over noninsurance subsidiaries.

NOTES

1. This definition of systemic risk is analogous to the definition proposed in Group of Ten (2001, 126). Similar definitions have been proposed by other organizations. See, for example, Financial Stability Board (2009).
2. The exception is a single paper on P-C insurance by Park and Xie (2011), which is briefly discussed here. Life insurance counterparty relationships have not previously been analyzed. Cummins and Weiss (2014) also look at reinsurance counterparty relationships.
3. Prudential was omitted from the analysis to obtain this result. See Cummins and Weiss (2014).
4. Our primary indicators are based on those identified in Financial Stability Board (2009). The International Association of Insurance Supervisors (IAIS) (2009) proposes a fourth factor, *timing*, based on the argument that systemic insurance risk propagates over a longer time horizon than systemic risk in banking. The International Monetary Fund (IMF) considers size, interconnectedness, leverage, and (risky) funding structure in assessing the systemic importance of institutions (IMF 2009). Our taxonomy also considers leverage and funding structures but classifies these as contributing factors rather than primary indicators.
5. As pointed out in Financial Stability Board (2009, 9), "While size can be important in itself, it is much more significant when there are connections to other institutions. The relevance of size will also depend on

the particular business model and group structure, and size may be of greater systemic concern when institutions are complex ... for example, well-capitalized large institutions with simpler business models and exposures can be a source of stability in times of stress."

6. The shadow banking system consists of financial intermediaries that provide banking-like services without access to central bank liquidity or explicit public-sector credit guarantees. Shadow banks are less stringently regulated than commercial banks. Shadow banks include finance companies, structured investment vehicles, hedge funds, asset-backed commercial paper conduits, money market mutual funds, securities lenders, and government-sponsored enterprises. For further information see Pozsar et al. (2010).

7. With a 10-to-1 assets-to-equity ratio, a 5 percent decline in asset values would wipe out half of equity. If liabilities remained unchanged, the firm would need to sell about 47.4 percent of assets and use the proceeds to pay off liabilities in order to restore its assets-to-equity ratio to the preshock level.

8. The other three megabanks are Bank of America, Citigroup, and Wells Fargo, each of which had more than $1 trillion of assets in 2012 (Standard & Poor's 2012a). The bank data are for March 2012.

9. The failure rate is defined as the number of failures divided by the total number of institutions.

10. An insolvent insurer is defined as an insurer that is in receivership or liquidation.

11. In other words, life guaranty funds often replace policyholders' coverage, not policyholders' cash.

12. Policyholder claim/benefit payments are typically frozen for a period of time, except for death and financial need.

13. New York is an exception. The rationale for *ex post* assessments is that, unlike the obligations of the Federal Deposit Insurance Corporation (FDIC), insurance payments under policies are spread over many years in the future as claims arise.

14. In the United States, small policyholders are typically protected by guaranty funds. Commercial insurance is covered also, but more than half of the states have a net worth restriction, such that if a company has net worth above some threshold (usually $25 million to $50 million) it is excluded from coverage. In addition, workers' compensation insurance is always covered, while a few lines such as title insurance and mortgage guaranty insurance are not covered.

15. Life guaranty fund capacity is from the National Organization of Life & Health Insurance Guaranty Associations, www.nolhga.com/factsand figures/main.cfm/location/assessmentdata. P-C guaranty fund capacity is from NCIGF (2011), www.ncigf.org.

16. For example, in a life insurer insolvency, the shortfall in assets relative to liabilities is typically in the 5 to 10 percent range and seldom is as high as 15 percent (Gallanis 2009, 7).

17. The data in this paragraph and the following paragraph are from NAIC (2011) and unpublished NAIC data.

18. Cross-holdings between banks and insurers can be substantial in Europe, and the bank insurance model (BIM) or *bancassurance* is more common there than in the United States. Thus in Europe a systemic link can exist between insurers and banks such that a large event for an insurer can spread to an affiliated bank and vice versa. For example, Allianz owned Dresdner Bank from 2001 to 2008. Multibillion write-downs by Dresdner Bank adversely affected Allianz's equity and balance sheet as well as some of its key capital ratios (Baluch, Mutenga, and Parsons 2011).

19. Based on international data, Swiss Re (2003) also concludes that reinsurance failures historically have not been an important cause of insolvencies in the primary insurance industry.

20. Some have likened the retrocession market to interbank lending and borrowing in the banking industry. As such, it is sometimes thought to be a transmission mechanism for contagion and systemic risk within the reinsurance industry. But unlike MBSs in the recent crisis, retroceders still retain part of the risk (to reduce adverse selection).

21. In a primary insurer cession, business underwritten by the insurer is ceded (or sold) to a reinsurer, with the primary insurer paying a fee (premium) to the reinsurer. In reinsurance assumed, the assuming insurer purchases business underwritten by another insurer for a premium.

22. The term *reinsurance receivables* is used to refer to asset page item 16 in the NAIC life and P-C annual statements. It includes amounts receivable from reinsurers, funds held by or deposited with reinsured companies, and other amounts receivable under reinsurance contracts.

23. U.S. insurers can take balance sheet credit for reinsurance as long as the reinsurer is "authorized" (i.e., licensed in the ceding insurer's state of domicile, accredited in the ceding insurer's state of domicile, or licensed in a state with substantially similar credit for reinsurance laws). Insurers can take credit for unauthorized reinsurance only if the reinsurer posts collateral, in the form of funds held in the United States or letters of credit from U.S. banks. The NAIC and several individual U.S. states have begun to liberalize collateralization rules, and the process is ongoing.

24. The difference between receivables, on the one hand, and reserve credit taken and net amount recoverable, on the other hand, is that receivables represent amounts currently owed and payable, whereas reserve credit taken and net amount recoverable largely represent estimated reserve liabilities for future losses. Reserve credit taken data for life insurers

are from Schedule S of the NAIC annual statement, and reinsurance recoverables from P-C insurers are from Schedule F of the NAIC annual statement.

25. The SNL database used in compiling the reinsurance data nets out intragroup transactions.

26. The Gramm-Leach-Bliley (Financial Services Modernization) Act repealed part of the Glass-Steagall Act of 1933, opening up the market among banks, securities firms, and insurers. The Glass-Steagall Act had prohibited any one institution from acting as any combination of an investment bank, a commercial bank, and an insurance company.

27. Banks have also expanded into insurance and annuity markets. However, banks primarily serve as distributors of insurance products underwritten by unaffiliated insurance companies and not as insurance underwriters (Insurance Information Institute 2012). Therefore, such expansion does not seem to have systemic implications.

28. Research by Chen et al. (2014) uses Granger causality tests to determine whether insurers create crises that spread to banks or vice versa. The results indicate that insurers are much more significantly susceptible to crises that spread from banks rather than the other way around. The results show that shocks spreading from banks to insurers are possible based on the data analysis and that the impact is economically significant.

29. The SRISK data are from the website: http://vlab.stern.nyu.edu/analysis/RISK.USFIN-MR.MES.

30. All of the variables contained in Table 7.4 could not be included in the regressions because of the limited number of observations of these variables vis-à-vis other variables. Notably, the variables with limited numbers of observations are the off-balance-sheet and customer deposits (bank) variables. Although the bivariate analysis is conducted on no fewer than 150 observations, when the off-balance-sheet variables were included in the regression analysis, the number of observations for the regressions was reduced to only about 50. Hence, the firms with off-balance-sheet data have missing values for other regression variables.

31. The t-statistics in the regressions are robust to heteroskedasticity.

32. The regression finding with respect to the life insurance dummy variable differs from the univariate correlation analysis, where this variable was not significantly related to SRISK.

33. Other lines of business variables were also tested—both for life and for P-C—but these were never significant in either regression.

34. AIG Financial Products was under the regulatory authority of the U.S. Office of Thrift Supervision (OTS). In retrospect, it is clear that OTS oversight was not adequate to prevent AIG FP's financial difficulties.

35. The revised model laws have been put out for comment until the end of 2012. Whether the revised model laws become a requirement for accreditation will be decided after that.
36. The webpage listing nonbank SIFIs as of September 19, 2013 is www .treasury.gov/initiatives/fsoc/designations/Pages/default.aspx#nonbank.
37. The Financial Stability Board (FSB) has the responsibility of identifying *global systemically important insurers* (G-SIIs). The Financial Stability Board was established to coordinate at the international level the work of national financial authorities and international standard–setting bodies and to develop and promote the implementation of effective regulatory, supervisory, and other financial sector policies. It brings together national authorities responsible for financial stability in significant international financial centers, international financial institutions, sector-specific international groupings of regulators and supervisors, and committees of central bank experts. The FSB is working with the International Association of Insurance Supervisors (IAIS) and other groups to identify G-SIIs. The assessment of G-SIIs involves three steps: collection of data, methodological assessment of the data, and a supervisory judgment and validation process. As of July 2013, the Financial Stability Board had identified the following firms as Global Systemically Important Insurers (G-SIIs): Allianz, American International Group, Assicurazioni Generali, Aviva, Axa, MetLife, Ping An Insurance Group of China, Prudential Financial (U.S), and Prudential (U.K.). Further analysis of the identification of G-SIIs is provided in IAIS (2012) and Geneva Association (2011).

REFERENCES

Acharya, Viral V., John Biggs, Matthew Richardson, and Stephen Ryan. 2009. "On the Financial Regulation of Insurance Companies." Working paper, NYU Stern School of Business, New York.

Acharya, Viral V., Robert Engle, and Matthew Richardson. 2012. "Capital Shortfall: A New Approach to Ranking and Regulating Systemic Risks." *American Economic Review* 102:59–64.

Acharya, Viral V., Lasse H. Pedersen, Thomas Philippon, and Matthew Richardson. 2010. "Measuring Systemic Risk." Working paper, Federal Reserve Bank of Cleveland, Cleveland, OH.

A.M. Best Company. 2012a. *Best's Aggregates and Averages: Life/Health—2012 Edition.* Oldwick, NJ: A.M. Best.

A.M. Best Company. 2012b. *Best's Aggregates and Averages: Property/Casualty—2012 Edition.* Oldwick, NJ: A.M. Best.

A.M. Best Company. 2012c. *U.S. Life/Health—1969–2011 Impairment Review*. Oldwick, NJ: A.M. Best.

A.M. Best Company. 2012d. *U.S. Property/Casualty—1969–2011 P/C Impairment Review*. Oldwick, NJ: A.M. Best.

Baluch, Faisal, Stanley Mutenga, and Chris Parsons. 2011. "Insurance, Systemic Risk, and the Financial Crisis." *Geneva Papers* 36:126–163.

Bank for International Settlements (BIS). 2007. *Triennial Central Bank Survey: Foreign Exchange and Derivatives Markets in 2007*. Basel, Switzerland: BIS.

Bell, Marian, and Benno Keller. 2009. *Insurance and Stability: The Reform of Insurance Regulation*. Zurich, Switzerland: Zurich Financial Services Group.

Berry-Stölzle, Thomas R., Gregory P. Nini, and Sabine Wende. 2011. "External Financing in the Life Insurance Industry: Evidence from the Financial Crisis." Working paper, University of Georgia, Athens, GA.

Billio, Monica, Mila Getmansky, Andrew W. Lo, and Loriana Pelizzon. 2012. "Econometric Measures of Connectedness and Systemic Risk in the Finance and Insurance Sectors." *Journal of Financial Economics* 104:535-559.

Brunnermeier, Markus K. 2009. "Deciphering the Liquidity and Credit Crunch: 2007–2008." *Journal of Economic Perspectives* 23:77–100.

Brunnermeier, Markus K., and Lasse Heje Pedersen. 2009. "Market Liquidity and Funding Liquidity." *Review of Financial Studies* 22 (6): 2201–2238.

Chen, Hua, J. David Cummins, Krupa S. Viswanathan, and Mary A. Weiss. 2014. "Systemic Risk and the Inter-Connectedness between Banks and Insurers: An Econometric Analysis." *Journal of Risk and Insurance*, forthcoming.

Cummins, J. David. 2007. "Reinsurance for Natural and Man-Made Catastrophes in the United States: Current State of the Market and Regulatory Reforms." *Risk Management and Insurance Review* 10:179–220.

Cummins, J. David. 2008. *The Bermuda Insurance Market: An Economic Analysis*. Hamilton, Bermuda: Bermuda Insurance Market. www.bermuda-insurance.org.

Cummins, J. David, and Mary A. Weiss. 2000. "The Global Market for Reinsurance: Consolidation, Capacity, and Efficiency." *Brookings-Wharton Papers on Financial Services* 2000:159–222.

Cummins, J. David, and Mary A. Weiss. 2014. "Systemic Risk and the Insurance Industry." *Journal of Risk and Insurance*, forthcoming.

Financial Stability Board. 2009. *Guidance to Assess the Systemic Importance of Financial Institutions, Markets and Instruments: Initial Considerations*. Basel, Switzerland: Financial Stability Board.

Gallanis, Peter G. 2009. "NOLHGA, the Life and Health Insurance Guaranty System, and the Financial Crisis of 2008–2009." Available at www.nolhga.com/factsandfigures/main.cfm.

Geneva Association. 2010. *Systemic Risk in Insurance: An Analysis of Insurance and Financial Stability.* Geneva, Switzerland: Geneva Association.

Geneva Association. 2011. *Considerations for Identifying Systemically Important Financial Institutions in Insurance.* Geneva, Switzerland: Geneva Association.

Geneva Association. 2012. *Insurance and Resolution in Light of the Systemic Risk Debate.* Geneva, Switzerland: Geneva Association.

Grace, Martin F. 2010. "The Insurance Industry and Systemic Risk: Evidence and Discussion." Working paper, Georgia State University, Atlanta.

Group of Ten. 2001. *Report on Consolidation in the Financial Sector.* Basel, Switzerland: Bank for International Settlements.

Group of Thirty. 2006. *Reinsurance and International Financial Markets.* Washington, DC: Group of Thirty.

Harrington, Scott E. 2009. "The Financial Crisis, Systemic Risk, and the Future of Insurance Regulation." *Journal of Risk and Insurance* 76 (4): 785–819.

Insurance Information Institute. 2012. *Financial Services Fact Book.* New York: Insurance Information Institute.

International Association of Insurance Supervisors (IAIS). 2009. *Systemic Risk and the Insurance Sector.* Basel, Switzerland: IAIS.

International Association of Insurance Supervisors (IAIS). 2012. *Global Systemically Important Insurers: Proposed Assessment Methodology.* Basel, Switzerland: IAIS.

International Monetary Fund (IMF). 2009. *Global Financial Stability Report, Responding to the Financial Crisis and Measuring Systemic Risks.* Washington, DC: IMF.

Kaufman, George G., and Kenneth E. Scott. 2003. "What Is Systemic Risk, and Do Bank Regulators Retard or Contribute to It?" *Independent Review* 7 (3): 371–391.

MacMinn, Richard, and James Garven. 2000. "On Corporate Insurance." In *Handbook of Insurance*, ed. Georges Dionne. Boston: Kluwer Academic Publishers.

National Association of Insurance Commissioners (NAIC). 2011. *Capital Markets Special Report.* New York: NAIC Capital Markets Group, May 20.

National Conference of Insurance Guaranty Funds (NCIGF). 2011. "Testimony for the Record on the National Conference of Insurance Guaranty Funds before the House Financial Services Subcommittee on Insurance, Housing, and Community Opportunity." Washington, DC, November 16. www.ncigf.org.

Neyer, J. Steven. 1990. "The LMX Spiral Effect." *Best's Review* 91 (July): 62ff.

O'Neill, William, Nilam Sharma, and Michael Carolan. 2009. "Coping with the CDS Crisis: Lessons Learned from the LMX Spiral." *Journal of Reinsurance* 16:1–34.

Park, Sojung C., and Xiaoying Xie. 2011. "Reinsurance and Systemic Risk: The Impact of Reinsurer Downgrading on Property-Casualty Insurers." Working paper, California State University, Fullerton.

Pozsar, Richard, Tobias Adrian, Adam Ashcraft, and Hayley Boesky. 2010. "Shadow Banking." Federal Reserve Bank of New York Staff Report No. 458.

Standard & Poor's. 2012. *Industry Surveys: Banking.* New York: S&P.

Standard & Poor's. 2012. *Industry Surveys: Insurance—Life & Health.* New York: S&P.

Swiss Re. 2003. "Reinsurance—A Systemic Risk?" *Sigma* 5/2003.

U.S. Department of Commerce, Bureau of Economic Analysis (BEA). 2012. *National Economic Accounts.* Washington, DC: BEA. http://bea.gov/national/nipaweb/Index.asp.

U.S. Department of the Treasury, Financial Stability Oversight Council (FSOC). 2012. *2012 Annual Report.* Washington, DC: FSOC.

CHAPTER 8

Designation and Supervision of Insurance SIFIs

Scott E. Harrington
The Wharton School, University of Pennsylvania

The 2007–2009 U.S. financial crisis and its aftermath pose fundamental challenges in formulating regulatory and policy responses, to reduce the likelihood and severity of future crises while avoiding overly restrictive, stringent constraints on financial institutions that would lessen the availability and/or increase the price of valuable financial services. The question of whether the Dodd-Frank Wall Street Reform and Consumer Protection Act of 2010 will achieve that goal has generated extensive and ongoing debate.

Key Dodd-Frank Act provisions created the Financial Stability Oversight Council (FSOC), with the authority to designate systemically important nonbank financial institutions (nonbank SIFIs) for enhanced supervision by the Federal Reserve "if the Council determines that material financial distress at the U.S. nonbank financial company, or the nature, scope, size, scale, concentration, interconnectedness, or mix of the activities of the nonbank financial company could pose a threat to the financial stability of the United States." The FSOC subsequently promulgated a three-stage quantitative and qualitative process for designating nonbank SIFIs.

As of August 2013, the FSOC had designated American International Group (AIG) as systemically important, with AIG accepting the designation without challenge. The FSOC justified this decision based largely on the rationale that AIG was vulnerable to destabilizing runs by policyholders with potentially large spillovers on other insurers and financial markets. A second insurance entity, Prudential Financial, had requested a hearing over its proposed designation as systemically important.[1] The FSOC had advanced a third insurance entity, MetLife, to Stage 3 for SIFI designation, and MetLife had indicated that it would contest any ultimate designation.

The Federal Reserve was in the process of developing rules for enhanced prudential supervision of insurance SIFIs.

The Dodd-Frank Act's regime for designating nonbank SIFIs for enhanced supervision was in significant part motivated by the financial problems and subsequent federal government bailout of AIG. AIG's liquidity crisis was not attributable to its core insurance activities, but instead reflected its large and unique exposure to collateral calls associated with its credit default swap portfolio and, to a lesser extent, with its securities lending.[2] It remains uncertain how an AIG failure would have affected its noninsurance counterparties, which were the ultimate recipients of the bulk of federal assistance to AIG. Without federal assistance, there clearly was sufficient capital in AIG's property-casualty insurance subsidiaries to meet their obligations to policyholders, and in its property-casualty and life insurance subsidiaries combined to meet their aggregate obligations. Whether the capital in each of its life subsidiaries was sufficient to meet those entities' obligations on a stand-alone basis is less clear. The general view, however, is that AIG's financial distress did not reflect significant shortcomings in state regulation of its insurance subsidiaries. Because it owned a savings and loan, AIG had been subject to a form of consolidated supervision at the federal level by the Office of Thrift Supervision, which was abolished by the Dodd-Frank Act.

The financial distress and federal government bailout of AIG, due predominantly to its noninsurance activities, represent singular events in the financial history of the United States. Given those events and authorizing provisions in the Dodd-Frank Act, the FSOC's designation of AIG as systemically important and subject to enhanced prudential supervision by the Federal Reserve was almost certainly a foregone conclusion.

This chapter considers the broader issues of whether insurance entities pose systemic risk and the challenges and potential adverse consequences of designating additional insurance entities for enhanced supervision by the Federal Reserve. It makes four principal arguments.[3] First, AIG notwithstanding, core insurance activities and organizations that predominantly specialize in those activities pose little or no systemic risk. Second, the potential benefits of designating additional insurance organizations as systemically important are correspondingly modest compared with the potential direct and indirect costs. Third, enhanced capital, leverage, and other prudential requirements for AIG and any additional insurers that could be designated as systemically significant (despite the third argument) should be designed to reflect the distinct operations and risks of those entities. Fourth, there exist significant advantages to basing enhanced capital requirements for any insurers designated as systemically important on the existing state system of insurance company risk-based capital requirements.

The chapter begins with an overview of research and analyses of whether insurance activities and entities pose systemic risk. It then summarizes the FSOC process for designating nonbank SIFIs and the FSOC's stated rationale for designating AIG as systemically important. Three issues are then briefly considered: (1) regulatory and compliance costs and potential undesirable market disruptions from designation of insurance entities as SIFIs subject to enhanced supervision, (2) the design of enhanced capital requirements for insurer SIFIs, and (3) the risk that designation of insurer SIFIs would ultimately reduce market discipline by expanding "too big to fail" policy. The concluding section reiterates the chapter's main arguments.

INSURANCE AND SYSTEMIC RISK

The 2007–2009 financial crisis in general and the 2008 funding crisis at AIG in particular have stimulated significant research and analysis into the extent to which insurance involves systemic risk.[4] Although there is no common definition, systemic risk generally encompasses the risk of any large, macroeconomic shock that affects financial stability and risk arising from interdependencies or interconnectedness among firms, with an attendant risk of contagion and significant economic spillovers on the real economy. As an example, Cummins and Weiss (2013) define systemic risk as "the risk that an event will trigger a loss of economic value or confidence in a substantial segment of the financial system that is serious enough to have significant adverse effects on the real economy with a high probability."

The risk of common shocks to the economy, such as widespread reductions in housing prices or large changes in interest rates or foreign exchange, which have the potential to directly harm large numbers of people and firms, is conceptually distinct from risk that arises from interconnectedness and contagion.[5] It is often difficult, however, to sort out any contagion effects from the effects of common shocks, and broad definitions of systemic risk encompass both sources of risk.[6]

Regardless of the specific definition, qualitative analyses generally have concluded that core insurance activities pose little systemic risk, especially compared with banking (Swiss Re 2003; Harrington 2004a; Geneva Association 2010, 2012; IAIS 2011; Cummins and Weiss 2013).[7] An obvious implication is that insurance organizations that focus predominantly in those activities would not pose significant systemic risk. Compared with banks, financial distress of insurers, whether life or property-casualty, does not threaten the payment system or short-term lending. Banking crises have much greater potential to produce widespread harm to economic activity. Life insurers have longer-term and much less liquid liabilities, much more time to resolve financial distress, more extensive duration/matching of assets and liabilities, and substantial separate account assets and liabilities where most if not all investment risk is borne directly by customers.

Quantitative research on financial institutions' stock prices has provided evidence of interconnectedness among insurers and other financial firms and developed equity-based metrics for measuring systemic risk at the firm level with stock price data. Billio et al. (2012), for example, used principal components analysis and Granger causality tests to analyze stock returns for insurers, banks, securities brokers, and hedge funds during 1994–2008. They found evidence of causal relationships between the sectors during 2001–2008 but not 1994–2000, and argued that several insurers were systemically important.[8] Acharya et al. (2010) developed a measure of systemic risk (marginal expected shortfall) that reflects a firm's tendency to lose value when the overall equity market suffers large losses. Their analysis of stock returns for insurers and other financial firms during 2006–2008 suggested that insurance firms were the least systemically risky. Insurers with the largest equity-based systemic risk measures had significant activity in credit derivatives and financial guarantees.

Building on or related to Acharya et al. (2010), several additional measures have been used to rank individual entities by systemic risk potential, usually related to historical correlations of the firm's stock returns with equity market returns in down markets. The measures are based on elegant conceptual and empirical frameworks and often reflect considerable sophistication in estimating correlations with down markets. While seemingly precise, however, the Acharya et al. and related measures are not necessarily very accurate indicators of systemic risk. Different quantitative measures of systemic risk produce significantly different rankings (Benoit et al. 2013). In addition, the measures are not closely tied to analysis of the underlying drivers of potential contagion, and the assumptions on which they are based are not tailored to specific sectors.

Perhaps the best-known measure is SRISK (or SRISK%), which is published by the NYU Stern School (http://vlab.stern.nyu.edu/welcome/risk/) and described by Acharya, Engle, and Richardson (2012). SRISK is a measure of a firm's expected capital shortfall relative to a presumed prudent level of capital, conditional on the occurrence of a large drop in aggregate stock market value. The calculation reflects a firm's estimated (long-run) marginal expected shortfall and leverage in relation to an assumed prudent capital ratio. The measure has generally ranked several life insurance entities relatively highly among large, publicly traded financial institutions. SRISK, however, is very highly correlated with a firm's total liabilities (Benoit et al. 2013), making large firms inherently prone to high rankings, regardless of whether their underlying operations pose a risk of significant spillovers from financial distress. The calculation of SRISK also assumes the same (and bank-centric) prudent capital ratio for different types of financial institutions, which is inconsistent with heterogeneity in risk, systemic or otherwise, across banks, insurers, and other types of companies. There is no consideration of the nature or duration of liabilities, and no distinction of separate account liabilities for life insurers. As a result, while quantitatively sophisticated, SRISK values (and related measures) provide limited and potentially misleading guidance about whether financial distress at individual insurance entities could threaten the financial stability of the United States.

FSOC DESIGNATION OF NONBANK SIFIS

The Dodd-Frank Act charged the FSOC with (1) identifying risks to financial stability from "the material financial distress of large, interconnected bank holding companies or nonbank financial companies, or that could arise outside the financial services marketplace"; (2) promoting market discipline "by eliminating expectations on the part of shareholders, creditors, and counterparties that the Government will shield them from losses in the event of failure"; and (3) responding to "emerging threats to the stability of the U.S. financial system." The FSOC has 10 voting members from member agencies, including, among others, the Federal Reserve chair, Treasury secretary, Securities and Exchange Commission (SEC) chair, Federal Deposit Insurance Corporation (FDIC) chair, Comptroller of the Currency director, and a presidential appointee with expertise in insurance, and five nonvoting members, including the Office of Financial Research director, the Federal Insurance Office director, a state insurance commissioner, a state banking commissioner, and a state securities commissioner.

Section 113 of the Dodd-Frank Act provides the FSOC with the authority by a two-thirds vote to designate a nonbank financial company, including an insurance company, as systemically important (capable of imposing a threat to the financial stability of the United States) and subject to enhanced regulation and supervision by the Federal Reserve. The Federal Reserve is required to establish, with input from the FSOC, enhanced risk-based capital requirements, leverage rules, resolution standards, and other requirements for systemically important nonbank financial companies. Section 113 specifies factors the FSOC must consider in determining whether a company will be designated as systemically important, including its leverage; its off-balance sheet exposure; its importance as a source of credit and liquidity for households, businesses, state and local governments, and low-income communities; the nature, scope, size, and interconnectedness of its activities; the amounts and nature of its assets and liabilities; the degree to which it is already regulated by one or more primary regulators; and "any other risk-related factors that the Council deems appropriate."

FSOC regulatory rules and guidance for designating nonbank financial companies as systemically important set forth six broad risk categories for determining systemic importance: size, lack of substitutes for the firm's services and products, interconnectedness with other financial firms, leverage, liquidity risk and maturity mismatch, and existing regulatory scrutiny. The size, lack of substitutes, and interconnectedness criteria "seek to assess the potential for spillovers from the firm's distress to the broader financial system." The leverage, liquidity risk and maturity mismatch, and existing regulatory scrutiny criteria "seek to assess how vulnerable a company is to financial distress." The rules establish a three-stage process for determination of whether a nonbank financial company poses a threat to the financial stability of the United States.

Stage 1 employs publicly available information and information from member regulatory agencies to identify nonbank financial companies for more detailed evaluation in Stage 2. A company is evaluated further in Stage 2 if its global consolidated assets are U.S. $50 billion or greater and it meets at least one of five additional quantitative thresholds. Stage 2 entails a review and prioritization of Stage 2 entities based on analysis of each company using information available to the FSOC through existing public and regulatory agencies and information obtained from the company voluntarily. Based on this analysis, the FSOC notifies companies it believes merit further evaluation in Stage 3, including analysis of additional information collected directly from the company. The evaluation considers the company's resolvability in the event of financial distress and includes consultation with the company's primary regulator. Following Stage 3 analysis, a "Proposed Determination" of a company as systemically significant requires a two-thirds vote of the FSOC, followed by a hearing if the company requests and, if so, a final vote.

As noted in the introduction, as of August 2013 the FSOC had designated AIG as systemically important, Prudential Financial was contesting a proposed designation, and MetLife had been notified that the firm had advanced to Stage 3 of the designation process. The FSOC had published an explanation for the AIG designation. It had not released any conclusions regarding Prudential Financial pending a hearing and final FSOC decision.

The FSOC's published explanation (FSOC 2013) for the AIG designation states that "many of AIG's life insurance and annuity products, while intended to be long-term liabilities, have features that could make them vulnerable to rapid and early withdrawal by policyholders." If financial distress "were sufficiently severe, funds . . . might be withdrawn regardless of the size of associated surrender charges or tax penalties." That in turn could "compel the company to liquidate a substantial portion of its large portfolio of relatively illiquid" assets, which could "have disruptive effects on the broader financial markets." The explanation further states that "wide-ranging and rapid withdrawals by AIG policyholders" and associated distress at AIG could cause financial contagion if "negative sentiment and uncertainty" at AIG were to increase surrender activity at other insurers.[9] It notes that the state insurance guaranty system could reduce potential policyholder losses from failure of AIG's insurance subsidiaries, but that such failure "could put unprecedented strain on the system, potentially exhausting its capacity to cover other policyholders at other firms and undermining confidence in other insurers, particularly in the context of broader financial stress across the insurance industry."

It seems likely that the FSOC's vulnerability to runs explanation of the AIG designation would also be used to support any final designation of Prudential Financial or MetLife. Be that as it may, and the unique circumstances of AIG aside, the designation of one or more major insurance companies as systemically important would be difficult to reconcile with much of the academic and policy research on systemic risk potential in insurance, or with evidence that financial difficulties at individual insurance entities have not produced significant negative spillovers on other insurers or their policyholders (see, e.g., Fenn and Cole 1994; Brewer and Jackson 2002).

POTENTIAL CONSEQUENCES OF SIFI DESIGNATION

It might be argued that FSOC designation of one or more large insurers as systemically important and subject to enhanced supervision by the Federal Reserve is prudent, given the potentially large costs associated with systemic events and the goal of making sure that any noninsurance activities of major insurance entities do not escape meaningful regulatory supervision. Those arguments should be weighed against the potential direct and indirect costs of such designation. Evaluation of the benefit-cost trade-off also should consider the likelihood that enhanced supervision would effectively reduce risk, as well as alternatives for reducing potential gaps in insurance regulatory authority (for example, through possible modifications in state insurance regulation).

Any additional insurance entities designated as systemically important and subject to enhanced supervision will face significant costs in complying with new and potentially duplicative regulation. Depending on the details, and as elaborated here, such entities' operating decisions could be affected in ways that reduce their ability to provide insurance coverage and services at attractive prices and disrupt normal competition within the insurance sector. Enhanced supervision also requires the costly development by the Federal Reserve of rules and expertise, which could involve some diversion of resources and effort from activities that would add more value than developing and administering enhanced supervision for a few insurance entities. While some of those costs will necessarily be incurred due to the AIG designation, it seems plausible that they could be significantly higher if other insurers are designated. The designation of additional insurers as systemically important could also lead to changes in the political dynamic associated with regulation in general and capital requirements in particular by, for example, expanding the number and political clout of opponents of more stringent capital standards and supervision for systemically important institutions.

The design of enhanced capital and leverage requirements for insurance SIFIs represents a critically important and challenging issue. Subtitle C of the Dodd-Frank Act provides a broad framework for federal regulation of bank and nonbank SIFIs. Section 165 in particular requires the Federal Reserve to develop prudential standards for such institutions, including risk-based capital requirements and leverage limits, which reflect organizational and risk differences between bank and nonbank SIFIs.

Section 165 provides the Federal Reserve with guidance and broad discretion in prescribing more stringent capital standards. Section 165(a)(2)(A) allows the Federal Reserve on its own or based on recommendation by the FSOC to "differentiate among companies on an individual basis or by category, taking into consideration their capital structure, riskiness, complexity, financial activities (including the financial activities of their subsidiaries), size, and any other risk-related factors that the Board of Governors deems appropriate." Section 165(b)(3)(D) requires the Federal Reserve to "adapt the required standards as appropriate in light of any predominant line of business of such company, including assets under management or other activities for which particular standards may not be appropriate." Sections 171(b)(1) and 171(b)(2) (aka the Collins Amendment) require federal agencies to establish minimum leverage and risk-based capital requirements on a consolidated basis for insured depository institutions, bank holding companies, savings and loan holding companies, and nonbank SIFIs that cannot be less than the generally applicable requirements for insured depository institutions, or lower than the "requirements that were in effect for insured depository institutions as of the date of enactment of this Act."

Subsequent proposals by federal regulatory agencies to impose bank-centric capital rules (based on Basel III) on insurance organizations with savings and loan subsidiaries have generated substantial push-back from insurance trade groups. Similar concerns arise from the potential application of bank-centric capital regulation to insurance SIFIs, and the extent to which the Collins Amendment constrains Federal Reserve authority for prescribing enhanced prudential standards that reflect the specific operations and risks of insurer SIFIs under Section 165 is being debated.[10]

Core insurance activities and existing insurance capital and leverage requirements are fundamentally different from banking. Bank capital rules focus heavily on asset risk. Insurance risk-based capital requirements are tailored to the specific risks of insurance operations, including the risk that claims may turn out to be higher than predicted when policies were priced and that reported liabilities for unpaid claims may prove inadequate.

Enhanced capital requirements for insurance SIFIs (and capital requirements for insurance organizations with savings and loan subsidiaries) should be designed to reflect the distinct operations, risks, and business models of such entities. One approach for the Federal Reserve to achieve that objective would be to start with the Basel rules and substantially modify those rules to reflect the distinct risks of insurance organizations. That patchwork approach would necessarily add substantial complexity to an already complex framework—without necessarily producing capital and leverage ratios that would be truly comparable across banking and insurance organizations.

A second and potentially far simpler (but not simple) approach would be for the Federal Reserve to base enhanced capital standards for insurance SIFIs on existing state-based risk-based capital requirements, with appropriate tailoring to address risks of any noninsurance activities.[11] This approach would lever existing risk-based capital requirements for insurers, which have evolved over two decades. It would likely involve lower administration and compliance costs and entail significantly less risk of unintended consequences. By maintaining fundamental distinctions between banking and insurance, it also might mitigate the risk of further expansion of bank-centric rules to insurers, such as the development of a federal guarantee of insurer obligations based on the deposit insurance model.

PROMOTING MARKET DISCIPLINE AND AVOIDING TOO BIG TO FAIL

A potentially important unintended consequence of designating individual insurance organizations as systemically important, regardless of other language and provisions of the Dodd-Frank Act, is that it might imply that the entity is too big (important) to fail. The designation could cause some potential creditors and policyholders to infer that the federal government would intervene to protect them from losses they otherwise would suffer in the event the entity experienced severe financial distress, especially in an environment of broad financial turmoil. The FSOC's prevention of runs and contagion rationale for its AIG SIFI designation could encourage that inference.

As a result, and other things being equal, a SIFI designation could allow a designee to obtain funding at lower cost and have a competitive advantage in attracting risk-sensitive policyholders. Thus, while enhanced prudential standards for an insurance SIFI would increase regulatory compliance costs and potentially harm its ability to compete for clients, perceptions of possible implicit federal backing of the entity's obligations would tend to reduce market discipline for its safety and soundness. Neither effect is consistent with achieving a level playing field for competition within the insurance sector.

A lack of market discipline contributed significantly to the 2007–2009 financial crisis. A primary objective of legislative and administrative responses to crisis should be to encourage market discipline to promote safety and soundness in all types of financial institutions. A significant objective of parts of the Dodd-Frank Act is to reduce the likelihood of future government bailouts of financial firms. There exists an uneasy tension between that objective and designation of insurance entities as systemically important.

Insurance markets generally have been characterized by relatively strong market discipline from policyholders, bondholders, insurance intermediaries, and rating agencies, and by the desire of many insurers to protect against loss of franchise value that would follow financial distress.[12] Consistent with much lower systemic risk potential in insurance than in banking, policyholder protection provided by state guaranty associations is relatively narrow, reducing moral hazard and helping preserve market discipline. The designation of insurance SIFIs by the FSOC and the prevention of runs and contagion rationale could ultimately contribute to pressure for more comprehensive and explicit federal guarantees of insurers' obligations to policyholders, perhaps patterned after bank deposit insurance, as well as an expanded perception of implicit guarantees. The ultimate result could be reduced market discipline in insurance, excessive risk taking, and another round of reforms to deal with the consequences.

CONCLUSION

The financial collapse and subsequent federal government bailout of AIG due predominantly to its noninsurance activities represent singular events in the financial history of the United States. Given those events and authorizing provisions in the Dodd-Frank Act, the FSOC's subsequent designation of

AIG as systemically important and subject to enhanced prudential supervision by the Federal Reserve was inevitable. AIG notwithstanding, however, core insurance activities pose little or no systemic risk, and financial distress at organizations that focus predominantly on insurance would be unlikely to threaten the financial stability of the United States. The potential benefits of designating additional insurance organizations as systemically important are therefore modest compared with the potential direct and indirect costs. Enhanced capital, leverage, and other prudential requirements for AIG and any other insurers that nonetheless may be designated as systemically important should be designed to reflect the distinct operations and risks of those entities. There are significant advantages to basing enhanced capital requirements on existing risk-based capital requirements for insurers.

NOTES

1. The FSOC also designated GE Capital as a nonbank SIFI without challenge by the company. On the international front, the Financial Stability Board had proposed nine insurance organizations, including AIG, MetLife, and Prudential Financial, for designation as systemically important.
2. Harrington (2009) contains detailed discussion.
3. Several of these or similar arguments have been made previously (Harrington 2009, 2011, 2013).
4. Parts of this section draw from Dionne and Harrington (in press). The systemic risk issue for insurance received some attention before the financial crisis. Harrington (2004a), for example, contrasted systemic risk potential among property-casualty insurers, life insurers, reinsurers, and banks.
5. There are at least four sources of potential contagion that could contribute to systemic risk (e.g., Kaufman 1994), including: (1) asset price contagion (fire sales), (2) counterparty contagion, (3) information-based contagion (the revelation of financial problems at some institutions creates uncertainty about the effects on counterparties), and (4) irrational contagion (investors and/or customers withdraw funds without regard to risk). Ellul, Jotikasthira, and Lundblad (2011) provide evidence of regulatory-induced fire sales of downgraded corporate bonds by life insurers.
6. Harrington (2009) discusses uncertainty about whether AIG's credit default swaps and securities lending presented significant risk of contagion and the extent to which an AIG bankruptcy would have had significant adverse effects beyond its counterparties, or the extent to which

its counterparties had hedged or otherwise reduced their exposure to AIG.

7. The detailed review and analysis by Cummins and Weiss (2013), for example, concluded that "the core activities of U.S. insurers do not pose systemic risk."

8. Chen et al. (2012) used Granger causality tests to examine interconnectedness between banks and insurers using data on credit default swap spreads. Also see Grace (2010).

9. The explanation also noted that AIG's commercial insurance services would be "difficult for policyholders to replace in a short time frame" if AIG were to exit the market for those services and that complexities of resolving financial distress at AIG would increase the threat to U.S. financial stability.

10. Sarfatti (2013) provides a detailed critique of problems associated with applying Basel rules to insurers.

11. MetLife has outlined a proposal along these lines.

12. See, for example, the detailed discussion in Harrington (2004b) and evidence provided by Epermanis and Harrington (2006). Also see Eling (2012).

REFERENCES

Acharya, V., R. Engle, and M. Richardson. 2012. "Capital Shortfall: A New Approach to Ranking and Regulating Systemic Risks." *American Economic Review* 102:59–64.

Acharya, V. V., L. H. Pedersen, T. Philippon, and M. Richardson. 2010. "Measuring Systemic Risk." Working paper, Federal Reserve Bank of Cleveland, Cleveland, Ohio.

Benoit, S., G. Colletaz, C. Hurlin, and C. Perignon. 2013. "A Theoretical and Empirical Comparison of Systemic Risk Measures," February 14. http://ssrn.com/abstract=1973950.

Billio, M., M. Getmansky, A. W. Lo, and L. Pelizzon. 2012. "Econometric Measures of Connectedness and Systemic Risk in the Finance and Insurance Sectors." *Journal of Financial Economics* 104:535–559.

Brewer, E., and W. Jackson. 2002. "Intra-Industry Contagion and the Competitive Effects of Financial Distress Announcements: Evidence from Commercial Banks and Insurance Companies." Federal Reserve Bank of Chicago Working Paper No. 2002-23.

Chen, H., J. D. Cummins, K. S. Viswanathan, and M. A. Weiss. 2012. "Systemic Risk and the Inter-Connectedness between Banks and Insurers: An Econometric Analysis." *Journal of Risk and Insurance*, in press.

Cummins, J. D., and M. A. Weiss. 2013. "Systemic Risk and the Insurance Industry." In *The Handbook of Insurance*, 2nd ed., ed. G.Dionne (New York: Springer, in press).

Dionne, G., and S. E. Harrington. In press. "Insurance and Insurance Markets." In *Handbook of the Economics of Risk and Uncertainty*, ed. M. J.Machina and W. K.Viscusi, 203–262 (Oxford, UK: North-Holland/ Elsevier).

Eling, M. 2012. "What Do We Know about Market Discipline in Insurance?" *Risk Management and Insurance Review* 15:185–223.

Ellul, A., C. Jotikasthira, and C. T. Lundblad. 2011. "Regulatory Pressure and Fire Sales in the Corporate Bond Market." *Journal of Financial Economics* 101, issue 3 (September): 596–620.

Epermanis, K., and S. E. Harrington. 2006. "Market Discipline in Property/ Casualty Insurance: Evidence from Premium Growth Surrounding Changes in Financial Strength Ratings." *Journal of Money, Credit and Banking* 38:1515–1544.

Fenn, G. and R. Cole. 1994. Announcements of Asset-Quality Problems and Contagion Effects in the Life Insurance Industry." *Journal of Financial Economics* 35:181–198.

Financial Stability Oversight Council. 2013. "Basis of the Financial Stability Oversight Council's Final Determination Regarding American International Group, Inc.," July 8.

Geneva Association. 2010. *Systemic Risk in Insurance: An Analysis of Insurance and Financial Stability*. Geneva, Switzerland: Geneva Association.

Geneva Association. 2012. *Insurance and Resolution in Light of the Systemic Risk Debate*. Geneva, Switzerland: Geneva Association.

Grace, M. F. 2010. "The Insurance Industry and Systemic Risk: Evidence and Discussion." Working paper, Georgia State University.

Harrington, S. E. 2004a. "Capital Adequacy in Insurance and Reinsurance." In *Capital Adequacy beyond Basel: Banking, Securities, and Insurance*, ed. Hal S. Scott. Oxford, UK: Oxford University Press.

Harrington, S. E. 2004b. "Market Discipline in Insurance and Reinsurance." In *Market Discipline: The Evidence across Countries and Industries*, ed. C. Borio et al. Cambridge, MA: MIT Press.

Harrington, S. E. 2009. "The Financial Crisis, Systemic Risk, and the Future of Insurance Regulation." *Journal of Risk and Insurance* 76:785–819.

Harrington, S. E. 2011. "Insurance Regulation and the Dodd-Frank Act." Networks Financial Institute Policy Brief 2011-PB-01, March.

Harrington, S. E. 2013. "The Dodd-Frank Act, Solvency II, and U.S. Insurance Regulation." *Journal of financial Perspectives* 1:1–12.

International Association of Insurance Supervisors (IAIS). 2011. "Insurance and Financial Stability." IAIS, November.

Kaufman, G. 1994. "Bank Contagion: A Review of Theory and Evidence." *Journal of Financial Services Research*, 123–150.

Sarfatti, Aaron. 2013. "Too Big to Insure: A Review and Commentary on the Capital and Liquidity Rules of Non-Bank SIFI Insurers." Presentation, American Risk and Insurance Association Annual Meeting, Washington, DC, August 6.

Swiss Re. 2003. "Reinsurance—A Systemic Risk?" *Sigma* 5/2003.

CHAPTER 9

Is the Insurance Industry Systemically Risky?

Viral V. Acharya and Matthew Richardson[1]

Stern School of Business, New York University

As a result of the financial crisis, the Congress passed the Dodd-Frank Wall Street Reform and Consumer Protection Act and it was signed into law by President Barack Obama on July 21, 2010. The Dodd-Frank Act did not create a new direct regulator of insurance but did impose on nonbank holding companies, possibly insurance entities, a major new and unknown form of regulation for those deemed systemically important financial institutions (SIFIs)—sometimes denoted "too big to fail" (TBTF)—or presumably any entity that regulators believe represents a contingent liability for the federal government in the event of severe stress or failure.

In light of the financial crisis and the somewhat benign changes to insurance regulation contained in the Dodd-Frank Act (regulation of SIFIs aside), how should a modern insurance regulatory structure be designed to deal with systemic risk?

The economic theory of regulation is very clear: Regulate where there is a market failure. It is apparent that a major market failure in the financial crisis of 2007–2009 was the emergence of systemic risk. More concretely, systemic risk emerged when aggregate capitalization of the financial sector became low. The intuition for why this is a problem is straightforward. When a financial firm's capital is low, it is difficult for that firm to perform financial services; and when capital is low in the aggregate, it is not possible for other financial firms to step into the breach. This breakdown in financial intermediation is the reason severe consequences occurred in the broader economy.

When financial firms therefore ran aground during the crisis period, they contributed to the aggregate shortfall, leading to consequences beyond the firm itself. The firm has no incentive to manage the systemic risk, and the negative externality associated with such risks implies that private markets cannot efficiently solve the problem, so government intervention is required. In other words, regulators now need to focus not just on a financial institution's own losses, but also on the cost that its failure would impose on the system.

The question is whether this applies to the insurance sector. Some academics and others have argued with good reason that there are fundamental differences between the insurance and banking sectors; for example, see Cummins and Weiss (2013); Harrington (2009, 2010, 2013); and Tyler and Hoenig (2009).[2] The argument basically rests on the fact that traditional insurers do not write and retain large and concentrated amounts of non-traditional insurance or similar risk management products with exposure to macroeconomic variables. That is, traditional insurance usually protects policyholders against risks that they deem significant but that are at least reasonably idiosyncratic and thus diversifiable from the insurers' perspective.[3] Moreover, insurance companies have much longer-term and less liquid liabilities, which makes them less susceptible to a run on their liabilities of the sort that plague financial firms during typical financial crises.

It does not follow, however, that systemic risk cannot emerge in what is typically defined as the insurance sector. One of the main reasons is that researchers misunderstand the meaning of systemic risk. As described earlier, the emergence of systemic risk is that financial firms will no longer be able to provide intermediation, causing knock-on effects to households and businesses.

The purpose of this chapter is to explain why the insurance sector may be a source for systemic risk. In brief, we argue that the insurance industry is no longer traditional in the above sense and instead (1) offers products with nondiversifiable risk, (2) is more prone to a run, (3) insures against macro-wide events, and (4) has expanded its role in financial markets. This can lead to the insurance sector performing particularly poorly in systemic states, that is, when other parts of the financial sector are struggling. We provide evidence using publicly available data on equities and credit default swaps. As an important source for products to the economy (i.e., insurance) and a source for financing (i.e., corporate bonds and commercial mortgages), dis-intermediation of the insurance sector can have dire consequences. Indeed, the recent decision by the Financial Stability Oversight Council (FSOC) to name American International Group (AIG) and Prudential Financial (and potentially MetLife) as SIFIs is related to this point.

The chapter is organized as follows. The first section that follows describes the arguments for and against systemic risk regulation of the insurance sector. Given the Dodd-Frank Act's required regulation of insurance companies that are designated SIFIs, there is perhaps no greater controversy in insurance regulation. Next, we provide an empirical analysis of the systemic risk of insurance companies based on a specific systemic risk measure. The following two sections address specific issues related to systemic risk, and in the last section of this chapter we analyze broader issues with respect to regulation at the federal versus state level.

ARE INSURANCE COMPANIES SYSTEMICALLY RISKY?

Our argument is that systemic risk emerges when aggregate capitalization of the financial sector is low. In the recent crisis, full-blown systemic risk emerged only when, in the early fall of 2008, the government-sponsored enterprises (GSEs) Fannie Mae and Freddie Mac, Lehman Brothers, AIG, Merrill Lynch, Washington Mutual, Wachovia, and Citigroup, among others, effectively failed. The result—as we have seen painfully in several crises over past 40 years around the world—was loss of intermediation to households and corporations. It is from this breakdown in financial intermediation that severe consequences occurred in the broader economy.

For insurance companies, disintermediation can take several forms. For example, the willingness of insurance companies to supply insurance products may suffer, leading to higher prices and an overall loss of economic welfare. There is growing evidence that capital-constrained financial firms, including insurance companies, may reduce the supply of capital in the face of losses. For example, in the catastrophe insurance area, Froot (2001) and Froot and O'Connell (1999) find that insurance premiums not only appear high relative to expected losses in these markets, but increase dramatically after a catastrophe.[4] Interestingly, this increase spills over to insurance markets not affected by the catastrophe. Garmaise and Moskowitz (2009) find that the supply of credit for catastrophe-susceptible properties in California fell after the earthquakes in the 1990s.[5] It is an open question whether these supply shocks extend beyond the catastrophe insurance area.

In addition, as an important player in the financing of credit-linked activities, insurance companies are an essential part of the economic system. Almost all financial firms have in common the characteristic that they are holders of long-term assets. Through the flow of funds within the economic system, these firms provide financing to real economy firms. These firms are in effect all financial intermediaries, such as banks holding retail, commercial, and mortgage loans, insurance companies holding corporate bonds, money market funds buying commercial paper, mutual funds and hedge funds holding equity and other securities, structured investment vehicles pooling loans into asset-backed securities, and so forth. In addition, some financial firms provide additional functions to real economy participants such as payment and clearing, liquidity, insurance against catastrophic risks, and so on. The important point is that all firms are potentially important. As we will make clear, the key factor in their systemic risk determination is whether the firm contributes to the aggregate capital shortfall.

Life insurance companies are one of the largest investors in the U.S. capital markets and therefore an important source of funding for the U.S. economy. See, for example, Cummins and Weiss (Chapter 7 in this volume) and Paulson, Plestis, Rosen, McMenamin, and Mohey-Deen (Chapter 6 in this volume). For example, the American Council of Life Insurers (ACLI) estimates that, at the end of 2010, life insurers held almost $5 trillion in total assets, and were the largest single investor in U.S. corporate bonds (17 percent) and a significant player in the commercial mortgage market (9.5 percent). If these firms are in distress and can no longer play their role as financiers for corporate America, then this is precisely the concern about systemic risk. In particular, if AA-rated and AAA-rated firms find it punitively expensive to issue corporate bonds, then they would draw down on their bank lines of credit as a form of last-resort financing, triggering massive liabilities for their relationship banks. While the healthier banks with adequate capital and deposit bases might be able to meet the sudden drawdowns of credit lines, moderately risky banks could experience distress, and the already weakened ones could run aground as they scramble for liquidity to avoid a shortfall between loan demand and their available funding.

Even leaving aside such a transmission of risk from the insurance sector to the banking sector via the flow-of-funds nexus between corporate bonds and lines of credit, it is clear that at a minimum the corporate bond market, which is not that liquid to start with, would experience further pressure on its liquidity. There is substantive evidence, for example, that the liquidity of the corporate bond market dropped after the onset of the crisis; for example, see Dick-Nielsen, Feldhutter, and Lando (2012).[6] In Chapter 6 of this book, Paulson, Plestis, Rosen, McMenamin, and Mohey-Deen describe the liquidity of the insurance industry's asset holdings.[7] In particular, they analyze stress scenarios in which the insurance industry would have to liquidate some of its assets. They find that, relative to runnable liabilities, these firms would have to dip fairly deeply into their holdings of corporate bonds and other less liquid securities (i.e., nonagency and nongovernment securities).

Manconi, Massa, and Yasuda (2012)[8] document that in the second half of 2007, bond mutual funds and insurance firms contributed to the illiquidity of the corporate debt market as losses on the holdings of securitized bonds and commercial mortgage-backed securities (CMBSs, which insurers hold more than securitized bonds, in contrast to bond mutual funds) transmitted in the form of asset sales or reduced purchases in other holdings, notably of lower-rated securitized and corporate bonds. The authors also document that the sales during the crisis were associated with widening yields, in contrast to the reverse association in the precrisis period. While bond mutual funds contributed more to this illiquidity due to their shorter horizons of investment, insurance firms did so due to the capital requirements they faced, especially if they were close to their risk-based capital threshold. Indeed, the authors conclude that "insurance companies did not act as strategic liquidity providers at the onset of the crisis and that at best, there is only weak evidence that their trades partially offset the net sales of corporate bonds by mutual funds."

Interestingly, this brings to the fore the role of risk-based capital requirements for insurance firms. Stanton and Wallace (2010)[9] attribute the precrisis rise in holdings of CMBSs on balance sheets of regulated financial firms to a "regulatory arbitrage" of risk weights, including by insurance companies. Since the crisis, insurance companies have indeed become dominant purchasers of securitized and tranched collateral loan obligation (CLO) and collateralized bond obligation (CBO) products, due to the reduced interest from the banking sector, which has come under tighter scrutiny of regulation and prudential norms. In other words, the insurance sector is now an increasingly important player not just in the corporate bond market but also in the securitized bond markets.

It is an open question what role financial disintermediation on the part of distressed insurers played in the credit crunch in the corporate bond market in the fall of 2008. More research examining this issue directly would be highly informative and important for understanding the transmission of insurance-sector distress to the real economy. Nevertheless, the impact of the insurance sector's unwillingness to intermediate in the corporate bond market is now well-documented, even when it is outside of a common shock to the economy. For instance, Ellul, Jotikasthira, and Lundblad (2010)[10] investigate fire sales of downgraded corporate bonds induced by regulatory constraints on insurance companies. Using transaction data from 2001 to 2005, they find that insurance companies more constrained by regulation are more likely to sell downgraded bonds. They show that these bonds exhibit significant price declines and subsequent reversals, effects that are stronger during periods when insurance companies as a group are more distressed and when other potential buyers' capital is relatively scarce. It would be natural to conclude that such fire-sale effects would be only stronger if the insurance sector was distressed coincidentally with a wave of downgrades in the economy, and especially so in a time when the banking sector was experiencing severe distress, too—an outcome we would call systemic risk, as it would imply limited capacity to reintermediate funding in the economy.

We have discussed two ways insurance companies might disintermediate in the face of losses. To this point, in declaring AIG to be a SIFI, FSOC argued that AIG poses a threat to financial stability through three related channels: "(1) the exposures of creditors, counterparties, investors, and other market participants to AIG; (2) the liquidation of assets by AIG, which could trigger a fall in asset prices and thereby could significantly disrupt trading or funding in key markets or cause significant losses or funding problems for other firms with similar holdings; and (3) the inability or unwillingness of AIG to provide a critical function or service relied upon by market participants and for which there are no ready substitutes."[11] The specifics of each of these channels are described by FSOC in its document, and map closely to our discussion. Note that in deciding that AIG is a SIFI, FSOC looked at the nature, scope, size, scale, and interconnectedness of AIG's activities, its leverage, its reliance on short-term funding, and whether AIG is a source of credit for the economy, among other things.

In this chapter, we have a somewhat different take on how much a firm contributes to systemic risk. To a first approximation, we argue that a systemic financial crisis occurs if and only if there is a capital shortfall of the aggregate sector. Of course, the source for an aggregate capital shortfall can take many forms. To coincide with FSOC's description of AIG, we illustrate this point in the context of AIG.

First, financial firms could all be highly leveraged and face aggregate market exposure. A large shock to the economy could therefore cause large aggregate losses and a capital shortfall. With respect to the financial crisis of 2007–2009, many financial firms had broad exposure to nonprime residential real estate through either loans or asset-backed security (ABS) holdings.

For example, a major factor in AIG's collapse was the $40.5 billion loss on AIG Capital Markets (AIG CM, a division of its Financial Services business), out of the total loss of over $100 billion (see page 116 of the 10-K). Much of this loss was due to AIG CM's selling of $527 billion worth of credit default swap (CDS) protection on super-senior ABSs (page 122, AIG quarterly filings, February 2008). In addition, AIG's Life Insurance and Retirement Services segment had serious losses in 2008, of $37.5 billion, almost as much as AIG Financial Services' loss of $40.8 billion. These losses came from its failed securities lending businesses, aggressive variable annuity death benefit provisions, and investment losses on its over $500 billion asset portfolio ($489.6 billion as of December 31, 2008). Securities lending is typically not considered a very risky business, as the collateral is invested in safe short-term assets. Other life insurance companies, such as MetLife, also run similar businesses. In AIG's case, however, state filings show that roughly two-thirds of its cash collateral was invested in mortgage-backed securities very similar to the AAA-rated tranches they were insuring in its Financial Products group.

Second, the financial sector, possibly starting from a weak point, could suffer a capital shortfall if a highly interconnected firm fails and losses reverberate throughout the sector. From our standpoint, the relevant issue is not only that the highly interconnected firm is systemically risky, but that its counterparties are as well by being exposed to that firm.

In AIG's case, the degree of interconnectedness to the financial system was a great contributor to systemic risk. Through its Capital Markets unit, AIG had $1.6 trillion in notional derivatives exposures, linking itself to over 1,500 corporations, governments, and institutional investors. The problem with over-the-counter (OTC) derivatives markets, like the ones AIG participated in, is that bilateral collateral and margin requirements in OTC trading do not take into account the counterparty risk externality that each trade imposes on the rest of the system, allowing systemically important exposures to be built up without sufficient capital to mitigate the risks. To get an idea of the magnitude of the losses and the depth of the counterparties, Acharya, Biggs, Le, Richardson, and Ryan (2010) document the 10 largest payments of AIG to its various counterparties from September 16, 2008, to December 31, 2008, as a result of government aid.[12] The payments are broken down into (1) collateral postings under credit default swap contracts, (2) the outright purchase of collateralized debt obligations that AIG had written CDS contracts on via Maiden Lane III, and (3) guaranteed investment agreements held by municipalities. They show that, without government support, the losses across the financial community from these three sources alone during the three-month period would have been staggering, reaching a total of $61.6 billion. The resulting market and funding liquidity conditions of these and other firms would have likely led to even greater aggregate capital shortfalls, exacerbating the financial crisis.[13]

Third, the financial sector, again possibly starting from a weak point, could suffer a capital shortfall if a large financial firm fails and liquidation of illiquid assets leads to fire sales that pose funding problems for other financial firms, which in turn lead to greater liquidations and more funding problems, et cetera. The result is a financial sector death spiral. In our view, the relevant point is not only that this large firm with concentrated holdings is systemically risky, but also that other financial firms are as well as long as these firms are exposed to similar risks.

With respect to AIG, its holdings of $1.6 trillion in derivatives would have led to an unwinding of positions that could have created a deathlike spiral. An additional question is whether AIG's failure at the parent level could lead to fire sales on its vast holdings of assets beyond the derivative products mentioned earlier. Going into the crisis, AIG was the fifth-largest institutional asset manager worldwide. If one were to include all of AIG's investments, AIG was the largest investor in corporate bonds in the United States and the second largest holder of U.S. municipal bonds through its Commercial Insurance (AIG CI) business, worth $50 billion. Any significant forced sale of these bond portfolios would have put substantive stress on the respective financial markets. Since the assets of AIG's insurance companies were legally separated from AIG CM, however, it is not clear that a failure at the parent level would indeed have caused a fire sale of its asset holdings elsewhere in the organization. In case of default, the AIG parent company had guaranteed the contracts at AIG CM, which effectively meant the counterparties had a claim on the underlying businesses owned by AIG though not ahead of the policyholders. It is quite possible that the businesses would have continued as normal. Finally, as mentioned earlier, there were significant losses from AIG's investments in the cash collateral derived from its securities lending business in which it lent out securities held in its life insurance and retirement service businesses. These losses were mostly attributable to AA and AAA tranches of nonprime mortgage-backed securities. Acharya, Cooley, Richardson, and Walter (2010) show that many financial firms were exposed to the exact same tail risk associated with these securities.[14]

Fourth, the financial sector, again possibly starting from a weak point, could suffer a capital shortfall if there is a run on a financial firm that encounters trouble and is funded via short-term liabilities. Given the uncertainty about other likewise financial institutions, an aggregate capital shortfall could result because these other institutions might suffer a similar run on their liabilities. The end result is a run on the financial sector. As before, from our standpoint, the relevant matter is not only that the failing firm is systemically risky, but likewise financial firms are as well given that they are also subject to a run even if solvent.

Even if AIG were not failing at the individual insurance company level, it is possible that its failure at the parent level, and weaknesses described previously at the insurance company level, could cause a classic "run on the bank." Since AIG has more than 81 million life insurance policies worldwide with a face value of $1.9 trillion, a large-scale run could have wide effects. For example, in one scenario, policyholders would cash in their policies, forcing AIG to raise cash, primarily through asset sales, leading to the type of spillover risk described earlier. The only protection AIG would have in this case would be the surrender charges or cancellation penalties, or untapped value of the policies. In another scenario, the sudden jump in uninsured would put temporary pressure at least on the ability of other life insurance companies to meet the insurance demands of these potential new customers. Of course, the largest concern of a "bank" run is that it leads to a systemwide run on the sector. A systemwide run is catastrophic as it leads to a freezing of the market these institutions operate in, and causes severe externalities toward related individuals and businesses. Given the importance of the life insurance sector to the overall economy, a system-wide run would be very damaging. It remains an open question whether a run on some of AIG's insurance businesses would lead to a run on other insurance companies. To many analysts, AIG was a unique company, so its troubles may be seen as specific to its circumstances—the failure of AIG CM and the collateral investments of its securities lending business—and not a more endemic characteristic of life insurance companies such as investment-oriented life insurance policies with minimum guarantees.

What should be clear from these examples is that systemic risk is really a statement about codependence. While the approach to regulation may be different in all of these cases, the bottom line is that firms that contribute to an aggregate capital shortfall are systemically risky. Earlier, we argued why the insurance sector is an important part of the economy-wide financial intermediation process. It follows that significant capital shortfalls of the insurance sector would contribute to systemic risk. We used the case of AIG to illustrate how an insurance company can potentially impact the aggregate shortfall of the financial sector. In the next section, we apply this intuition to a particular methodology for estimating and measuring systemic risk. That said, it is certainly reasonable to argue that AIG is a special case and that, for the most part, insurance companies do not add significantly to aggregate capital shortfalls and are not systemic. From this perspective, it is useful to compare traditional insurers with banks, and they differ in two important respects.

First, the underwriting risks of traditional insurers' claim liabilities usually are better diversified than are the credit risks of banks' loan assets, which typically are exposed to the macroeconomy, geographical regions, industries, or lines of business. When this is the case, traditional insurers can hold smaller amounts of capital relative to the face amount of insurance and still maintain an adequate solvency cushion against adverse claim outcomes.

Second, traditional insurers typically experience illiquidity only when they make poor business decisions rather than as an inevitable result of their business model.[15] In contrast, banks' illiquidity risk arises from their business model of investing in less liquid assets than liabilities. Traditional insurers, though, tend to write insurance policies that (1) require premiums to be received before claims are paid and have fairly high policy renewal rates; (2) naturally link the insurers' assets and liabilities because, when policyholders cancel their insurance policies, the insurer both refunds any unused premiums and eliminates any related claim liabilities; and (3), even for investment-oriented life insurers with accumulated policy values, often require policyholders who cash out those policies early to be subject to surrender charges or have the investment values of the policies paid out over prolonged periods (e.g., as annuities).

Because of these distinct features, most traditional insurers weathered the financial crisis considerably better than did most banks and other financial institutions. It is therefore difficult to make a case that traditional insurance firms, even large ones, cause systemic risk. For example, Park and Xie (2011) analyze systemic risk among interconnected property-casualty (P-C) insurers around rating downgrades.[16] While they do find evidence of spillover effects, the probability that these effects could lead to a systemwide impact is seen as small.

The argument that the insurance sector poses systemic risk, however, relies on the view that the insurance industry is no longer traditional in the above sense and instead (1) offers products with nondiversifiable risk, (2) is more prone to a run, (3) insures against macro-wide events, and (4) has expanded its role in financial markets.

First, the product offerings of insurance companies may contain aggregate, nondiversifiable risk. For example, some large life insurers, notably AIG, Hartford Financial Services Group (HFSG), and Lincoln National, aggressively wrote investment-oriented life insurance policies with minimum guarantees and other contract features that exposed them to equity and other investment markets. These policies expose the insurers to potentially large losses when markets decline. Moreover, the investment decisions of insurance companies may also include aggregate market exposures. If these risks materialize (and the risks by nature are more likely to do so during a financial and economic crisis), then insurance companies collectively will suffer investment losses. Some recent studies include Brewer, Carson, Elyasiani, Mansur, and Scott (2007), which examines the interest rate sensitivity of life insurers' holdings, and Baranoff and Sager (2009), which investigates life insurers' exposures to mortgage-backed securities.[17] Both of these papers show sensitivity to marketwide exposures.

To some degree, it is an empirical question whether insurance companies face aggregate exposures. Due to marked-to-market losses in their asset holdings or product offerings (like guaranteed investment contracts) becoming underwater, all tied to common macroeconomic events, the equity and subordinated bonds' value of insurance companies will (as it did in the financial crisis of 2007–2009) come under pressure. For example, the credit default swap (CDS) spreads—the cost of buying protection against default of senior, subordinated bonds—of MetLife, Hartford, and Lincoln National, among others, all rose well above 500 basis points in the fall of 2008 after Lehman's collapse.

Second, insurance products and markets have shifted in major ways. There has been a rapid rise in annuities—particularly variable annuities, some with imprudent macroeconomic guarantees. Most annuities are now purchased as withdrawable investment accounts (albeit with cash-out penalties) and represent almost 75 percent of all premiums. The standard assumption that the liabilities of distressed insurance companies cannot be run on no longer holds.

In Chapter 6 of this volume, Paulson, Plestis, Rosen, McMenamin, and Mohey-Deen provide a detailed analysis of this issue.[18] They provide evidence that approximately 50 percent of liabilities are in a moderately to highly liquid category, allowing for some type of withdrawal. Projected onto stress scenarios, they estimate that 43 percent or 31 percent of the life insurance industry's liabilities are subject to withdrawals in an extreme or moderate stress environment, respectively. In light of the possibility that life insurance premiums are no longer as sticky, one can look at evidence from the P-C industry (which are generally short-term contracts) to see that an insurer's distress can impact its ability to intermediate. See, for example, Cummins and Lewis (2003) and Epermanis and Harrington (2006).[19]

Third, over the past few decades, some insurers have deviated from the traditional insurance business model by providing so-called insurance or similar financial products protecting against loss due to macroeconomic events and other nondiversifiable risks. For example, in the years leading up to the financial crisis, the monoline insurers and American International Group (AIG) wrote financial guarantees on structured financial products tied to subprime mortgages.[20] If these nontraditional insurers become distressed, as they did during the most recent financial crisis, then their losses can be passed on to their counterparties, thus causing possible contagion throughout the financial sector at large.

Fourth, more broadly, the line between insurance companies and other financial services companies has become blurred over time. For example, some insurance companies, in particular AIG, ran large securities lending businesses. Securities lending is simply a form of shadow banking—that is, lightly regulated and subject to significant liquidity and run risks when underlying security or counterparty risks materialize. Another example is detailed in Koijen and Yogo (2013) and is reminiscent of the special purpose vehicles of large complex banks during the financial crisis.[21] Koijen and Yogo show that some of the larger life insurance companies are now using reinsurance to move liabilities from operating companies that sell policies to less regulated (i.e., less capitalized) "shadow insurers" in regulation-friendly U.S. states (e.g., South Carolina and Vermont) and offshore locales (e.g., Bermuda and the Cayman Islands). Since the liabilities stay within the insurer's holding company, there is not the usual risk transfer between the insurer and reinsurer. The authors show that this type of regulatory arbitrage has grown from $10 billion to $363 billion over the past decade, and, when accounted for, expected losses are almost $16 billion higher in the industry.

In another sign of blurring of the insurance industry's functional form, annuities are now the product of choice within the insurance sector, and can be considered investment products with certain features not unlike those offered by asset management companies. In surveys of these changes, Brown (2008) and Cummins and Weiss (2009) both provide descriptions of the convergence of financial services across different parts of the financial sector.[22] Of course, if different types of financial companies are offering similar products, then this suggests that regulation should be by function and not form, and also contradicts the often-stated claim that insurance companies are fundamentally different.

If systemic risk can indeed emerge from the insurance sector, what is the likelihood that insurance companies will fail en masse during a financial crisis period? Systemic risk should be broadly conceived as the potential failure of a significant part of the financial sector—one large institution or many smaller ones—leading to reductions in the availability of credit and/ or critical risk management products such as insurance, thereby adversely affecting the real economy. And, because of the interconnectedness of the modern financial sector, for the purposes of systemic risk regulation one must view the financial sector also broadly as composed of not just commercial banks taking deposits and making loans, but also investment banks, money market funds, mutual funds, insurers, and potentially even hedge funds and private equity funds.

In terms of measuring systemic risk of the insurance sector, however, there is not uniformity in the academic literature. For example, Billio, Getmansky, Lo, and Pelizzon (2012) find, through a battery of tests, that hedge funds, banks, broker-dealers, and insurance companies have become more interconnected over the past decade, giving support to the aforementioned thesis.[23] In contrast, Chen, Cummins, Viswanathan, and Weiss (2012) find that, while there is some bidirectional evidence of systemic risk between banks and insurers, the majority of this risk derives from banks.[24] Similarly, Grace (2010) argues that the insurance industry is less impacted, and provides some evidence around potentially systemic events during the recent financial crisis.[25]

All of this evidence, in favor and against, however, falls into the potential trap of measuring systemic risk incorrectly. Instead, the relevant issue is whether an insurer, and (when aggregated) the insurance sector, contributes to an aggregate capital shortfall of the financial sector and whether financial disintermediation results from this shortfall.[26] In Chapter 7 of this book, Cummins and Weiss (2013) relate particular insurance characteristics to such a measure, and find that systemic risk measured this way is more likely to show up in noncore activities of the insurance sector. In contrast, in Chapter 8 of this book, Harrington questions the efficacy of some of these methods applied to the insurance sector. In the next section, we provide an analysis of systemic risk based on aggregate capital shortfall.

SYSTEMIC RISK EVIDENCE

Why is measuring systemic risk so important?

The current problem with financial regulation is that the regulation seeks to limit each institution's risk in isolation. Unless the external costs of systemic risk are internalized by each financial institution, however, these institutions will have the incentive to take risks that are not borne just by the institution but instead by society as a whole. In other words, individually, firms may take actions to prevent their own collapse, but not necessarily the collapse of the system. It is in this sense that the financial institution's risk is a negative externality on the system.

Formal economic theory can be a useful guide to help measure systemic risk. Specifically, in (1) a model of a financial system in which each firm has limited liability and maximizes shareholder value, (2) the regulator provides some form of a safety net (i.e., guarantees for some creditors such as deposit or too-big-to-fail insurance), and (3) the economy faces systemic risk (i.e., systemwide costs) in a financial crisis when the financial sector's equity capitalization falls below some fraction of its total assets; these costs are proportional to the magnitude of this shortfall, and the costs of each financial firm are equal to the sum of two components:[27]

Costs to society of the financial firm
= Expected losses of the firm's guaranteed debt upon default
+ Expected systemic costs in a crisis per dollar of capital shortfall
× Expected capital shortfall of the firm if there is a crisis

In this framework, the systemic risk of a firm therefore is equal to:

Expected real social costs in a crisis per dollar of capital shortage
× Expected capital shortfall of the firm in a crisis

The first term reflects the product of the large bailout costs and real economy welfare losses associated with financial crises times the probability of such crises. The second term deals with the relative contribution of each financial firm to systemic risk though the firm's expected losses in a crisis.

The advantage of the above formula for a firm's systemic risk is that it is precise in nature. To measure a financial firm's contribution to systemic risk involves measuring the firm's expected capital shortfall in a crisis. This immediately provides the regulator with a quantifiable measure of the relative importance of a firm's contribution to overall systemic risk. The measure also captures in one fell swoop many of the characteristics considered important for systemic risk such as size, leverage, concentration, and interconnectedness, all of which serve to increase the expected capital shortfall in a crisis. But the measure also provides an important addition, most notably the comovement of the financial firm's assets with the aggregate financial sector in a crisis. The other major advantage of this measure is that it makes it possible to understand systemic risk, not just in terms of an individual financial firm but in the broader context of financial subsectors. For example, since the measure is additive, it is just one step to compare the systemic risk of, say, the regional banking sector versus the life insurance sector.

Can we quantify and measure the systemic risk of financial institutions? In this section, we argue that significant progress can be made even by relying exclusively on market information. The basis behind these calculations are provided in Acharya, Pedersen, Philippon, and Richardson (2010) and Brownlees and Engle (2010).[28] A detailed analysis is given at NYU Stern's Systemic Risk website, http://vlab.stern.nyu.edu/welcome/risk. Indeed, the results that follow are extracted from this site.

In brief, the procedure is to calculate the losses in market value of equity of a financial firm in a crisis, defined as the marginal expected shortfall (MES) associated with a market decline of at least c:

$$MES_{i,t} = E_{t-1}(-R_{i,t} \mid R_{m,t} < c) \tag{9.1}$$

The MES can be estimated in a variety of ways using either a structural model (e.g., an asymmetric general autoregressive conditional heteroscedasticity [GARCH] and dynamic conditional correlation model as in Brownlees and Engle [2010]) or a tail distribution model (e.g., see Acharya, Pedersen, Philippon, and Richardson [2010]), among other methodologies. The key point is to estimate what a firm's losses will be in the aggregate crisis state, hence, building into the framework the idea of codependence. The estimate of these losses allows us to calculate the expected capital shortfall of each firm if there is a crisis. This is a simple calculation based on the leverage of the firm.

$$SRISK = -\min[0, E - k(E + D)] \tag{9.2}$$

where E is the market value of equity in crisis, D is the book value of debt, and k is a prudential capital requirement, which is taken to be 8 percent in accordance with current regulatory standards. The expected value of equity is simply:

$$E = (1 - MES)E_0 \tag{9.3}$$

where E_0 is today's market value of equity. The contribution to systemic risk then is simply:

$$SRISK\%_{i,t} = \frac{SRISK_{i,t}}{\sum\limits_{i=1}^{N} SRISK_{i,t}} \tag{9.4}$$

A few observations on the procedure are in order. First, note that there is an implicit assumption that the capital ratio at which firms disintermediate (i.e., k) is the same for all firms, bank or no bank. It has been suggested that this may not be appropriate for insurance companies (e.g., see Chapter 8 of this book, by Scott E. Harrington). While this is true, it is not clear whether k should be higher or lower for insurance companies. Indeed, there is evidence to suggest that a ratio of $k = 8$ percent is conservative for property-casualty insurance companies.[29] That is, in equilibrium, these companies tend to be less leverage than their bank counterparts. Since their market value of equity covers a higher fraction of total assets, if a property-casualty insurance company were to fall to a capital ratio as low as 8 percent, this level would be far from normal. Second, the theory outlined in Acharya, Pedersen, Philippon, and Richardson (2010) would apply a negative SRISK to safe, well-capitalized financial firms. In a crisis, these firms would be natural buyers of struggling financial firms and therefore would reduce aggregate systemic risk. The current analysis at NYU Stern's Systemic Risk website ignores this element and could impact some of the results analyzed in the following pages. Third, and perhaps most important, a dollar of capital shortfall for any firm is treated the same in its contribution to aggregate capital shortfall. This issue was discussed in detail in the previous section, and in particular with respect to a comparison between the insurance sector and the banking industry. While the discussion pointed to insurance companies being systemic, whether their capital shortfalls are equal to those of other financial institutions is an open and reasonable question.

Figure 9.1 describes the SRISK (i.e., the total estimated expected aggregate capital shortfall [CS] in a future crisis) of the total financial sector and the insurance subsector over the years 2003 to 2013. Up until the occurrence of the financial crisis, the estimate of the financial sector and insurance subsector, respectively, hovered around $200 billion and $40 billion. As the crisis took root in the summer of 2007 and peaked in the fall of 2008 (with the failure of Lehman Brothers), SRISK increased to around $1 trillion for the financial sector and $200 billion for the insurance subsector. Interestingly, as the financial sector worked through the financial crisis, with various peaks

FIGURE 9.1   Total Systemic Risk of U.S. Financial Sector and Insurance Subsector

and valleys, SRISK of the financial sector in 2013 has gone down to around $400 billion whereas the insurance subsector has also declined, albeit less on a percentage basis, to approximately $100 billion. The relative improvement of the rest of the financial system compared to the insurance subsector can be attributed to reductions in market leverage relative to the insurance subsector.

This point is highlighted in Figure 9.2. Figure 9.2 describes the insurance subsector's percentage of the U.S. financial sector's total quasi market value (QMV) of assets and SRISK (i.e., total systemic risk).[30] Prior to the crisis, the insurance sector was approximately 20 percent in terms of both percentage shares. In other words, the insurance sector's SRISK was commensurate with its share of total assets. Starting in 2005 and going through the financial

FIGURE 9.2   Insurance Subsector Percentage of U.S. Financial Sector's Assets and Systemic Risk

crisis, its share was less, reaching a low of 10 percent in terms of systemic risk. This is not surprising since the financial crisis was very much a banking crisis, even putting aside the fact that insurance companies had broken into nontraditional businesses. By the spring of 2009, however, insurance had become on a relative basis, in terms of its total assets, a more systemically risky financial subsector. Whether it is due to regulation or to conscious behavior, the banking sector has become better capitalized and less risky relative to the insurance sector on a per dollar basis. In particular, Figures 9.1 and 9.2 show that this reduction in systemic risk is less true of the insurance sector. In fact, the insurance sector's percentage contribution to overall systemic risk is generally between 25 percent and 30 percent, in contrast to the insurance sector's 22 percent to 23 percent share of overall assets.

The preceding analysis uses historical equity market data to back out systemic risk estimates of individual financial companies and then aggregates up these estimates to the overall financial sector and the insurance subsector. We will extend this analysis in two ways: (1) by focusing on a particular snapshot of the insurance sector, namely June 2007, just prior to the emergence of the financial crisis, and (2) by measuring systemic risk using credit default swap (CDS) data.

Insurance firms experienced significant stress during the financial crisis of 2007–2009. Figure 9.3 shows the time series of daily levels of the Center for Research in Security Prices (CRSP) value-weighted index and the daily average levels of CDS spreads for 20 insurance firms whose spread data is available from Bloomberg.[31] Noticeably, the stock market declined gradually from the onset of the crisis in the middle of 2007, only to take a big plunge in the summer of 2008. Meanwhile, insurance firms showed serious signs of stress from as early as the fourth quarter of 2007, when their CDS spreads remarkably widened from around 20 basis points to over 600 basis points. These spreads remained considerably high throughout the crisis, peaking at around 1,200 basis points right before the trough of the stock market.

An important question is thus posed: How can we measure *ex ante* which insurance firms are relatively more systemic than others and thus will undergo greater stress during a systemic crisis? We show that information from the credit default swaps market can offer a good answer to this question. In particular, we find that a measure of systemic risk computed from CDS spreads, namely CDS marginal expected shortfall (CDS MES), could have successfully predicted the performance of insurance firms during the 2007–2009 financial crisis.

The idea of using marginal expected shortfall (MES) based on stock market data as a measure of firm-specific systemic risk is employed and discussed in the preceding paragraphs. Given that information from CDS data is informative about the level of stress experienced by insurance firms over the

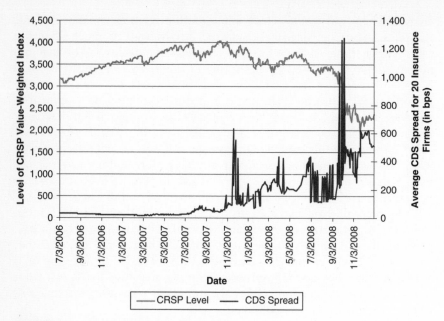

FIGURE 9.3   CDS Spread versus CRSP Index Level
Source of data: Bloomberg.
The graph depicts a plot of the daily average CDS spread for 20 insurance firms included in the sample, and CRSP index level over the July 2006 to December 2008 period.

crisis, we employ a similarly defined measure of MES computed from CDS spread data. Acharya, Pedersen, Philippon, and Richardson (2010) argue that this measure can approximate expected systemic risk contribution given that the change in CDS spreads attaches smaller weights to safer firms.[32]

As a proxy for the market of insurance firms, we initially consider the 102 U.S. financial firms with at least $5 billion in market capitalization (as of June 2007). Data on CDS spreads are available from Bloomberg for 40 of these firms, 20 of which are insurance firms, which are the focus of this section. To compute CDS MES for each insurance firm, we take the 5 percent worst days over the one-year precrisis period (from July 1, 2006, to June 30, 2007) for an equally weighted portfolio of CDS returns on the 40 financial firms, and then calculate CDS MES for each individual firm as the average daily logarithmic returns on CDS spreads over these days.[33] The CDS MES obtained is our measure of systemic risk for each of the 20 insurance firms examined. Table 9.1 provides the ranking for these 20 firms based on their CDS MES. These rankings can be viewed as systemic risk on a per dollar basis. At the

TABLE 9.1 CDS MES Ranking of 20 Insurance Firms

Name of Company	Ticker	Assets ($ Billions)	CDS MES Ranking	Realized CDS SES (July 2007–June 2008)	Realized CDS SES (July 2007–Dec. 2008)	CDS MES
Genworth Financial Inc.	GNW	111.94	1	145.38%	403.03%	16.40%
Ambac Financial Group Inc.	ABK	21.06	2	424.10%	389.12%	8.05%
MBIA Inc.	MBI	43.15	3	383.11%	303.44%	6.71%
American International Group	AIG	1,033.87	4	277.42%	369.20%	3.40%
Allstate Corp.	ALL	160.54	5	183.66%	271.38%	2.97%
Loews Corp.	L	79.54	6	136.79%	175.47%	2.67%
Prudential Financial Inc.	PRU	461.81	7	240.25%	394.44%	2.33%
Lincoln National Corp. Inc.	LNC	187.65	8	234.94%	403.58%	2.27%
Aon Corp.	AOC	24.79	9	32.41%	55.10%	2.26%
Hartford Financial Svcs. Group	HIG	345.65	10	212.09%	368.41%	2.03%
Travelers Companies Inc.	STA	115.36	11	124.68%	171.62%	1.95%
Chubb Corp.	CB	51.73	12	164.91%	192.52%	1.73%
Unum Group	UNM	52.07	13	118.33%	165.43%	0.98%
Safeco Corp.	SAF	13.97	14	123.95%	155.92%	0.85%
CNA Financial Corp.	CNA	60.74	15	105.34%	218.89%	0.84%
MetLife Inc.	MET	552.56	16	220.59%	362.62%	0.75%
Torchmark Corp.	TMK	15.10	17	24.69%	182.45%	0.34%
Aetna Inc.	AET	49.57	18	127.42%	192.96%	-0.12%
Cigna Corp.	CI	41.53	19	124.73%	267.69%	-0.56%
Marsh & McLennan Cos. Inc.	MMC	17.19	20	31.82%	33.43%	-0.63%

This table contains the list of 20 U.S. insurance firms with a market cap in excess of $5 billion as of June 2007. The firms are listed in descending order according to their CDS marginal expected shortfall (MES) at the 5 percent level, calculated over the July 2006 to June 2007 period. Realized CDS systemic expected shortfall (SES) is the return on the CDS spread during the crisis.

top of the list is Genworth Financial Inc., whose systemic risk measure is as high as 16.40 percent. Ambac Financial Group Inc., MBIA Inc., and AIG are next. Of course, because AIG has considerably more assets than either MBIA or Ambac ($1.0333 trillion versus $43 billion and $21 billion, respectively), AIG's overall systemic risk is an order of magnitude higher. On the other hand, Aetna Inc., Cigna Corporation, and Marsh & McLennan Companies Inc. are the least systematically risky firms, with CDS MESs being negative.

Results from Table 9.1 reveal at a preliminary level the success of CDS MES as a predictor of how stressful each firm was during the crisis. Figures 9.4 and 9.5 show at a more detailed level how well CDS MES could have predicted the realized systemic risk contribution of the 20 insurance firms during the July 2007 to June 2008 crisis period. This realized contribution is measured using both the percentage change in CDS spreads and the total percentage change in stock returns. As can be seen from the figures, CDS MES as an

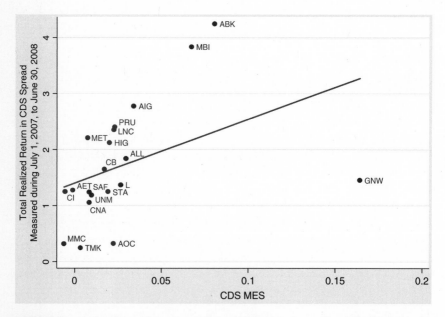

FIGURE 9.4   CDS Marginal Expected Shortfall (MES) versus Total Realized Return in CDS Spread Measured during the Period July 1, 2007, to June 30, 2008
The graph depicts a scatter plot for 20 insurance firms of the CDS MES computed during the July 1, 2006, to June 30, 2007, period versus the total realized return on CDS spread during the period from July 1, 2007, to June 30, 2008. CDS MES is the average CDS returns on the worst 5 percent days from July 1, 2006, to June 30, 2007, when the average CDS returns of the 40 companies were the highest.

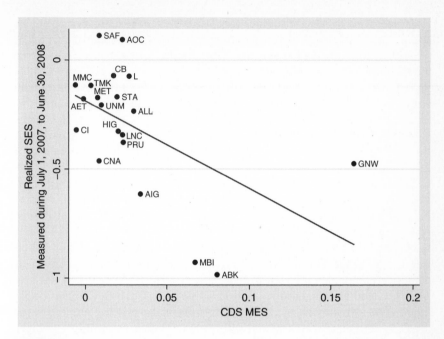

FIGURE 9.5 CDS Marginal Expected Shortfall (MES) versus Total Realized Stock Return Measured during the Period July 1, 2007, to June 30, 2008
The graph depicts a scatter plot for 20 insurance firms of the CDS MES computed during the July 1, 2006, to June 30, 2007, period versus the total realized stock return during the period from July 1, 2007, to June 30, 2008. CDS MES is the average CDS returns on the worst 5 percent days from July 1, 2006, to June 30, 2007, when the average CDS returns of the 40 companies were the highest.

ex ante measure of systemic risk contribution does very well *ex post*. There is indeed a clear positive association between CDS MES as a measure of systemic risk and realized systemic costs over the crisis. Firms that had higher systemic risk *ex ante* were under greater stress *ex post*; that is, they experienced larger increases in CDS spreads and lower stock returns over the crisis.[34]

STATE VERSUS FEDERAL REGULATION OF INSURANCE COMPANIES

As described in the introductory remarks of this chapter, unlike other financial regulation, most insurance regulation is carried out by the states, as has been the case since the nineteenth century. Several legal attempts have been made over time to bring insurance regulation under the federal government as part of its power to regulate interstate commerce. Notably, in *Paul v. Virginia* in 1869, the Supreme Court ruled that insurance was not commerce and thus not subject to federal regulation. In *United States v. South-Eastern Underwriters Association* in 1944, the Supreme Court ruled that insurance was commerce, overruling *Paul v. Virginia*, and thus the regulation of insurance was a federal responsibility. In response to this ruling, in 1945, Congress passed the McCarron-Ferguson Act, which deferred insurance regulation to the states. This act reserved the federal government's right to oversee and, if necessary, to take greater responsibility for insurance regulation.

The previous sections focused on one particular type of insurance regulation, namely systemic risk. Those sections provided an analysis of whether the insurance sector can impose significant systemic risk on the economy. If the insurance sector is systemically risky (as we have argued), then it is inconceivable that there would not be federal regulation of this sector. Indeed, the Dodd-Frank Act allows for identification and regulation of insurance companies through a dedicated systemic risk regulator such as the FSOC and its enhanced regulation of SIFIs. In Chapter 8 of this book, Harrington provides an excellent description of the existing procedure for FSOC to determine whether nonbank companies such as insurance companies should be designated as SIFIs.

Systemic risk aside, this leads to the question of whether federal regulation is necessary beyond the creation of the Federal Insurance Office, stipulated by the Dodd-Frank Act. In the long term, would the U.S. financial architecture be better off by creating a national insurance regulator and an associated federal charter, and by establishing a national insurance guaranty fund? Chapters 3, 4, 10, and 11 of this book address this issue.

Note that insurance regulation comprises several other activities. Specifically, insurance regulation focuses on accounting and disclosure requirements and also the formation and licensing of companies, affiliation and holding company considerations, the licensing of agents and brokers, product approval, marketing methods, on-site examinations, and investment restrictions.

Each state has an insurance department and a commissioner of insurance. The commissioner usually is appointed by the governor of the state, but is elected in 10 states. The National Association of Insurance Commissioners (NAIC) promotes the effective performance of state regulation by developing model state laws and regulations, by codifying Statutory Accounting Principles, and in various other ways. The NAIC also rates investments for regulatory purposes. The NAIC's efforts have reduced, though not eliminated, the frictions resulting from state-level regulation of interstate insurers.

Interstate insurers and others have criticized the high cost and inefficiency of state-level regulation, preferring the option of a national insurance charter and federal insurance regulation. However, Congress generally has resisted changing the existing system except when faced with force majeure issues, such as terrorism and Hurricane Katrina. The states vigorously defend their performance in regulating local issues (consumer protection, complaints, etc.), and they point to the far fewer failures of insurers than of partly or wholly federally regulated banks.

The states have a point. State regulators argue that their proximity to the ground helps them better regulate insurance companies. Perhaps an even stronger argument is the generally dismal performance of federal regulators, across various agencies, to regulate banks, securities dealers, and other shadow banks during financial crises. See Kimball and Boyce (1958) and Tyler and Hornig (2009) for discussions of why state regulation is preferred.[35] For instance, a striking example is the regulation of mortgages (or lack thereof) leading up to the recent financial crisis even though many federal regulations were at the disposal of regulators. To the extent there are inefficiencies within the state system, pro-state advocates argue that the NAIC has, and will continue, to address these over time (e.g., Webel and Cobb [2005]).[36]

That said, the federal government does intervene in states' insurance regulation. For example, the Employee Retirement Income Security Act (ERISA) preempted state supervision of pensions and health plans administered by insurers. The Securities and Exchange Commission (SEC) regulates insurers' offerings of variable annuities and other performance-based investment products, as well as the financial reporting of publicly traded insurers. When insurance industry capacity is challenged by large unexpected shocks or ongoing uncertainty, the federal government may take actions to free up industry capacity or provide insurance itself. For example, the terrorist attacks of September 11, 2001, yielded large property liability claims that reduced insurers' capital and, more importantly, very high uncertainty about potential future terrorist events that effectively froze terrorism reinsurance markets. The Terrorism Risk Insurance Act (TRIA) solved the latter problem by providing government reinsurance of losses from a terrorist attack if and when the industry's aggregate losses reached a certain level.[37]

Moreover, the Federal Liability Risk Retention Act of 1986 does allow some insurers, known as risk retention groups (RRGs), to do nationwide business under one license. These RRGs allow for a controlled experiment to compare RRGs to other more standard state-regulated commercial liability insurers. Leverty (2011) documents substantial costs associated with duplicative regulation across states, providing strong support (albeit using limited data) for national regulation.[38] See also Waterfield (2002) for a more general analysis of state versus federal regulation of insurance companies.[39]

Putting aside the issue of efficiency, there is also the question of whether states can reasonably be expected to address the systemic risks of insurers offering nontraditional insurance products. State insurance regulators are inherently limited in their ability to do so, for various reasons. These regulators generally will not have access to all of the relevant information about the insurers operating in multiple states and the overall financial system in which they operate, and so will not be able to see the potential magnitude of and avenues for insurers' systemic risk. With considerable variation across states, state regulators lack the financial resources and technical skills to measure the systemic risk contributions of individual insurers, as well as the ability to levy premiums for these contributions or even ban systemically risky products. Were a state to levy higher premiums, treat insurers' systemic risk contributions more onerously, or ban certain insurance products, insurers would have the incentive to redomicile in more lenient states (i.e., engage in regulatory arbitrage). An example of regulatory arbitrage was given previously in this chapter—see Koijen and Yogo (2013).[40] Of course, it is an open question whether the Dodd-Frank Act's Consumer Financial Protection Bureau or the FSOC will be capable of filling this void.[41]

CONCLUSION

As a final comment, there are clear reasons to question the existing regulatory architecture of the insurance industry. First, if systemic risk is indeed present within the insurance sector, then there must be a role for federal regulation. The question is whether the FSOC is sufficient to address this issue. Second, wherever the regulation takes place, the current system is antiquated in terms of its current regulatory architecture. Cummins and Phillips (2009), for example, argue that, even though the insurance industry appears to have been prudently managed by state regulators, the current system is vastly out of date, especially when compared to regulation in Europe.[42] Third, others, such as Brown (2008), go even further and suggest that the debate regarding state versus federal regulation misses the point.[43] Her argument is that insurance is no longer a unique financial service, and that the boundaries between insurance and financial services products have converged so much that regulation must really be at the risk and product level of these institutions; see also Cummins (2005).[44] Of course, this argues both against state regulation and against having a national insurance regulator.

NOTES

1. The authors are at the New York University Stern School of Business. E-mail: vacharya@stern.nyu.edu, mrichar0@stern.nyu.edu. Some of this essay is based on "Systemic Risk and the Regulation of Insurance Companies," by Viral V. Acharya, John Biggs, Hanh Le, Matthew Richardson, and Stephen Ryan, published as Chapter 9 in *Regulating Wall Street: The Dodd-Frank Act and the Architecture of Global Finance*, ed. Viral V. Acharya, Thomas Cooley, Matthew Richardson, and Ingo Walter (Hoboken, NJ: John Wiley & Sons, 2010).

2. J. David Cummins and Mary A. Weiss, "Systemic Risk and Regulation of the U.S. Insurance Industry," Chapter 7 in this volume; Scott Harrington, "The Financial Crisis, Systematic Risk, and the Future of Insurance Regulation," *Journal of Risk and Insurance* 76 (2009): 785–819; Scott Harrington, "Insurance Regulation and the Dodd-Frank Act," working paper, Wharton School at the University of Pennsylvania, 2010; Scott E. Harrington, "Designation and Supervision of Insurance SIFIs," Chapter 8 in this volume; Ralph Tyler and Karen Hornig, "Reflections on State Regulation: A Lesson of the Economic Turmoil of 2007–2009," *Journal of Business & Technology Law* 4, no. 2 (2009): 349–370.

3. This is not to say that different types of policies do not differ in the diversifiability of claim payments. For example, automobile claims are more diversifiable than product liability claims. Moreover, some policies with generally diversifiable risks exhibit specific risks that are not diversifiable. For example, life insurers are exposed to pandemics, which occur rarely but can devastate life insurers when they do occur.

4. Kenneth A. Froot, "The Market for Catastrophe Risk: A Clinical Examination," *Journal of Financial Economics* 60 (2001): 529–571; Kenneth A. Froot and Paul G. J. O'Connell, "The Pricing of U.S. Catastrophe Reinsurance," Chapter 5 in *The Financing of Catastrophe Risk*, ed. Kenneth A. Froot, 195–232 (Chicago: University of Chicago Press, 1999).

5. Mark J. Garmaise and Tobias J. Moskowitz, "Catastrophe Risk and Credit Markets," *Journal of Finance* 64 (2009): 657–707. The evidence of supply effects in capital markets is not just related to catastrophe reinsurance markets. For example, Ivashina and Scharfstein (2010) document a sharp decline in bank loans with the onset of the financial crisis and show that some of this drop is supply driven; see Victoria Ivashina and David Scharfstein, "Bank Lending during the Financial Crisis of 2008," *Journal of Financial Economics* 97 (2010): 319–338.

6. Jens Dick-Nielsen, Peter Feldhutter, and David Lando, "Corporate Bond Liquidity before and after the Onset of the Subprime Crisis," *Journal of Financial Economics* 103, no. 3 (2012): 471–492.

7. Anna Paulson, Thanases Plestis, Richard Rosen, Robert McMenamin, and Zain Mohey-Deen, "Assessing the Vulnerability of the U.S. Life Insurance Industry," Chapter 6 in this volume.

8. A. Manconi, M. Massa, and A. Yasuda, "The Role of Institutional Investors in Propagating the Crisis of 2007–08," *Journal of Financial Economics* 104, no. 3 (2012): 491–518.

9. R. Stanton and N. Wallace, "CMBS Subordination, Ratings Inflation, and the Crisis of 2007–2009," unpublished manuscript, University of California at Berkeley, 2010.

10. A. Ellul, P. Jotikasthira, and C. Lundblad, "Regulatory Pressure and Fire Sales in the Corporate Bond Market," working paper, Indiana University Bloomington, 2010.

11. FSOC, "Basis of the Financial Stability Oversight Council's Final Determination Regarding American International Group, Inc.," July 8, 2013.

12. Viral V. Acharya, John Biggs, Hanh Le, Matthew Richardson, and Stephen Ryan, "Systemic Risk and the Regulation of Insurance Companies," Chapter 9 in *Regulating Wall Street: The Dodd-Frank Act and the Architecture of Global Finance*, ed. Viral V. Acharya, Thomas Cooley, Matthew Richardson, and Ingo Walter (Hoboken, NJ: John Wiley & Sons, 2010).

13. For a detailed discussion of the cycle of market and funding liquidity, see Marcus K. Brunnermeier and Lasse H. Pedersen, "Market Liquidity and Funding Liquidity," *Review of Financial Studies* 22 (2009): 2201–2238.

14. Viral V. Acharya, Thomas Cooley, Matthew Richardson, and Ingo Walter, "Manufacturing Tail Risk: A Perspective on the Financial Crisis of 2007–2009," *Foundations and Trends in Finance* 4 (2010): 247–325.

15. An exception to this statement occurs when insurers experience rare and extremely adverse underwriting outcomes. For example, epidemics that kill large numbers of people in short periods of time are rare—the last significant one in the United States was the Spanish flu in 1918–1919—but when they occur, they can devastate life insurers.

16. Sojung Carol Park and Xiaoying Xie, "Reinsurance and Systematic Risk: The Impact of Reinsurer Downgrading on Property-Casualty Insurers," working paper, California State University, Fullerton, 2011.

17. E. Brewer, J. M. Carson, E. Elyasiani, I. Mansur, and W. L. Scott, "Interest Rate Risk and Equity Values of Life Insurance Companies: A GARCH-M Model," *Journal of Risk and Insurance* 74, no. 2 (2007): 401–423; E. G. Baranoff and T. W. Sager, "The Impact of Mortgage-Backed Securities on Capital Requirements of Life Insurers in the Financial Crisis of 2007–2008," *Geneva Papers on Risk and Insurance* 34, no. 1 (2009): 100–118. See also the earlier-cited papers, A. Ellul, P. Jotikasthira, and

C. Lundblad, "Regulatory Pressure and Fire Sales in the Corporate Bond Market," working paper, Indiana University Bloomington, 2010; A. Manconi, M. Massa, and A. Yasuda, "The Role of Institutional Investors in Propagating the Crisis of 2007–08," *Journal of Financial Economics* 104, no. 3 (2012): 491–518; Anna Paulson, Thanases Plestis, Richard Rosen, Robert McMenamin, and Zain Mohey-Deen, "Assessing the Vulnerability of the U.S. Life Insurance Industry," Chapter 6 in this volume; and J. David Cummins and Mary A. Weiss, "Systemic Risk and Regulation of the U.S. Insurance Industry," Chapter 7 in this volume.

18. Paulson, Anna, Thanases Plestis, Richard Rosen, Robert McMenamin, and Zain Mohey-Deen, "Assessing the Vulnerability of the U.S. Life Insurance Industry," Chapter 6 in this volume.

19. J. D. Cummins and C. M. Lewis, "Catastrophic Events, Parameter Uncertainty and the Breakdown of Implicit Long-Term Contracting: The Case of Terrorism Insurance," *Journal of Risk and Uncertainty* 26, no. 2–3 (2003): 153–178; K. Epermanis and S. Harrington, "Market Discipline in Property/Casualty Insurance: Evidence from Premium Growth Surrounding Changes in Financial Strength Ratings," *Journal of Money, Credit, and Banking* 38 (2006): 1515–1544.

20. AIG also incurred larger losses on its insurance subsidiaries in 2008 than on the Financial Products group, and these losses were due largely to its securities lending, certain repurchase agreement transactions, and its direct purchase of the super-senior tranches of subprime mortgage-based CDOs, which were the same type as those insured by the CDSs sold by the Financial Products group.

21. Ralph S. J. Koijen and Motohiro Yogo, "Shadow Insurance," working paper, London Business School, 2013.

22. Elizabeth F. Brown, "The Fatal Flaw of Proposals to Federalize Insurance Regulation," Research Symposium on Insurance Markets and Regulation, 2008, 1–84; J. D. Cummins and M. A. Weiss, "Convergence of Insurance and Financial Markets: Hybrid and Securitized Risk-Transfer Solutions," *Journal of Risk and Insurance* 76, no. 3 (2009): 493–545.

23. M. Billio, M. Getmansky, A. W. Lo, and L. Pelizzon, "Econometric Measures of Connectedness and Systemic Risk in the Finance and Insurance Sectors," *Journal of Financial Economics* 104 (2012): 535–559.

24. Hua Chen, J. David Cummins, Krupa S. Viswanathan, and Mary Weiss, "Systemic Risk and the Inter-Connectedness between Banks and Insurers: An Econometric Analysis," working paper, Temple University, 2012.

25. Martin F. Grace, "The Insurance Industry and Systemic Risk: Evidence and Discussion," working paper, Georgia State University, 2010.

26. For example, Grace (2010) looks at excess returns of P-C insurers, life insurers, AIG, and distressed insurers around seven events relevant to

the financial crisis. Grace reasons that, because the excess returns are not particularly negative around these events, little systemic risk emerged. But he also reports extraordinarily high market betas, especially for the struggling insurance companies, which suggests very large losses during extreme market downturns. The question is whether these losses were broad enough across the insurance sector that they resulted in financial disintermediation.

27. See Viral V. Acharya, Lasse Pedersen, Thomas Philippon, and Matthew Richardson, "Measuring Systemic Risk," working paper, NYU Stern School of Business, 2010.

28. Viral V. Acharya, Lasse Pedersen, Thomas Philippon, and Matthew Richardson, "Measuring Systemic Risk," working paper, NYU Stern School of Business, 2010; Christian Brownlees and Robert F. Engle, "Volatility, Correlation and Tails for Systemic Risk Measurement," working paper, NYU Stern School of Business, 2010.

29. See Giuseppe Corvasce, "The Role of Capital in Financial Institutions and Systemic Risk," working paper, 2011. Corvasce calculates the assets-to-market value of equity ratio for the cross-section of financial institutions over the past decade. He documents the median and tail ratios for insurance companies and other financial companies for five years prior to the financial crisis, during the crisis, and subsequent to the crisis. Corvasce generally documents higher ratios for property-casualty companies and lower ratios for life insurance companies than, for example, the regional banking sector. Ceteris paribus, this might suggest that property-casualty or life insurance companies should have a k higher or lower, respectively, than 8 percent.

30. Quasi market value of assets is equal to the book value of assets plus the difference between the market value and book value of equity.

31. CDS data for this study is the spread on the five-year senior unsecured credit default swaps.

32. Viral V. Acharya, Lasse H. Pedersen, Thomas Philippon, and Matthew Richardson, "Measuring Systemic Risk," working paper, NYU Stern School of Business, 2010.

33. CDSs are not as frequently traded as stocks. Hence, to eliminate the effect of CDS return on a given day being the aggregated return over many nontrading days, we use only returns on days where CDS spread information is available for that day and the previous trading day. No return is used for a day when no spread information can be obtained for the trading day immediately preceding it. The worst days of the CDS index are defined as days when returns on the CDS index are the highest.

34. In unreported results, we also measured realized performance over the July 2007 to December 2008 period. We argue that CDS MES should explain *ex post* performance better when the realized systemic risk contribution is measured for the July 2007 to June 2008 period, as the government bailout programs introduced during the latter part of 2008 could have had a stabilizing effect on CDS spreads and stock returns. In fact, we document the same patterns as in Figures 9.4 and 9.5. To confirm our conjecture, these effects are, nevertheless, weaker when realized CDS spreads or stock returns are measured up until December 2008.

35. Spencer L. Kimball and Ronald Boyce, "The Adequacy of State Insurance Rate Regulation: The McCarran-Ferguson Act in Historical Perspective," *Michigan Law Review* 56, no. 4 (1958): 545–578; Ralph Tyler and Karen Hornig, "Reflections on State Regulation: A Lesson of the Economic Turmoil of 2007–2009," *Journal of Business & Technology Law* 4, no. 2 (2009): 349–370.

36. Baird Webel and Carolyn Cobb, "Insurance Regulation: History, Background, and Recent Congressional Oversight," CRS Report for Congress, 2005.

37. To be precise, the insurer pays all losses up to a deductible and pays coinsurance of 15 percent for losses above the deductible up to an aggregate event limit of $100 billion. Above the event limit, the government covers all losses at no charge.

38. J. Tyler Leverty, "The Cost of Duplicative Regulation: Evidence from Risk Retention Groups," *Journal of Risk and Insurance* 79, no. 1 (2011): 105–127.

39. Danielle F. Waterfield, "Insurers Jump on Train for Federal Insurance Regulation: Is It Really What They Want or Need?," *Connecticut Insurance Law Journal* 9, no. 1 (2002): 283–337.

40. Ralph Koijen and Motoriho Yogo, "Shadow Insurance," working paper, London Business School, 2013.

41. Currently, insurance products are exempted from oversight by the Consumer Financial Protection Bureau.

42. J. D. Cummins and R. D. Phillips, "Capital Adequacy and Insurance Risk-Based Capital Systems," *Journal of Insurance Regulation*, 28, no. 1 (2009): 25–72.

43. Elizabeth F. Brown, "The Fatal Flaw of Proposals to Federalize Insurance Regulation," Research Symposium on Insurance Markets and Regulation, 2008, 1–84.

44. J. David Cummins, "Convergence in Wholesale Financial Services: Reinsurance and Investment Banking," *Geneva Papers* 30 (2005): 187–222.

CHAPTER 10

Modernizing the Safety Net for Insurance Companies

John H. Biggs

Stern School of Business, New York University

The Dodd-Frank law did not create any direct changes in the state system of regulation of insurance. But it did create a new Federal Insurance Office (FIO) to gather information on the insurance industry and to negotiate and enter into international agreements concerning insurance. Furthermore, the law called upon its director to make a proposal to Congress for "modernizing insurance regulation."

A further Dodd-Frank action, of potentially great significance to large insurers, is the creation of the Financial Stability Oversight Council (FSOC), including coverage of nonbank holding companies, which could clearly bring some form of Federal Reserve regulation to major insurance entities.

This chapter addresses the important aspect of insurance regulation that deals with rehabilitating or liquidating a stressed or failing company, and in particular policyholder protection in the event of a failure.

The current state system of guaranty associations (GAs) was developed in the 1970s for property-casualty (P-C) companies and in the 1980s for life and health (L/H) companies. Although they have purposes that are similar to those of the Federal Deposit Insurance Corporation (FDIC), established for banks in the 1930s, they have major differences in operation, especially due to the fact that each association is based in and operates under the law of the state establishing the association.

Congress did not take up the safety net needs of insurers in the 1930s in spite of the dramatic failure of one major company.[1] At that time, insurance legally was not "interstate commerce" and therefore was subject solely to regulation by the states. The Supreme Court declared insurance to be interstate commerce in 1944, but Congress quickly passed the McCarran-Ferguson

Act that gave the states primary authority for insurance regulation, subject to that regulation not being found deficient.

After the failure of a number of specialized P-C companies in the 1960s, Congress became concerned and proposed a federal guaranty system patterned on the FDIC. This led to a state response through the National Association of Insurance Commissioners (NAIC), which proposed a model statute creating the first GAs for P-C companies. The history of that statute was derived from a single state's (Wisconsin) answer to insurance insolvencies, drafted in the 1960s by the legendary insurance professor Spencer L. Kimball.

Kimball was dean and law professor at a number of Midwestern universities, ending his career at the University of Chicago Law School. His perspective was focused on what could be done that would be compatible with state regulation, and reflected industry views at that time. Those views included extraordinary aversion to federal regulation. Also, it must have seemed impossible, politically if not constitutionally, for the individual states to set up a prefunded premium-based system with a statutory backing from the state taxpayers. Accordingly, no consideration appears to have been made for a federal role.[2] The NAIC used Wisconsin as the recommended model, and most states adopted it or a close variant over the decade of the 1970s.

Predictably, congressional concern waned.

But again, in the 1980s and early 1990s, after several significant failures of insurers, including several large life companies, Congress again proposed a federal bill. And, again, the NAIC responded with a model bill creating L/H GAs, similar to the Wisconsin and NAIC bills for P-C companies. By the late 1980s all states had finally passed both types of GAs, with structures similar to the model bills but with many different specific provisions. This difficulty in state regulation has been a characteristic of all attempts to achieve uniformity, especially important for large companies doing business in all or many states. There is an obvious tension between the states' mutual interests and their individual sovereignty.[3]

In the P-C field there are many lines of insurance, ranging from auto insurance and workers' compensation to marine to malpractice, and not all lines of insurance business are covered in the state GAs.

When an insurer is stressed or fails, the insurance regulator of the state of domicile takes responsibility and conserves, rehabilitates, or liquidates the insurer. Federal bankruptcy for insurers is expressly prohibited by the federal statute. However, the receivership function is roughly equivalent to a Chapter 11 bankruptcy reorganization, with the state insurance commissioner triggering the action and with a state judge comparable to the federal bankruptcy judge. Significantly, there is no role for the GAs in the reorganization level. Insolvency, however, does bring the GAs into what is akin to a Chapter 7 liquidation bankruptcy.[4]

In the event of liquidation, policyholders are guaranteed benefits up to a cap, with significant variations by state. The costs of providing these benefits are covered through post hoc assessments against the surviving insurers licensed in that state, with the share of each insurer based on a percentage of the company's premiums in the state. There is no backup guarantee by any state in the event that the GAs are insufficient, unlike the FDIC, which is guaranteed by the federal government.

The state guarantee funds do not charge *ex ante* premiums, except in the single case of the New York P-C fund, and, therefore, no preexisting fund exists before these assessments. With considerable variation among states, insurers typically pay their assessments in the year assessed, but they often earn credits over a period of years against their state premium taxes. To the extent insurers earn such credits, state taxpayers ultimately bear the costs of insurer insolvency. The capacity of each state's GA is roughly 2 percent of the premiums paid by those insured in the state. Additional amounts can be assessed in later years, giving the impression of a very large potential amount, but most of it is deferred.

It is important to keep in mind the significant link between the usual 2 percent premium tax imposed by the states on insurance premiums and the 2 percent maximum premium assessment on surviving insurers, which can then over time offset the standard premium tax. In effect, the cost of the GA programs offsets a burdensome premium tax assessed by all states against insurance products. The estimated amount in 2011 was $16.7 billion.[5]

Accordingly, given the post hoc assessment system, there are no funds available to the insurance commissioner in the conservatorship, or rehabilitation plan for helping to finance a merger or reinsurance transaction. This is a major limitation compared to the process available to banks through the FDIC or through the "window of last resort" at the Federal Reserve, especially in halting a panic run from an otherwise sound company.

The NAIC and the two national organizations—the National Organization of Life & Health Insurance Guaranty Associations (NOLHGA) and the National Conference of Insurance Guaranty Funds (NCIGF)—have been vital in making the state system work for large national insolvencies. Also, the NAIC has proposed model bills for state legislatures and set up national systems to assist insurance commissioners, particularly in solvency regulation, through the following: risk-based capital requirements, the Insurance Regulatory Information System, and an early-warning financial analysis system.[6]

However, none of these national organizations has enforcement powers. Insurers have perennially, for decades, criticized the slow pace of state adoption of sensible plans for efficiency—for example, licensing of agents and policy form approvals. (See comments by Governor Dirk Kempthorne, Chapter 2 in this volume.)

Commissioners have also tried to create interstate compacts to strengthen insurance regulation.[7] Such compacts have been created for several of the most criticized regulatory areas, but their success has been limited by not achieving total coverage, especially in losing key large states.

The next part of this chapter describes criticisms of the state GA system from consumer, industry, and public policy points of view.

CRITIQUE OF THE GA SYSTEM

The preceding description of the state GA system suggests several fairly obvious shortcomings that the states and the NAIC have recognized and tried to cure.

The system has a serious problem of lack of uniformity. This is not surprising since it is based on required legislation in 50 states and the District of Columbia. The maximum benefits and categories of benefits vary significantly across states, cause considerable confusion to cautious consumers who are concerned about financial protections, and are also inconsistent with other national safety nets for similar benefits.

Second, the system's post hoc assessment feature limits its ability to deal with liquidity crises (runs), does not provide for even rough justice in assessing costs to companies, and cannot promptly deal with some claims. The system is also procyclical in its charging effect by making assessments against the industry at the same time it is recovering from an insurance financial shock.

Third, it is questionable whether the system could deal with a major failure (e.g., that of one of the top 25 multistate companies) without invoking help from federal resources.

And, fourth, the system played no role in protecting policyholders in major insurance companies in the financial panic of 2008 and 2009 (e.g., Hartford and Lincoln National were protected by Troubled Asset Relief Program [TARP] funds, and AIG by the Federal Reserve), thereby placing all risks and costs of such shocks on the federal taxpayer and none on the insurance industry or the states.

Each is discussed in the following sections.

Lack of Uniformity

Table 10.1 describes the wide variation in amounts guaranteed by the different state guaranty associations. These statutes contain different provisions

TABLE 10.1   Number of States and Jurisdictions: Amounts Guaranteed by the Life and Health Insurance Guaranty Associations

Type of Coverage	$100,000	Up to $300,000	Up to $500,000
Cash withdrawal values	43	6	3
Annuity benefits	8	40	4
Life insurance death benefit	0	46	6
Long-term care	14	31	8
Health insurance	11	14	27

that are quite confusing to a consumer trying to understand his or her coverage. Contrast them with the identical national benefits, widely publicized, by the FDIC or the Pension Benefit Guaranty Corporation (PBGC). The state GA amounts guaranteed for life insurance vary from $100,000 to $500,000, with few states at the highest level. These amounts also vary for annuity benefits, and for health, long-term care, and disability insurance. Information is available on the individual state websites but by law cannot be publicized.

The latter point is perhaps the most unusual and questionable, namely the advertising prohibition, known in the business as the "gag rule." A typical statement from one such law is: "No person, including an insurer, agent, . . . shall make, publish, . . . in any newspaper, magazine or . . . any advertisement, announcement . . . which uses the existence of the insurance guaranty association of this state for the purpose of sales, solicitation, or inducement to purchase any form of insurance. . . . " There is also a similar gag rule on publishing the ratio of a company's actual capital to the minimum required amount specified by the NAIC. Ironically, these provisions seem to reflect a view that it is not appropriate for a cautious consumer to monitor a prospective insurance company and thereby to be a part of market discipline.

The other best-known safety nets—the FDIC, the PBGC, and the Securities Investor Protection Corporation (SIPC)—have no such prohibitions. The purpose of the insurance industry in lobbying for this clause was presumably to prevent poorly capitalized insurers from using the guaranty associations as assurance in soliciting business. Given the difficulty of enforcement, it would seem rather to play into the hands of unscrupulous companies and sales representatives to violate the prohibition while agents of reputable companies would comply.

Interestingly, the opening statement of the president of the NCIGF in a congressional hearing was: "While they may not know it, American insurance consumers are protected by a nationwide system of insurance guaranty associations (sometimes also called 'guaranty funds')."[8] Their ignorance is not surprising since it is against the law, in almost all states, to tell consumers about the GAs.

The guaranteed amounts vary both significantly across states and across several kinds of benefits. This adds to the confusion and again is not found in the safety nets elsewhere in the financial sector.

The amounts shown in Table 10.1 guaranteed by the life and health insurance GAs seem out of line with other safety nets. The FDIC guarantees the well-known $250,000 per bank customer. (The NAIC is currently pushing states to raise the $100,000 minimum to $250,000.) As of 2013, the PBGC guarantees an annual income under the defined benefit pension plan of a bankrupt private pension sponsor of $55,841 at age 65, which, with actuarial adjustment for early or late retirement, provides a present value of $558,600. The PBGC benefit is indexed and changes uniformly with price increases. (However, note that the PBGC provides no coverage of amounts in excess of its guarantee, whereas the other safety nets use assets remaining in the estates, after the guaranteed benefits are paid, to distribute proportionally to those with claims in excess of the limits.)

The distinction is jarring: If an annuitant is in an employer-sponsored plan that fails, he or she is guaranteed by the PBGC a value up to $558,600. But for an annuity guaranteed by a life insurance company that fails, the guarantee today can be as low as $100,000 and never more than $500,000. Accordingly, in eight states a person receiving an annuity from a highly regulated financial institution specializing in making long-term financial guaranties is protected up to only $100,000.

This distinction has drawn particular attention recently in the purchase of annuities from the Prudential Insurance Company by General Motors for retirees under GM's defined benefit plan. The employees accepting the Prudential annuities lose their PBGC protection but gain the Prudential's GA protection, which varies dramatically from state to state. Of course the GA protection depends on the annuitants' home state, not on the Prudential's domiciliary state, New Jersey, with its generous amount. The GM offer also includes a lump-sum option that may be selected by some who want clear, unambiguous freedom from any risk of a corporate default. However, they would be taking on their own longevity risk by sacrificing the advantage of an annuity guarantee.

Another confusion: Much of the growth in annuity premiums has come from deposits to withdrawable personal annuities in the accumulation phase, with few of such accounts ever being converted to a classic lifetime annuity. If a company failed, would a request for a withdrawal be deemed to be cash withdrawal or an annuity benefit? It would depend on the judge in the local state court. And the decision could produce a significant variance.

Also consider the risk-averse consumer of financial products. Many bank depositors use multiple banks to protect their $250,000 FDIC coverage. A person who wanted to have the same security in purchasing an annuity would have to spend a great deal of time exploring websites to find out the GA coverage and even then could not count on a simple national standard of administration and interpretation.

In addition, in the event of a stressed company, there could be widely varying actions taken by different insurance commissioners (who have very short average tenures and are usually political appointments) and the state court overseeing the rehabilitation or insolvency.

Post-Insolvency Assessments

Compared to the financing of the FDIC bank guarantees, the insurance GA system is weak on several counts. The FDIC pre-insolvency funding gives consumers confidence in the system, makes it possible to base the premiums on risk-based characteristics of the banks, and has a federal statutory guarantee backing it. The insurance GAs have no preexisting funds, no risk-based funding in their assessments capability, and no guarantees from any of the states.

The PBGC has higher caps on its guarantees but, as a federally sponsored institution, has the implicit federal guarantees that are similar to those of Fannie Mae and Freddie Mac. And it has an *ex ante* fund, with premiums charged to pension sponsors that are roughly risk based (taking into account, at least, the amount of the plan's benefits that have not been funded).

The second weakness of the GA system is the delay in raising funds to cover the guaranteed caps. It is argued by many that this is not serious since the usual liabilities under most insurance policies have a long payout structure.[9] In the case of a typical life insurance policy, no cash must be raised until the insured dies. If an annuity is in the payout phase, the monthly payments are relatively small and stretch out over the remaining life of the annuitant. In the middle decades of the twentieth century, this may have been a legitimate defense for the assessment system's capacity.

For many companies, and especially the largest ones, the structure of the liability side has shifted dramatically toward immediate payouts. Since 1980, the premium structure of the industry has virtually reversed the relationship between life and annuity premiums. Annuity premiums are now almost three times the premiums for life insurance policies. In 1980, they were little more than half the size of the life premiums.[10]

Additionally, a large part of what is reported as "annuity" premiums would be better characterized as tax-advantaged "retirement investment accounts." Such accounts have cashability at any time (with a modest penalty in most cases) and with a rarely used option to convert them into a typical annuity at retirement. The special tax advantage of these accounts is that no tax is imposed on the investment income until the payout. Accordingly, many buyers keep them as accumulation vehicles with minimal withdrawals.

Another common and popular annuity form is the variable annuity, invested in stocks but with a minimum guaranteed amount by the life insurance company. These annuities were seriously threatened by the 2008–2009 stock market collapse and were a part of the need by several companies for TARP protection. It is not clear what would be guaranteed by the GA system if the insurance company were unable to pay the full amount guaranteed minus the underlying market value. If the state system is unclear, it could well depend on the interpretation of the state insurance commissioner or the state court.

P-C companies have many different liability structures, given the wide variety of risks they insure. In most cases the state insurance commissioner will seek a buyer for the defaulting company since it takes time to run out the full liabilities. Most auto and homeowners' claims would be known within a year, but medical malpractice claims are notorious for having a very long "tail," taking many years to know the full liability.

There is a broad literature on the desirability and means to provide risk-based premiums on government-based safety nets. Congress has considered over the years the desirability of risk-based premiums for the FDIC and the PBGC. For example, in the case of the PBGC, premiums are based on the unfunded liability of a pension fund but not on the credit rating of the sponsor, which would be an easy measure of the risk of corporate failure to support its pension plan. One might call this rough justice. One of the reasons that Congress has not extended the risk recognition method to take into account company creditworthiness is the "procyclicality" argument. If the company is stressed financially, the additional premiums called for might tend to push the company into bankruptcy.

In the case of the FDIC, the system charges premiums graded by the CAMELS rating, where C represents capital adequacy, A asset quality, M management effectiveness, E earnings, L liquidity, and S sensitivity to markets. If the regulators get these elements right, it would seem an ideal way to set premiums on a risk-based basis. Something similar for insurers would give a clear incentive to managers to reduce any excessive risk taking and thereby mitigate the moral hazard derived from the existence of the safety net.

GAs have is no relationship between the risk and assessments. Since the failed company has paid nothing or very little prior to insolvency, all the burden falls on the surviving solvent companies. Since the assessment is based simply on the volume of premiums of the surviving companies, there is little relationship to risk for the P-C companies, and none at all for the surviving life companies. For the latter there might be some rough justice if the assessments were based on assets or liabilities.

The academic literature has looked at risk-based premiums and other effects of the post hoc assessment system. In "Risk-Based Premiums for Insurance Guaranty Funds," Cummins (1988) outlines the benefits for P-C insurers of risk-based premiums instead of the usual flat amount. Ligon and Thistle (2007) argue that *ex ante* assessments are more incentive compatible for reducing excess risk taking. Bernier and Mahfoudi (2010) show that contagion is more likely to be the result in a system based on *ex post* assessments.[11]

In the case of a general industry financial shock, the GA represents a serious procyclicality problem, since no funds were built up in good time and all the extra charges (up to 2 percent of total premiums) are assessed immediately after the shock, thus aggravating its effect.

A standard advantage of life insurers competing in the huge market for retirement savings is their very conservative brand as long-term managers in investments. Such conservative investors will value guarantees, and the banks and private pensions will have a superior product element in the FDIC and PBGC systems versus the limited state GAs.

The aforementioned GM transfer of liabilities to Prudential illustrates the issue. Well-informed and cautious corporate managers, and their auditors, will take seriously the defeasement of their pension liability. They would take into account the change in their retirees' guaranty. The accumulation of a significant fund behind the GAs would add to the credibility of the system as well as its capability to act quickly. A federal sponsorship, if not an explicit guarantee, would also strengthen the system.

Clearly, moral hazard is a danger under any explicit governmental guaranty system. Implicit government guarantees are more insidious in that they are expected and based on past regulator behavior, and usually protect creditors and shareholders rather than participants. They have become a serious concern since the experience of 2008–2009 has introduced "systemic" and "too big to fail" concepts into regulation. (See more extensive discussion in a later section dealing with mitigating effects of risk-based premiums.)

Sheila Bair, chair of the FDIC throughout the financial crisis, in congressional testimony during the Dodd-Frank consideration of how to finance a strong resolution authority for nonbank holding companies, argued for prefunding:

"To be credible, . . . [w]e believe that a pre-funded . . . [resolution authority] has significant advantages over an ex post funded system. It allows all large firms to pay risk-based assessments into the [fund], not just the survivors after any resolution, and it avoids the pro-cyclical nature of requiring repayment after a systemic crisis."[12] See Bair, *Bull by the Horns* (2012).

A further important advantage for banks over insurers in distress is the explicit access to the liquidity window of the Federal Reserve, the lender of last resort in the event of a run or panic. An insurer remaining solvent with good collateral has no such option in the event of a run.

Large Company Failures

Finally, there has been interest in the capacity of the state guaranty associations in the event of a major collapse. A way of measuring the capacity is to compute the maximum percentage in each of the jurisdictions (generally 2 percent of premiums paid in each state) for one year, and to sum them over all jurisdictions. The guaranty associations can then assess a similar amount the next year and so on indefinitely. These assessments would only be available over time and could not deal with any immediate liquidity needs.

During a long workout on an orderly basis, a significant amount could be raised. However, a major life company failure requiring such high assessments would surely be accompanied with policyholder panic and a likely run, demanding immediate cash payouts of the now-prominent annuity accumulations that have immediate withdrawal rights.

NOLHGA has estimated its current capacity by this measure as $10 billion in year 1 and, if one allows for growth over the years, the total 10-year capacity is quite high, over $100 billion. NOLHGA has historically coordinated guaranty association protection for 80 multistate insurers, and the individual guaranty associations have done the same for 326 smaller or single-state liquidations. The largest one-year assessment was over $900 million in 1994, but the assessments in the decade 2000 to 2009 were extremely low, with a zero dollar amount in two of the years and the largest year being just $200 million.

NCIGF estimates, on the same basis, that its one-year capacity is now $6.7 billion. Its losses were quite high during the years from 2000 to 2005. However, its assessment over those years came to $5 billion, with a cumulative capacity over those six years of $33 billion.[13]

The record is impressive, but the total capacity amounts do not match the scale of the AIG numbers, which came to over $100 billion in losses in one year, 2008.[14] Of course, under the state laws, the holding company losses would not have been covered, and it can be argued that the insurance units, if forced into liquidation, would have had estates that were adequate to meet most obligations. However, $41 billion of those 2008 losses came from the insurance company losses and most of the rest from credit default swaps. (And $19.6 billion in the Maiden Lane II vehicle for direct Federal Reserve injection of cash into AIG was for the liquidity concerns of the state-regulated life insurance business. That number alone dwarfs the one-year capacity of the life insurance GAs.)

There are now life companies that exceed the size of AIG life companies at the time of default—see the following. Also, the total funds extended to AIG by the Federal Reserve and Treasury ultimately came to $175 billion.

It is more useful to consider the size of the largest companies that the GA system is expected to cover. The general account of an insurance company includes the assets that back up long-term financial guarantees. Table 10.2 includes the amounts of these assets for the largest 10 companies. Consider the size of these exposures for the GAs compared to the maximum one-year assessments.

Table 10.3 sets out the amounts of the top 10 life insurer issuers of individual annuities, creating the chief potential liabilities that could be immediately cashed out.

Note that for several companies the individual annuity reserves represent one-half of the guarantees made by the general accounts. In the case of TIAA, however, most of the annuities can only be withdrawn on a 10-year annuity format.

Given the extreme size of the current insurance companies and the additional and greater risks now facing such entities, there would seem to

TABLE 10.2 Ten Largest Life Insurers, by General Account Assets, 2011 (in Billions)

MetLife	$398.3
TIAA	212.9
New York Life	195.3
Prudential Financial	186.2
AIG	182.5
Northwestern Mutual	171.0
Manulife Financial	111.1
Aflac	103.9
Massachusetts Mutual	101.4
Aegon USA	97.2

Source: Data from tabulations by the American Council of Life Insurers (ACLI) based on NAIC data, used by permission. The NAIC does not endorse any analysis or conclusions based on use of its data.

TABLE 10.3   Ten Largest Life Insurers, by Individual Annuity Reserves, 2011 (in Billions)

MetLife	$198.0
TIAA	157.9
AIG	111.9
Lincoln National	94.7
Hartford Life	82.6
Jackson National	80.2
Allianz	75.8
Riversource Insurance	73.3
Prudential Financial	71.9
New York Life	66.3

Source: Data from tabulations by the American Council of Life Insurers (ACLI) based on NAIC data, used by permission. The NAIC does not endorse any analysis or conclusions based on use of its data.

be a reasonable possibility that a major default could occur that would be beyond the capacity of the guaranty associations.

Perhaps the greatest risk is due to the dramatic shift in organization structure from mutual to stockholder owned in the past 20 years. The new risks are the kind revealed by the 2008 crisis from misused financial innovation, from pressure to raise risk levels to meet shareholder expectations, and due to the new global financial risks by which difficulties can migrate easily. The largest life companies are now mostly stockholder owned, with much more powerful incentives for management groups to take on excessive risk.

Of the top 10 general accounts in Table 10.2, only TIAA, New York Life, Northwestern Mutual, and Massachusetts Mutual are not stockholder owned. In the past 20 years MetLife, Prudential, and John Hancock (which was demutualized and purchased by stockholder-owned Manulife) have switched to stockholder ownership.

In addition to the three just cited, there was an extraordinary movement since 1990 in demutualizing other major life insurance companies: Canada Life Insurance, General American, Manufacturers Life (now owner of John Hancock as part of Manulife), Mutual Life Assurance of Canada, Mutual Life Insurance Company of New York (MONY), Phoenix Home

Life, Principal Life, Provident Mutual Life, Standard Insurance Company (Oregon), and Sun Life Assurance of Canada.

Why should this transformation of the ownership structure be of concern to the safety net?

First is the obvious change in appetite for risk when a company goes from mutual to stockholder ownership. Under mutual ownership there is a need for profit to the extent capital is needed to back up the policy guarantees. Under public stockholder ownership there is the obvious need, in addition to capital requirements, for returns to public outside owners. Most investors in financial institutions would seek a return on assets of roughly 1 percent on assets, to compensate for the risks they undertake in investing in such companies. This extra 1 percent must be earned from a portfolio of primarily fixed assets. Clearly, the managers have to seek that extra return on top of the return promised to policyholders. In this extended low-interest environment, that has been difficult to do, absent a significant increase in the riskiness of the portfolios.

There is a further constraint in managing a portfolio backing up a liability mix having a large component of withdrawable accumulating annuities, as has occurred in most of the large insurers. The most basic asset/liability management would dictate a very low-duration portfolio backing up such liabilities. Such an asset portfolio would have very low returns.

As investment products designed for accumulating retirement funds, their buyers are especially conscious of high annual expense charges. The usual mode of distribution is through commissioned agents and brokers. If one includes the all-in cost for their compensation, as well as the costs for investing and administering the deferred annuities, the insurers are fortunate if they can hold the total expense to 1 percent of the funds invested. With the addition of another 1 percent for the shareholders, the combined charge against investment earnings is 2 percent and sometimes more. Accordingly, there is a powerful incentive to reach for additional yield through acquiring more risky assets, especially in a low-yield environment on fixed-income investments as now. Managing a low-duration portfolio would induce the asset manager to reach even farther on the risk scale to get a return sufficient just to cover expenses and shareholder expectations.

It is significant that the two life insurance companies that took advantage of the TARP program (see a later section) were major writers of such deferred annuities.

The CEO of Aegon (number 10 in the list of largest life insurance general accounts) gave a stark warning on the riskiness of the insurers. Alex Wynaendts referred to "very dangerous" high guaranteed returns at a time of low interest rates. He summarized the concerns, saying, "It's very dangerous and you continue to see market players that are pricing products that are not aligned with the reality of today."[15]

Limited Role of GAs in the 2008–2009 Financial Crisis

The 2008–2009 financial crisis left a number of banks and insurance companies in a perilous financial position. In the fall and winter of 2008 the crisis seemed so desperate that extreme measures were initiated to protect the financial system, including individual companies and entire markets. Perhaps the most powerful argument for considering a new safety net structure for insurance companies during such a panic is the contrast between what the FDIC, Federal Reserve, and the Treasury (Office of the Comptroller of the Currency [OCC]) could do for banks and securities markets and what the insurance commissioners and GAs could do for insurers and their industry.

During the years from 2008 through 2011 the life and casualty GAs did protect policyholders in 35 small company insolvencies, with total net assessments of $1.12 billion.[16]

In the same period the FDIC resolved almost 414 banks with losses for the FDIC of $89.8 billion. Furthermore, the FDIC intervened in important and unprecedented ways, working with the OCC and the Federal Reserve to shore up major banking companies that were deemed systemic or too big to fail. In most cases the banks and markets were exposed, in fact or potentially, to destructive runs from depositors and foreign investors.

The FDIC roles in the federal interventions, which were not available to insurance commissioners or GAs, included guaranteeing loans to banks, ring-fencing assets in attempts to merge troubled banks into other banks, and temporarily lifting the guaranteed deposit caps as the crisis in confidence grew. These are all powers that an insurance regulator might well use to advantage in conservation or rehabilitation of a stressed insurer or in an industry-wide crisis. They would also be means to stop a panic run on withdrawable insurance company deposits such as unallocated pension funds or the popular individual investment type annuities in the accumulation phase.

Congress did enact the Troubled Asset Relief Program (TARP) that permitted, among other purposes, capital infusions into insurers as well as banks. This program dealt directly with insurers, not through the insurance regulators, and assisted AIG, Hartford, and Lincoln.

In the case of the attempt to merge Citi and Wachovia, the FDIC offered to ring-fence a block of stressed assets, extending maximum loss provisions on a group of questionable assets, for which it would have received Citi's preferred stock as compensation. The FDIC also guaranteed loans made to banks under the Temporary Liquidity Guarantee Program (TLGP). And, of course, the insurers, unlike the banks, had no direct access to the Federal Reserve's window of last resort.

The major federal interventions related to the insurance industry were the $175 billion for AIG, $3 billion for Hartford, and $915 million for Lincoln National. Given the demand for immediate action in the case of AIG, there was no possibility of using the GAs' assessment mechanism. Nor was it deemed a role for them to play in dealing with a financial holding company, even if the vast majority of the assets were insurance companies. And the amounts involved dwarfed the capability of the GAs.

The Federal Reserve was able to act under the 13(3) clause of the Federal Reserve Act that permits it to lend to nonbank companies only in the event of a major financial crisis.

AIG was the lead insurance entity requiring support during the crisis, but there were eight other major insurers that applied to be eligible for TARP emergency funds from the U.S. Treasury. Two of them, Hartford Life for $3 billion and Lincoln National for $900 million, actually took down the money. The latter two paid back the loans with interest within a year. AIG at this time (2013) has returned the majority of its borrowed funds with substantial interest to the Federal Reserve or the Treasury. Some of the insurers who qualified for TARP capital funds and others scrambled to acquire banks for themselves or their holding companies so as to be able to go to the Federal Reserve as a lender of last resort—a service that the GAs were not designed to provide.

A major, but not the largest, item in the AIG $100 billion loss reported in its 2008 10-K was the $40.8 billion loss in AIG's Financial Products (AIG FP) unit, which had written an enormous book of credit default swaps. Federal Reserve Chairman Ben Bernanke said in congressional testimony: "AIG had a financial products division which was very lightly regulated and was the source of a great deal of systemic trouble." He further called the AIG FP unit " a hedge fund basically that was attached to a large and stable insurance company that made large numbers of irresponsible bets, and took huge losses." He failed to highlight the very steep losses the AIG insurance entities had also suffered.

It is true that AIG FP had an operating loss of $40.8 billion in 2008, but the other businesses of AIG had losses of $67.9 billion, for a total of $108.8 billion. The insurance units of the "large and stable insurance company" had losses of $43.2 billion.[17] These losses include direct investment losses and those due to security lending, which is a normal part of the investment strategy of life insurance companies. Clearly, AIG, after such a loss in capital, would have had to join the other insurers applying for TARP support, even without the "hedge fund" losses.

It is also significant to contrast the very large 2008 loss suffered by AIG's insurance units of $43.2 billion with Citi's loss of $18.7 billion in the same year, 2008, which led to intense discussion of putting its underlying bank into receivership. Luckily, after 2008 and early 2009, the economy stabilized enough to reduce panic levels. AIG insurance units were not forced into insurance receivership, but, had it been necessary, the alarming numbers certainly might have squeezed the GAs' assessment capacity.

A FEDERAL OPTION FOR MODERNIZING THE INSURER SAFETY NET

The limitations of the state-based GAs could not be fully offset by a national version, combining the joint efforts of the NAIC, NOLHGA, NCIGF, and the insurance commissioners in the 50 states and the District of Columbia. Strenuous efforts over many decades leave the system as just described, with weaknesses in uniformity, lack of capability to deal with runs, and small resources considering the enormous growth in size and risk of the large insurers in recent decades.

As the imaginative designer of the GAs 50 years ago, Spencer Kimball, must have realized, he could not come up with a prefunded plan, given the widely varying positions of the 50 states, nor could he persuade the states to back up the GAs with their taxpayer resources. More importantly, the industry and Congress were not ready to create a federal system.

If the GA limitations and current scope and scale of the insurance business are seen as sufficiently severe and dangerous (not to mention systemic), then Congress, the federal regulators involved with FSOC, and even the insurance industry might support today a federal solution modeled on the FDIC and reflecting the annuity benefit structure of the PBGC.

National Consistency and *Ex Ante* Risk-Based Prefunding

A federal system could set uniform benefit caps for the various types of coverage, thereby eliminating the confusing questions facing consumers and, in particular, would be as open as the other federal plans, without a gag rule forbidding full disclosure of the caps on guarantees. The benefits for annuities could be synchronized with benefits guaranteed by the PBGC, and those for life insurance and cash withdrawals synchronized with the FDIC levels. All lines of insurance would be treated similarly without the current state variations.

Benefit caps would not depend on the insured's state of residency or the insurer's domiciliary state.

If there is a further rush to derisk corporate defined benefit plans by purchasing insurance company annuities, there would not be the large immediate drop in the safety net caps.

With pre-insolvency premiums in a federal system, with an explicit federal guarantee (as with the FDIC) or an implicit one (as with the PBGC), the fund could cope with an industry shock-driven run. It could also be a source to fund a merger with another company or, in a 2008–2009 type of panic, permit a fundamentally solvent company to survive.

As has been noted in the academic literature over the years, it would be possible to base the risk premiums for a pre-insolvency fund on the risk characteristics of the companies, on either a rough justice basis or one taking into account the regulators' capital requirements. It seems impossible to achieve any of these improvements with the states' system of post-insolvency funding.

The federal system would create a strong federal regulatory office that would oversee the insurance business, and would achieve a long-sought goal of many in the business of having a federal regulator that would protect the insurance industry in the event of a crisis, in which the interests of the banking and securities businesses might come ahead of protecting insurers.

A federal insurance regulator, with deep knowledge of the business and particularly of the major companies, with a substantial preexisting fund, could have played an important constructive role in the resolution of the AIG crisis. Since all the decision makers in resolving AIG's difficulties were bank regulators, the natural suspicion was that the extraordinary federal funds were expended to protect the banking system when other ways were open that would have better protected the insurance entities within AIG. One such solution could have been a bankruptcy proceeding for the holding company and its noninsurance holdings, with the underlying insurers sold or otherwise protected. Alternatively, an insurance regulator might have reduced dramatically the demand for the collateral by the banks through negotiation.

And, above all, well before the crisis, the AIG holding company would surely have been regulated by the federal insurance regulator, which could have stopped the reckless business growth of the poorly capitalized AIG Financial Products unit.

The state GAs could not possibly cope with the immediate liquidity needs of AIG, which at their peak came to $175 billion.

Also, the eight companies that sought TARP protection would have gone initially to their "first responder," the insurance regulator responsible for the federal safety net. Of the eight eligible for TARP funding, the two companies that required temporary liquidity could have been easily handled by the federal insurance fund or its backup federal resources. No call would have been made on the federal taxpayers.

At present the regulator overseeing an insurance holding company is the Federal Reserve, which has no actual insurance regulatory experience. Clearly, Congress could designate the new regulator of the safety net to replace the Federal Reserve in that role.

There is a recent insurer rehabilitation that could have been handled very differently under a system with a preexisting fund, or some form of access to a "lender of last resort for insurers."

General American Life Insurance Company entered into an imprudent contract of guaranteeing liquidity on a block of business that had immediate withdrawal rights in the event of a loss in its rating—similar to the guarantee made by AIG for the collateral of its obligations to purchasers of the credit default swaps.

When General American did in fact lose its rating, the company could not meet the immediate cash demands. Like AIG, it faced a classic run and there was no way the commissioner of insurance of Missouri could help it get through the liquidity crisis, short of liquidating the company. The only alternative was to merge the company into the giant MetLife, which could provide the liquidity.

General American was an otherwise well-capitalized company that could have entered into a temporary liquidity facility that would have been paid back in a few months or years and with excellent credit. The federal regulator could have exacted penalties through penalty interest charges, and possibly management changes and new board members. The company could have continued to serve its policyholders as it unwound the problematic contracts. The giant MetLife was certainly "too big to fail" before this transaction and was simply further engrossed.

Surely, insurance commissioners and the federal regulator could have superior outcomes in other forced liquidations and mergers. There is a great deal of attention paid to the desirability of prompt corrective action in the instances of the state insurance commissioner seeking court authority for placing a company under rehabilitation or liquidation. Clearly, the availability of a substantial existing fund would be useful in many such situations for a speedier solution and could be used as a basis for some form of lender of last resort.

The initial funding of the system could be built up slowly with nominal charges to the companies for the amounts of their liabilities protected by the system, with some offsetting against the very substantial premium taxes paid by the companies. With state premium taxes currently in the $16 billion to $20 billion range, the offset could be quite modest. And, of course, many states now permit credits against premium taxes for prior assessments.

Charging premiums before an industry shock would be anticyclical by raising defenses before the crisis. As with the banks' experience and the long-term low cost of insurance insolvencies, there may be few claims paid over several years.

If viewed over time, the costs to the industry will be the costs incurred due to insolvencies, and increased due to higher guarantees needed to make the system comparable to other safety net systems—especially the PBGC. There would of course be potential costs to the industry fund due to some insolvencies if those costs could, under the present GA system, have been shifted to the federal government. Examples of such costs were AIG, Hartford, and Lincoln in the 2008–2009 period (although all federal payments were repaid with interest, there was still risk assumed by the federal taxpayers). There would be more cost shifted to more risky firms under a risk-based premium regime, and less cost for less risky firms—in short, a fairer allocation of insolvency costs.

Mitigating the Moral Hazard Risk

The concern of moral hazard under such a system has become a concern of Congress, regulators, and academics. See especially Wallison (2009) and Harrington (1991, 1999).

Moral hazard appears in two forms. The first form, an *implicit* one, derives from market expectation created by the actions of regulators who in fact bail out firms that are deemed too big to fail or too systemic to fail. This form has an especially insidious effect since it leads investors to expect and rely on such bailouts for other firms and therefore damages market discipline. Those expecting such benefits include shareholders and other creditors of the companies as well as policyholders.

However, the FDIC, PBGC, and insurance GAs represent *explicit* guarantees and exist primarily to protect depositors, individual pension rights, and insurance policyholders. All of them are capped with maximum amounts. It is argued that such explicit guarantees create moral hazard since shareholders and managements can take on excessive risk with the rewards going to them, with a "put" to the government of the participant liabilities if the risks create losses. The experience with savings and loan companies in the 1980s was a severe example of the danger of moral hazard. It was created by extreme weakening, simultaneously, of investment standards and regulatory requirements for savings and loan companies by Congress. Almost immediately there were many instances of irresponsible and reckless investments, particularly in the most risky forms of real estate.

The moral hazard of such explicit guarantees has been illustrated as the creation of a valuable "put" for the shareholders and management in the event of the failure of the company,[18] and accordingly would create an incentive for equity holders to take on more risk.

A priori, one would expect a modest increase in moral hazard with the creation of the GA system or an increase in an existing system's benefit caps. The creation of the P-C GAs in the 1980s gave the opportunity to test this hypothesis. That the GAs created more risk taking is weakly supported by two Lee et al. papers (1997, 1999).[19] The papers also reject the idea that the GA system increased monitoring by other companies and find no effect on mutual companies. Intuitively, one would expect that the company governance structure (shareholder owned versus mutual) would provide an incentive to take on risk that would dwarf any such incentive due to moral hazard.

Cummins (1988) addresses risk-based pricing as a counter to the moral hazard created by the explicit guarantees for P-C companies.

Clearly, the adoption of a federally backed fund, with uniform and larger guarantees, as described here, would increase the value of the put, all else being equal. Also, the sharply increased visibility of the benefits would let customers, creditors, and investors in the companies know that the guarantees existed, thereby reducing their incentive to value quality in the company's finances (with no gag rule, there would be no need to go to websites to find out the level of the guarantee). Both of these effects would increase the value of the put.

However, all things would not be equal. Mitigating such an increase in moral hazard would be the effect of *ex ante* risk-based charges for insurers to a fund to cover future industry losses. Excessive risk taking, or weak capitalization, would be directly penalized by higher risk-based premiums. Also, a federal office overseeing the insurance insolvency risk would be able to see business trends and potential industry shocks, and could develop defenses against excessive risk taking. For instance, when insurers deviate from the classic actuarial reliance on idiosyncratic risks, capital requirements and even risk-based premiums could be adjusted. In the 2008–2009 crisis, these deviations, and consequent shocks, included broad industry exposure to a stock market decline when companies had guaranteed minimum returns of variable annuities invested in stocks. The monoline structure for guaranteeing municipal bonds suffered severe losses when firms broadened their market to include corporate debt.

CONCLUSION

Adoption of a federal system, as described in this chapter, would remedy most of the difficulties of the 50-state system of GAs described in the critique.

The federal system could produce easily understood and uniform guarantees for insurance policy owners and prospects, nationwide. They would be transparent to consumers, agents, and companies and surely not subject to state-imposed gag rules. After many years of effort by the companies and insurance commissioners, such a result does not seem possible under a state system.

The benefit level could be uniformly raised and made consistent with other levels in the economy, especially the PBGC.

Prefunding the federal system has many advantages. It permits risk-based premiums, it is anticyclical (unlike the GA post hoc assessment system), and it creates liquidity for the resolution process. Its existence brings credibility of the guarantees to policyholders.

Risk-based premiums would be fairer to the low-risk companies. They would be a strong deterrent to moral hazard, offsetting the increase in moral hazard due to higher transparent and explicit benefits.

The cumulative costs over time to the insurance industry would be equal to the losses incurred for insolvencies. These have been very modest for the GAs. Expected costs should be lower than bank losses due to the traditionally conservative long-range investment policies of insurers.

Of course, there may be further costs if the industry has to bear the costs that would otherwise be absorbed by the federal government in the absence of coverage by an industry system. That, however, represents an advantage of the system.

Having a well-informed and experienced federal regulator could be a significant benefit to the industry and would focus insurance regulation on industry-wide systemic issues. Intrusive bank-type limitations on management, likely under the bank regulation model of the FSOC provisions of the Dodd-Frank statute, could be avoided.

With the liquidity of the preexisting fund, the federal regulator would have more flexibility in finding a quick and optimal resolution of a failing company. This would reduce costs to other insurers. Furthermore, the regulator would have the capability to deal with runs and contagions, as well as general liquidity crises for otherwise well-capitalized companies.

Finally, the system would substantially eliminate the federal taxpayers' contingent liability for a major insurance failure. Costs of insurer failures would be borne by the industry itself, with some relief from the onerous state premium taxes.

Finally, and most importantly, the broader and more transparent federal system would strengthen the role of insurers in meeting the needs of American families.

NOTES

1. Most discussions of large insurance company failures look only at recent decades. Accordingly, they fail to include the largest life insurance failure in American history, the total collapse of the Missouri State Life Insurance Company in the 1930s. It was the seventh-largest company in the United States at the time (the seventh-largest today would represent more than $200 billion in assets). Missouri State's assets were valued at 50 percent of its liabilities when the insurance department took it over. No guarantee organizations were in existence, and insurance was regulated entirely by the states, to which the federal government deferred at that time since insurance by law was still not viewed as interstate commerce. Policy liens were established by the court of 50 percent of cash values, which were then deducted from the face amount upon death or withdrawal. The cause of the failure was the raiding of its assets by the bank holding company that owned it. See McFerrin (1939); also see Kimball, Denenberg, and Bertrand (1967) and Wilcox (1996) for an idea of the primitive character of procedures as late as 1967 in resolving insurers.

2. Christopher J. Wilcox, "The U.S. Guaranty Association Concept at 25," *Journal of Insurance Regulation* 14, no. 3 (Spring 1996): 370–372. This paper is a good source for what Spencer Kimball was trying to achieve in the 1960s: first, continuation of coverage for the policyholders; second, to be better than the recent record of "sufficiency of funds . . . average paid on liquidation being less than 50 cents on the dollar"; and third, the ending of unacceptable delays in payment, lasting typically more than seven years. Clearly, the GAs delivered on these limited but critical goals.

3. See Scott Harrington's "The History of Federal Involvement in Insurance Regulation" (1999) and Robert W. Klein's (1995) comprehensive description of insurance regulation, including guaranty associations.

4. See the description of the process in Gallanis (2009).

5. The total of insurance premium taxes paid creates the capability of the GAs to meet insolvencies. In the testimony of the two GA associations to the Federal Insurance Office, they estimate that their combined capacity was $16.7 billion a year in 2011. Accordingly, this is an estimate of the burden on insurance policyholders every year for taxes on their products, which are passed on to the buyers of all kinds of insurance. A very small fraction of this amount would be adequate to pre-fund a significant *ex ante* guaranty fund.

6. See NOLHGA and NCIGF papers and testimony and their websites, and also Peter Gallanis (2009), which explains the operation of NOLHGA and the resolution system for insurers in general.

7. See Manders, Vaughn, and Myers (1994). This paper was influential in persuading the NAIC to take the initiative in forming state compacts to encourage uniformity of state regulation.
8. See the discussion of both NOLHGA and NCIGF before the House Financial Services Subcommittee on Insurance, Housing and Community Opportunity, Insurance Oversight and Legislative Proposals (2011).
9. See Gallanis (2009) and the House Committee testimony of NOLHGA and NCIGF.
10. See premium data in the *Life Insurers Fact Book 2012* on the American Council of Life Insurers' website. In 1980, industry-wide life insurance premiums were $40.829 billion and annuity premiums $22.429 billion. In 2011, life premiums were $127.455 billion and annuity premiums $334.895 billion. The share of annuity premiums for the industry rose from 35 percent to 72 percent.
11. The Ligon and Thistle (2007) paper seeks an economic explanation of the survival of fleets of multiple P-C insurers under common ownership when combining in a multiline company would provide cost advantages. They see an economic motive in adding shareholder value by having multiple "puts" in the GA system rather than a combined one, with none of the assessments based on risk characteristics. The Bernier and Mahfoudi (2010) paper uses "contagion" for the effect that the postassessment process may weaken surviving companies. This is similar to the procyclicality concern expressed elsewhere in this chapter.
12. Sheila Bair, *Bull by the Horns* (2012, 196). Bair's testimony on the development of the Dodd-Frank bill before the House Committee on October 29, 2009, concerning the proposed but not adopted Financial Company Resolution Fund for nonbank financial institutions, including insurers.
13. See the Joint Comments of NOLHGA and NCIGF (2011).
14. See the AIG SEC Form 10-K filed for 2008.
15. The *Financial Times*, January 23, 2013.
16. See NOLHGA and NCIGF websites.
17. See page 71 of the AIG Form 10-K for 2008.
18. See Cummins (1995) on the relationship between the "put" created by the P-C GAs and proposed capital requirements muting the effects of the put.
19. Lee, Mayers, and Smith (1997) found that stockholder-owned P-C insurers modestly increased risk-based assets after the introduction of GAs but no change occurred for mutuals. Also, they found no evidence that companies monitored each other due to possible assessments under the GA system. Lee and Smith (1999) found a decrease in reserves by P-C companies after the GA introduction.

REFERENCES

American Council of Life Insurers (ACLI). 2012. *Life Insurers Fact Book 2012: Income, Premiums*. Washington, DC: ACLI. www.acli.com.

Bair, Sheila. 2012. *Bull by the Horns*. New York: Free Press.

Bernier, Gilles, and Ridha M. Mahfoudi. 2010. "On the Economics of Post Assessments in Insurance Guarantee Funds: A Stakeholders' Perspective." *Journal of Risk and Insurance* 77 (4).

Cummins, J. David. 1988. "Risk-Based Premiums for Insurance Guaranty Funds." *Journal of Finance* 43, no. 4 (September).

Cummins, J. David. 1995. "Risk Based Capital Requirements for Property-Casualty Companies: A Financial Analysis." In *The Financial Dynamics of the Insurance Industry*, edited by Edward I. Altman and Irwin T. Vanderhoof. New York: Salomon Center for the Study of Financial Institutions.

Gallanis, Peter G. 2009. "NOLHGA, the Life and Health Insurance Guaranty System, and the Financial Crisis of 2008–2009." Delivered at "Insurer Receivership and Run-Off: The Next Level," American Bar Association, June 5, New York.

Han, Li-Ming, Gene C. Lai, and Robert C. Witt. 1997. "A Financial-Economic Evaluation of the Insurance Guaranty Fund System: An Agency Cost Perspective." *Journal of Banking and Finance*.

Harrington, Scott E. 1991. "Should the Feds Regulate Insurance Company Solvency?" *Cato Review* 14:53–61.

Harrington, Scott E. 1999. "The History of Federal Involvement in Insurance Regulation." In *Optional Federal Chartering and Regulation of Insurance Companies*, edited by Peter J. Wallison. Lanham, MD: AEI Press.

House Financial Services Subcommittee on Insurance, Housing and Community Opportunity, Insurance Oversight and Legislative Proposals. 2011. Testimony of NOLHGA and NCIGF, November 16.

Kimball, Spencer L., Herbert L. Denenberg, and Robert J. Bertrand. 1967. "Rehabilitation and Liquidation of Insurance Companies." *Insurance Law Journal*, January.

Klein, Robert W. 1995. "Insurance Regulation in Transition." *Journal of Risk and Insurance* 62 (3).

Lee, Soon-Jae, David Mayers, and Clifford W. Smith Jr. 1997. "Guaranty Funds and Risk Taking: Evidence from the Insurance Industry." *Journal of Financial Economics* 44:3–24.

Lee, Soon-jae, and M. L. Smith Jr. 1999. "Property-Casualty Insurance Guaranty Funds and Insurer Vulnerability to Misfortune." *Journal of Banking and Finance* 23.

Ligon, J. A., and P. D. Thistle. 2007. "The Organizational Structure of Insurance Companies: The Role of Heterogeneous Risks and Guaranty Funds." *Journal of Risk and Insurance* 74:851–862.

Manders, John M., Therese M. Vaughn, and Robert H. Myers Jr. 1994. "Insurance Regulation in the Public Interest: Where Do We Go from Here?" *Journal of Insurance Regulation.*

McFerrin, John B. 1939. "Caldwell and Company, a Southern Financial Empire." Chapel Hill: University of North Carolina Press; reissued in 1969 by the Vanderbilt Press.

NOLHGA and NCIGF. 2011. "Joint Comments of NOLHGA and NCIGF in Response to Federal Insurance Office's Request for Public Input," December 16.

Wallison, Peter J. 2009. "Testimony on Regulating and Resolving Institutions Considered 'Too Big to Fail.'" Senate Banking Committee, May 6, American Enterprise Institute for Public Policy Research.

Wilcox, Christopher J. 1996. "The U.S. Guaranty Association Concept at 25," *Journal of Insurance Regulation* 14, no. 3 (Spring): 370–372.

CHAPTER 11

Policyholder Protection in the Wake of the Financial Crisis

Peter G. Gallanis*

National Organization of Life & Health Insurance Guaranty Associations

As this chapter is being completed, a number of financial journalists are publishing "fifth anniversary" retrospective analyses of the financial crisis that began in late 2007.[1] Strikingly absent from all of the articles is any mention of insurance consumers who suffered losses on their insurance contracts during the crisis.

The financial markets crisis of that period was indeed severe, as was the general recession associated with it. In many respects, it was the most serious challenge to the U.S. and global financial systems since the Great Depression. Even viewed solely as a U.S. financial markets phenomenon, the impact was striking. In the four-year period from the start of 2008 through the end of 2011, over 400 U.S. banks and thrifts failed;[2] the five largest investment banking firms either failed, were acquired, or converted to bank holding companies;[3] government-sponsored secondary mortgage entities Fannie Mae and Freddie Mac were placed in conservation; one of the largest money market funds "broke the buck"; various hedge funds and finance companies became insolvent; over 600 pension plans failed;[4] and most corporate equities plunged precipitously, as reflected broadly in the various stock market indexes.

*The author gratefully acknowledges the assistance of NOLHGA's General Counsel Bill O'Sullivan, Director of Communications Sean McKenna, and Manager of Insurance Services Joanna Akiyama, along with keen insights provided by Charles Todd Richardson and James Tsai of Faegre Baker Daniels (Washington, D.C.); Catherine M. Masters of Schiff Hardin (Chicago); and James R. Stinson of Sidley Austin (Chicago). Responsibility for any errors belongs solely to the author.

Besides the troubles of firms operating in the financial markets, the crisis was connected to a deep and long recession in the real economy, evidenced most strikingly by the bankruptcies of two of the three major U.S. auto manufacturers, prolonged high levels of unemployment, and the generally depressed situation of the U.S. housing markets and among homeowners, many of whom lost homes through mortgage foreclosures.

Consumers and institutions involved in the financial markets endured very large losses. Some of those may have been so-called paper losses, to the extent that investors held investment positions that declined in market value early in the crisis and recovered afterward. But for investors in firms that failed or fundamentally reorganized, investors who were compelled (or felt compelled) to dispose of investments at the nadir of the crisis, and people whose jobs were eliminated or whose homes were taken, the losses were real and permanent.

Interestingly, the turmoil that beset the financial services marketplace generally beginning in late 2007 did *not* have a material negative effect on insurance products purchased by consumers, and neither for the insurance companies writing those products did it cause the types of widespread company failures seen in other segments of the financial services field.

No nationally significant operating insurance companies in the business of writing conventional life and health or property-casualty products failed during the recent financial crisis. The handful of very small life and health insurance companies that were liquidated under state insurance receivership processes during the period 2008–2011 followed a pace very similar to the precrisis average annual failure rates,[5] and the same held true on the property-casualty side of the industry.[6]

More important, those few life and health insurance companies that were liquidated, in the aggregate, had nominal liabilities to policyholders of about $996 million, and virtually all of those amounts owed to policyholders were fully protected through existing resolution processes (the insurance receivership processes and guaranty association [GA] mechanisms discussed later).[7]

Stated differently, and despite occasional popular misconceptions to the contrary, the performance of the traditional insurance industry through the recent financial crisis and recession (and the effective protection of the relatively few consumers owning contracts issued by the several small insurers that did fail) was a highlight in an otherwise widespread display of failures and consumer losses relating to the financial sector.

Notwithstanding those facts, as the financial crisis postmortems continue, and as implementation of U.S. financial market regulatory reforms under the Dodd-Frank Act[8] slowly proceeds, a recurring question arises: How confident should purchasers and beneficiaries of insurance products (particularly life insurance and annuity contracts) be that the essential promises of their contracts will be fulfilled?

This chapter proposes the following answer to that question: Consumers should be confident that insurers' commitments to them will be honored. The basis for that confidence is the existence and operation of a comprehensive, interconnected complex of protective features that has served insurance consumers well for decades and that can be expected to do so under any reasonably foreseeable circumstances.

Four key factors now combine (as they have for decades) to enhance the likelihood that insurers' commitments to consumers will be satisfied. They are (1) the inherent financial and operational conservatism of the insurance industry; (2) effective financial regulatory and quasi-regulatory processes that constrain insurer risk taking; (3) a well-designed and generally effective process for administering the receiverships of the few insurers that do occasionally fail; and (4) a well-designed, tested, and proven financial safety net (the insurance guaranty system) that effectively provides a floor level of financial protection for consumers whose insurers do fail. This chapter addresses the interplay of those four factors, with particular emphasis on protections provided to life insurance and annuity purchasers through the life and health insurance guaranty system, a system that has been the subject of few comprehensive public essays to date.

When the author was an undergraduate, the late economist Milton Friedman used to challenge students by saying of a given student assertion, "That's all well and good in practice, but how does it work *in theory*?" He meant by that challenge not that real-world evidence should be ignored in favor of untethered abstractions, but rather that we should strive to understand not only the available evidence, but also *why* that evidence develops the way it does. An understanding of the four interrelated protective factors just described not only helps develop an appreciation of key empirical evidence regarding the historical satisfaction of insurance promises, but also helps develop the explanation of *why* insurers performed so much better than other financial services providers in the recent financial crisis (and in earlier periods of economic stress)—and why they can be expected to do so in the future.

A proper study of post–financial crisis reforms is testing how companies would perform when confronted with various assumed economic stress factors. In that vein, it should be recognized that the recent financial crisis *itself* was a remarkably probative live-fire stress test of financial institutions. It is no accident that, through that most real of stress tests, individual insurance companies and the industry as a whole performed well and consumers were well protected against the risks of insurance company failures.

To understand the operation of the multilayered system or complex of protections that guard insurance consumers, one must grasp the basic details of how the core insurance business model operates, how insurers are regulated for solvency, how insurance company resolution processes operate in the relatively rare cases when insurers fail, and how the insurance guaranty system works in tandem with the insurance regulatory and receivership processes.

BASIC ASPECTS OF THE U.S. DIRECT INSURANCE INDUSTRY

Many key aspects of the operations of U.S. direct writers[9] of insurance are summarized beginning at page 3 of an important recent report by the Government Accountability Office, *Insurance Markets: Impacts of and Regulatory Response to the 2007–2009 Financial Crisis* (June 2013), which is hereinafter referred to as the GAO Insurance Study.

Core Promises to Consumers: Insurance Contrasted to Banking

As discussed in the GAO Insurance Study and elsewhere, the business model for insurance companies is relatively straightforward, though it is also fundamentally different from the business model for banks, thrifts, and certain other types of financial services institutions.

An insurance consumer agrees to acquire insurance protection in exchange for the payment of one or more premiums for the insurance policy or contract. In exchange, the core promise of the insurer is to make agreed payments upon the occurrence of a specified contingency covered by the contract (if and when that contingency takes place). Depending on the type of policy, that contingency may be, for example, a property loss caused by natural events or human action, the amount of a judgment for legal liability or related legal expenses, medical expenses, death benefits under a life policy, or an agreed-upon stream of income payable if and when an annuitant reaches a specified age.

In contrast, the core promise to consumers of banking institutions is not a promise of protection against contingencies that may (or may not) occur at a later date, but rather a promise of funding *liquidity* whenever a consumer may request delivery of liquid funds that the consumer has deposited with an institution. Stated differently, the core promise of a bank is to make consumer deposits available upon demand, whenever demand may be made by consumers, while the core promise of an insurer is to pay against a contingency that (if it occurs at all) is always in the future, and often in the distant future. The contingency-driven obligations of an insurer are in some respects the obverse or opposite of the demand-based liabilities of depository institutions.

The nature of the core promise made by insurers to their consumers is the essential foundation for understanding how insurers do business, what their consumers expect (and how they behave in periods of economic stress), how insurance is regulated, how insurer receiverships are administered, and how the insurance safety net is designed and operates.

The Financial Model of Insurance Companies

Because fulfillment of an insurer's promise to its consumers involves payment at a later date of agreed financial protections, an insurers' basic financial model requires the availability of the necessary funds to make those payments at the times they must be made. Insurers do that by charging premiums for their contracts that are calculated by reference to the anticipated eventual costs of the contingency payments they commit to make, also factoring in projected earnings on funds invested in the interim, operating costs, and the maintenance of appropriate surplus funds to provide a cushion against unanticipated adverse developments.

Insurers generally pursue investment strategies that, when possible, match maturities of investments to anticipated contingency payments to consumers (predicted through actuarial modeling).[10] Insurers with liabilities expected to develop in the near future (sometimes referred to as "short-tail liabilities"), such as claims on auto insurance and under most health insurance policies, tend to have investment portfolios predominantly comprising short-term bonds and notes and similar instruments. Insurers with liabilities expected to develop further into the future ("long-tail liabilities"), such as issuers of life insurance and annuity contracts and of casualty products, typically have investment portfolios predominantly comprising long-term bonds, commercial mortgage loans, and other investments with similar characteristics.

Understanding the principal balance sheet components of an insurer (particularly a writer of life insurance and annuity business) requires an appreciation not only of the *quantitative* aspects of those components, but also the important, and very real, *qualitative* aspects.

The major liability component of an insurer is the set of accounts setting forth its reserves, which reflect the value today of the company's liabilities for honoring contractual commitments to policyholders when (and if) those commitments are due. The asset side, as noted, tends mostly to include fixed-income investments matched to anticipated liability maturation.

Grasping the quality of an insurer's assets is fairly straightforward, but for a given company, key questions are how well the maturities of investments match projected payment obligations on policies; whether the yield on the portfolio is sufficient to meet assumptions in place when policy premiums were established; and, most important, whether issuers of the financial instruments in the portfolio are likely to perform on their own obligations to the insurer.

That assessment in turn is intimately related to an appreciation of the qualities of the insurer's reserve liabilities—the value of honoring its contractual obligations to policyholders. Such an analysis includes, among other things, the predicted frequency and schedule of the development of claims and fixed payments on contracts; the quality of the underwriting on which payment frequency and scheduling assumptions were developed; and the likelihood that policies may be terminated, lapsed, or (where contractually permissible) made the subject of premature surrenders or withdrawals of account values, and the financial consequences for the insurer of such policyholder actions.

The fact that payment obligations on insurers' essential promises are triggered by the occurrence of contractually stipulated contingencies (rather than, e.g., depositor demands, as with banks) means that the bulk of insurer liabilities either cannot or will not be payable simply because economic prospects for the insurer, the financial sector, or the general economy have declined. Most consumers do not die, get sick, crash their cars, or lose their lawsuits because the gross domestic product (GDP) has turned south, although, if they are worried enough, they might be inclined to withdraw cash (at least amounts above Federal Deposit Insurance Corporation [FDIC] protection levels) from a bank.

Because insurance consumers are buying protection against contingencies, and not protection against illiquidity (otherwise they would simply put insurance premium dollars in the bank instead), the insurance marketplace has accepted the development and refinement of contract features that provide incentives to hold insurance contracts for the originally contemplated term. Such incentives include surrender or withdrawal penalties that wear off gradually the longer a contract is in force, interest rates on policyholder loans, and cash value calculations that make a whole life contract materially more valuable when held to maturity than if surrendered early.[11]

For all the foregoing reasons, instances of surrender and withdrawal activity by insurance consumers have traditionally been low, even in cases when a specific insurer is the subject of publicized financial difficulties, or when the financial and general economies are challenged.[12] In atypical cases when unexpected increases in surrender and withdrawal activity might appear to pose liquidity threats to an insurer, the insurer (and its receiver, should receivership be required) also has contractual and statutory powers to stabilize the book of insurance business, and thus protect the availability of assets to satisfy core insurance products to all consumers, by implementing a temporary moratorium on contract surrenders and withdrawals.

Stated differently, the quality of contingency-based insurer reserves—the value of their commitments to consumers—makes them "sticky" liabilities, fundamentally different in character from the type of demand liabilities thought to result in "run on the bank" behavior driven by consumer economic concerns.

In general, then, the two key characteristics of an insurers' balance sheet—and particularly an insurer writing long-tail liability business like life insurance or annuity contracts—are the sticky nature of its contingency-based long-tail liabilities and the conservative, long-term investments in its investment portfolio.

Implications of Insurers' Business and Financial Models

Because both the liabilities and the assets of traditional insurers are properly viewed as long-term in nature, traditional insurers (particularly life and annuity writers) are not in the business of *maturity transformation* and hence do not face the sorts of disintermediation risks that were at the heart of the problems faced in the recent financial crisis by other financial services providers (e.g., the repo risks of some investment banks, the mismatched mortgage portfolio risks of some large thrifts and other mortgage lenders, and the credit default swaps issued by American International Group [AIG] Financial Products).

In addition, quite apart from regulatory controls discussed later, the desire of insurers to operate at a profit and to be able to compete in an insurance marketplace that values financial stability, together with the desire of consumers to receive when due the insurance protection for which they contract and pay, converge to incentivize most insurance companies to strive—for business reasons rather than due to regulatory pressures alone—to develop well-underwritten and predictable books of insurance contracts (policyholder liabilities) and to invest in reliable, predictable, and safe investments. That set of consumer expectations has been translated through political and governmental processes into the basis for the financial regulation of insurance.

FINANCIAL REGULATION AND QUASI-REGULATION OF INSURERS

The primary concern of insurance regulators has long been the financial supervision of insurers and the enforcement of financial standards aimed at protecting insurers' ability to perform their contractual commitments to consumers.[13] Even frequent critics of insurance regulation concede that regulators historically have performed well at that job,[14] as they did through the recent financial crisis[15] and through prior adverse economic periods, including even the Great Depression.[16]

The Constitution of Insurance Regulation

Since shortly after the Civil War, the regulation of insurance in the United States has been recognized as a matter that is primarily the responsibility of the states.[17] Additionally, as further discussed in the following section, the resolution of failed insurers is also a matter of state law,[18] as is the provision of a financial safety net protecting consumers from losses they might otherwise suffer as the consequence of an insurer's failure.

Although the Dodd-Frank Act reconstituted various aspects of the regulation of the broad U.S. financial services sector, few substantive regulatory changes were made to the state-based insurance regulatory system.[19] Under Dodd-Frank, financial solvency regulation remains primarily a state matter, as are the resolution process and the consumer safety net. However, Title I of Dodd-Frank does establish the Financial Stability Oversight Council (FSOC), which is charged with identifying systemic financial risks and firms (potentially including insurers) that could pose threats to the stability of the financial system. Orderly liquidation procedures under Title II of Dodd-Frank could be applied to address the resolution of a holding company that has insurer subsidiaries (but generally not the insurers themselves). Additionally, Dodd-Frank establishes the Federal Insurance Office, which has no direct regulatory functions but which represents the United States federal government in the performance of specified international insurance regulatory efforts, and which generally serves as the "eyes and ears" of the federal government on matters relating to insurance.

In addition to U.S. regulatory oversight, insurers are affected directly and indirectly by various international regulators and regulatory bodies. U.S.-based insurers doing business in other countries are subject to direct supervision by regulators in those countries. In addition, U.S. insurers are affected (sometimes indirectly) by standards and rulings of international bodies such as the International Association of Insurance Supervisors (IAIS) and the Financial Stability Board, which was formed by the G-20 countries to address questions of systemic risk in the global financial system.[20]

The Substance and Processes of U.S. Insurance Regulation

As previously noted, the primary objective of insurance regulation is to ensure that companies maintain the financial and operational resources to meet their contractual commitments to consumers. Regulators pursue this objective through a combination of tools, standards, and processes.[21]

State laws and regulations, often drawn from and based on model legislation and regulation promulgated by the National Association of Insurance Commissioners (NAIC), establish standards that must be satisfied in order to form, acquire, and operate an insurance company. Key standards relating to the financial integrity of insurers include statutory accounting rules,[22] which conservatively limit the admissibility, valuation, and concentration of assets held for investment by an insurer, and reserving rules that similarly require a conservative valuation of the liabilities represented by an insurer's commitments under the policies and contracts it has issued.

In addition, all states have established a system for measuring risk-based capital of insurers, each of whom is required to maintain a custom-tailored capital cushion that takes into account the specific types of contracts and policies the insurer has in force, characteristics of that insurer's investment portfolio, and other risks. A graduated series of regulatory responses is permitted and mandated under risk-based capital rules as the level of an insurer's capital diminishes in relation to a specified "control level."

From a process standpoint, the chief insurance regulator (generically referred to as the commissioner) in an insurer's state of domicile is the party primarily responsible for monitoring that company's solvency, and the domiciliary commissioner and his or her staff do that through the review of filings mandated by statute and regulations, and through desk and on-site audits and other reviews. Since a series of solvency regulation improvement measures were adopted by the NAIC in the mid-1990s, certain substantive and procedural measures must be in place for a state to maintain accreditation by the NAIC.

Additionally, insurers writing business in multiple states—particularly insurers about which there may be solvency concerns—are reviewed regularly on a coordinated, multistate basis by the NAIC's Financial Analysis Working Group (FAWG), a standing body made up of experienced senior financial regulators from a number of states.

Finally, in addition to official regulatory oversight by the domiciliary and multistate regulatory processes, most insurers of any size also strive to maintain acceptable ratings from national rating agencies (which have done an effective job rating the creditworthiness of insurers, regardless of issues some agencies may have had administering other types of ratings). The rating agencies perform a quasi-regulatory function that usually complements— sometimes in very important ways—the official regulatory roles of state insurance regulators. Independent equity analysts and the financial and trade press also, to an extent, perform a quasi-regulatory function.

The rules, tools, and processes of insurer financial regulation are all aimed at providing early warning of solvency issues so that companies can work with regulators to develop remediation plans that may address the particular solvency pressures at issue so that a formal receivership proceeding may be avoided, if possible.

When remediation proves impossible, those same standards and processes are designed to result in early regulatory intervention in a company's decline, which benefits insurance consumers and the public generally by minimizing the shortfall (in receivership) of the insurer's assets, compared to its liabilities to policyholders. Put another way, early regulatory intervention maximizes the amount of assets that can be applied to reduce losses of policyholders and other stakeholders in the receivership process.

Receivership is the term used broadly to describe the process of resolving the affairs of a troubled insurer that cannot otherwise be remediated through voluntary or regulatory action.

THE U.S. INSURANCE RECEIVERSHIP AND GUARANTY SYSTEM

As noted previously, the principal objective of the insurance regulatory system is to protect the financial integrity of insurers so that their essential insurance promises to consumers will be fulfilled. In the relatively rare cases when insurers do fail, the law and practice of U.S. insurer insolvency administration are designed to further similar objectives: providing the best possible outcomes for insurance consumers while minimizing both direct losses to insurance contract owners and the negative externalities that can follow from the failure of an insurance company.

The insurance receivership system is the legal framework within which the rehabilitation or liquidation of a troubled insurer is managed and stakeholder claims are considered.

The insurance guaranty system and its constituent guaranty associations provide the financial safety net designed to minimize losses that consumers would otherwise suffer when an insurer is liquidated.

The primary focus of this chapter is on how the life and health insurance guaranty system, working in conjunction with insurance regulators and receivers, operates to protect consumers who own policies and contracts with troubled life and health insurers. Many of the same general principles and patterns apply to the protections afforded to owners of property-casualty insurance policies and other types of insurance contracts.[23]

From its inception in the early 1970s, the life and health insurance guaranty system has evolved into an effective national network that has fully performed its obligations to provide protection to consumers. The system has protected consumers in 84 insolvencies of insurers that wrote business in multiple states, and in another 332 instances where smaller single-state or regional carriers failed.[24] In those cases, the system has protected, in the aggregate, more than 2.83 million policyholders, and it has guaranteed policyholder values in an aggregate amount of about $28.3 billion.

Although, as noted earlier, the recent financial crisis laid waste to a number of financial services providers of many kinds, operating insurance companies stood up well to the many challenges of the period.[25] Only 15 life and health insurers (10 life and five health) were placed in liquidation from the start of 2008 through the end of 2011, with aggregate liabilities to policyholders of about $996 million.[26] And while the insurance industry fared comparatively well through the crisis, the guaranty system's financial and operational resources are greater now than they have ever before been, supporting the conclusion that the system can and would protect consumers in a challenging future financial environment, as it has done in the past.

Development of the Current Life and Health Insurance Guaranty System

There was no organized national consumer insurance safety net before the early 1970s, but by then a consensus had developed that such a system was needed. As a result, insurance regulators, legislators, and the industry developed guaranty association model legislation (the NAIC Life and Health Insurance Guaranty Association Model Act[27]) that states adopted widely in the 1970s and 1980s as the foundation of the current guaranty system.[28]

By 1991, life and health insurance guaranty associations had been established by the legislatures of all 51 of NOLHGA's current member jurisdictions (the 50 states and the District of Columbia).

NOLHGA was formed by the guaranty associations in 1983 to provide a process, facilities, and staff to coordinate and support the activities of the member guaranty associations, particularly in connection with the insolvencies of insurers writing business in multiple states.

How Guaranty Associations Work

Insurance guaranty associations provide protection to consumers; they do not provide rescue or bailout financing for financially troubled companies. The fundamental responsibility of an insurance guaranty association is to assure the provision of insurance protection to consumers, up to a statutorily established maximum level of guaranteed protection, once the duties of the guaranty association have been triggered by a judicial determination that an insurer is insolvent and should be liquidated under state insurance receivership laws.[29]

A working understanding of how guaranty associations protect consumers thus requires first a working understanding of the insurance receivership process.

The Conduct of Insurance Receiverships Domestic U.S. insurance companies are excluded from the definition of *debtor* under the U.S. bankruptcy code, and thus their financial failure is resolved outside of the federal bankruptcy process.[30] Rather, an insurer receivership is an insolvency proceeding conducted in a state court of the state where the insurer is chartered and primarily regulated (the domiciliary state).

Under the laws of most states, the receivership is commenced by the filing of a petition by the state's attorney general on the relation of the state's insurance commissioner, who is appointed as statutory receiver if the court grants the petition.

Receiverships are of several different types. For example, in Illinois (and many other states), the mildest form of receivership is *conservation*, under which the insurance commissioner is appointed conservator for purposes of securing the finances and records of the company, thus protecting the status quo pending a determination of whether a more serious form of receivership is required. If serious solvency concerns are raised, a company can be placed into *rehabilitation*, where the commissioner, as rehabilitator, is expected to develop and propose to the court a rehabilitation plan aimed at addressing the causes for concern about the company. If a company is financially troubled and cannot be rehabilitated, the commissioner petitions for *liquidation*, under which the commissioner is appointed liquidator and directed to marshal the assets of the failed company, evaluate claims against it, and distribute the assets to those with valid claims in the manner specified in the state's receivership law.[31]

Three aspects of the insurance receivership process are particularly relevant to how guaranty associations protect consumers.

First, insurance receivership judicial proceedings, like bankruptcy cases, generally provide for notice to and participation by creditors on material issues. While the development of a resolution plan for a failed insurer usually is proposed in the first instance by the domiciliary commissioner as receiver, this is done with knowledge that affected creditors will have opportunities to comment upon or object to all or part of the proposal.

Second, state receivership laws generally confer priority creditor status on claims against the estate of the failed insurer that arise from the insurer's direct policies of insurance. Since receiverships follow an absolute priority rule, all claims at the insurance policy level must be paid *in full* before any payments may be made on lower-ranking claims, such as general creditor claims, claims in respect of subordinated financing, or equity claims.

Third, guaranty associations are subrogated to the claims of the insurance policy and contract owners that the associations protect; that is, when guaranty associations protect consumers, the associations step into the shoes of those policyholders as creditors of the insolvent insurer at the (preferred) policyholder creditor level.[32] In effect, the associations are responsible—within statutory coverage levels—for the entire amount of covered policy liabilities to consumers, but if the estate has significant assets when the insurer is placed in liquidation, the associations' subrogation claims to those assets effectively become part of the associations' financing. If the consumer has a claim exceeding association coverage levels, that over-limits portion of the claim is *entirely* dependent on the availability of estate assets.

Viewed another way, since the obligation of a guaranty association is to assure that consumers are completely protected *up to* the association's limit of coverage, the amounts of assets that can be marshaled by the receiver are critically important not only to the guaranty associations and those paying or sharing the associations' costs (by reducing the expense of providing coverage within the associations' limits), but also to policyholders with large claims (by maximizing the assets available to cover any portion of a policyholder's over-limits claim). Accordingly, the comparative success of a receivership—and how well (or badly) policyholders with over-limits claims and other stakeholders fare in the receivership—is primarily a question of whether the receiver marshals assets covering a significant percentage of policy-level liabilities. (For a more detailed discussion of this issue, see Appendix 11A, "The Critical Role of Prompt Corrective Action.")

As a consequence of the three receivership aspects described, the activities and interests of insurance receivers and the guaranty system are closely interrelated, a fact recognized widely among state regulators and receivers.[33]

Operations of the Guaranty System in a Receivership Once a guaranty association is triggered by a judicial determination that an insurer is insolvent and should be liquidated, the association has two principal sets of duties to consumers. First, the guaranty association must pay, up to statutory coverage levels, any claims that are or become ripe for payment. Second, as to contracts that the failed insurer had no right to cancel prospectively (e.g., annuities, most life insurance contracts, and some types of health insurance contracts), the guaranty association must guaranty, assume, or reinsure the continuing insurance coverage. In other words, the association must make sure that the coverage continues, as long as the consumer pays any required premiums.

Regarding the first set of obligations—payment of ripe claims—the duties of life and health guaranty associations are substantially similar to those of property and casualty guaranty funds. The function of the triggered guaranty association is to process, adjudicate, and pay claims coming due in much the same way that the insurer would have done, had it not failed.

However, because noncancellable contracts, such as life and annuity contracts, are purchased to provide protection over an extended period of time, for contract terms and premiums that are often permanently established at the inception of the contract (unlike, for instance, property and casualty coverage, which is purchased annually and may be subject to annual repricing, reunderwriting, contract term changes, or even cancellation by either party), the policy owner has an investment or equity interest that cannot be fully protected unless the contract is, in effect, kept in force. For example, a policyholder might have been in good health when she purchased a life policy 10 years before the insurer entered liquidation, but at the time the insurer failed, her health might have deteriorated to the point where she might be unable to purchase replacement coverage on similar terms, or at any price.

Consequently, for the safety net to work in respect to most noncancellable contracts, the guaranty association must assure the continuing covered benefits promised by the contract on the terms originally agreed upon between the policyholder and the (now-failed) insurer. In many cases, this is accomplished by the negotiation of an arrangement known as an *assumption reinsurance* transaction. In such a transaction, a healthy carrier agrees to assume all or part of the policy liabilities of the failed insurer in exchange for a transfer of assets to support the liabilities—assets that are usually provided in part by the receiver from the estate of the insurer, and in part by guaranty associations. In other cases, affected guaranty associations simply assume the covered liabilities of the insolvent insurer for whatever period is required for the liabilities to run off. A combination of both approaches can also occur, in which the guaranty associations assume the covered liabilities for some period of time, after which a healthy carrier takes over the liabilities via assumption.

Coordination of Guaranty Association Responses   Guaranty association coverage responsibilities under current law are determined by the residence of the covered person: A covered person is protected by the guaranty association of the jurisdiction where the person resides at the time the insurer fails, even though the insurer whose liquidation triggers the association's coverage responsibility may be domiciled in a different jurisdiction.

In some cases, an insurer may be licensed to do business only in its state of domicile and may sell contracts only to individuals in that state. If such a company fails, that state's guaranty association provides all of the available guaranty association coverage.

In many other cases, a failed insurer may have been licensed in (and may have contracts with residents of) many states, in which case coordination of the coverage responses of multiple guaranty associations is necessary. The guaranty associations effect that coordination through NOLHGA and its processes, with the result that the receiver and potential assuming carriers can deal with a single point of contact and contracting instead of having to engage in multiple discussions, negotiations, and contracts with a variety of different associations. That said, and though the national coordination process is essentially invisible from a consumer standpoint, the protection afforded each contract owner and the related funding for that consumer's protection always come from the guaranty association of the jurisdiction where the contract owner is deemed a resident.

NOLHGA's offices are in Herndon, Virginia, where a permanent full-time staff of 15 insurance, finance, management information system (MIS), and legal professionals and administrative staff members support the work of the member guaranty associations. Its management is overseen by a 13-member board of directors, and all significant decisions regarding major insolvencies are made by NOLHGA's member guaranty associations.

Guaranty Association Powers and Duties   Each guaranty association is a creature of statute whose powers and duties are established by legislation adopted in its state.

Since all guaranty association enabling laws are drawn from the NAIC Life and Health Insurance Guaranty Association Model Act, many of the provisions are similar or identical from state to state, though there are some differences. In some cases, the differences exist because the state insurance commissioners, through the NAIC, have amended the Model Act several times since it was first promulgated, with the result that there is usually a time lag of several years before most states' legislatures will have had an opportunity to consider updating their guaranty associations' enabling statutes in light of Model Act changes.

For example, the Model Act was amended in 2009 to (among other things) raise the guaranteed coverage protection levels for annuities from $100,000 to $250,000. To date, the laws of 44 jurisdictions cover annuities to a level of $250,000 or more, and other states are considering amendments to that effect, but a few states currently are still at the old $100,000 coverage level. (See Appendix 11B for more detail on guaranty association coverage levels as of September 19, 2013.)

All insurers licensed to market covered lines of business in a jurisdiction are obliged to be members of the guaranty association of that jurisdiction. The costs of covering consumers and of operating the association that are not provided from assets of an insolvent carrier or any ongoing premiums in respect of contracts continued by the association are financed by assessments payable by member companies. Those assessments are levied in proportion to the insurers' market shares within the jurisdiction and are subject to an assessment cap each year (typically 2 percent of an insurer's gross premium in the assessed line of business—life, health, or annuity).[34]

Under Section 13 of the Model Act, a state's legislature has the option of providing a *premium tax offset* to guaranty association member companies for portions of the assessments a company pays to provide protection for consumers. Many state legislatures have provided such premium tax offsets, in recognition of the practical difficulties preventing a member from recovering assessment expenses from any other source.

Each guaranty association is subject to regulatory supervision and examination by the insurance commissioner of its jurisdiction, and its responsibilities are prescribed by its enabling statute and by a plan of operation approved by the insurance commissioner. Operations are governed by a board of directors elected by the membership in accordance with the enabling legislation, plan of operations, and bylaws of the association.

Daily operations of a guaranty association are primarily the responsibility of an executive director, sometimes referred to as an administrator, engaged on behalf of the association by its board of directors. Depending on the activity level of the association, the administrator may supervise staff of varying sizes; the administrator also typically oversees work done for the association by counsel or other professional advisers.

Historical Insolvency Performance of the Life and Health Insurance Guaranty Associations

Guaranty associations have protected consumers in 84 multistate insolvencies coordinated through NOLHGA. In addition, they have protected consumers in approximately 332 smaller or single-state insolvencies in which NOLHGA was not directly involved. Set forth in Figure 11.1 is a chart displaying by year the frequency and cost (by assessments "called," or collected from guaranty associations' member insurers) of the 79 insolvencies from 1988 to 2011 coordinated through NOLHGA.

As the chart suggests, insolvencies have tended to increase and decrease—both in frequency and in severity—in apparent waves or cycles that bear some relationship to broader economic and financial trends.

For example, the chart shows a marked increase in the frequency and cost of insurer failures in the first half of the 1990s, when the U.S. economy was emerging from a general recession and the financial sector was also still suffering the consequences of negative developments in the commercial real estate and corporate high-yield bond markets. A number of the more significant life company insolvencies in this period were precipitated by significant deteriorations in real estate or bond investments.

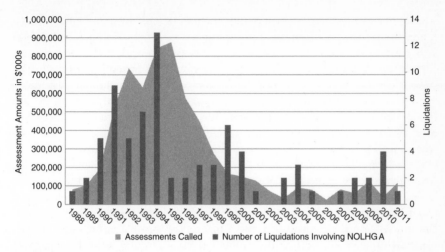

FIGURE 11.1   Assessments Called with Number of Liquidations, 1988–2011

Interestingly, the recent financial crisis—which saw the failure of over 400 commercial banks and thrifts, several major investment banking firms and hedge funds, finance companies, government-sponsored housing entities, and other firms—resulted in very few liquidations of operating life and health insurers. Of the 15 life and health companies that entered liquidation between the start of 2008 and the end of 2011, almost all were comparatively tiny regional writers; none were remotely systemically important, and their aggregate liabilities to policyholders were approximately $996 *million*—compared to, for example, the initial general creditor liability of Lehman Brothers alone, which was reported at the start of its bankruptcy filing as being approximately $613 *billion*.

To be sure, the financial crisis is never discussed without reference to the federal rescue of AIG, nor should it be. Along with Lehman Brothers, AIG is commonly viewed as a poster child financial institution at the heart of the crisis. Because AIG is most commonly known for its insurance company subsidiaries, it is easy for casual observers to conclude, first, that AIG's near failure was centrally related to its insurance operations and, second, that because AIG collapsed, other insurers must have been similarly affected by the crisis.

The truth, though, was recognized early on by Federal Reserve Chairman Ben Bernanke, who described AIG as "a hedge fund basically that was attached to a large and stable insurance company."[35] He attributed the problems of the entity not to the regulated insurance operations, but to the noninsurance entity AIG Financial Products, over which he said there was "no oversight."[36] The core financial problems at AIG were, primarily, the sale through the Financial Products division of naked credit default swap (CDS) contracts, and secondarily, the adoption of a corporate-wide, nontraditional, and unusually risky approach to securities lending transactions.[37] Little or no evidence developed during or after the crisis suggesting that any of AIG's insurance operations caused or resulted in problems for AIG or its insurance customers.

AIG aside, the primary negative impact of the financial crisis on the life insurance industry was to depress the surplus of some large companies that had issued variable annuity contracts involving guaranty features linked to the financial markets. When equity markets reached their lowest point in the crisis in March 2009, the reserve liabilities in respect of such contracts increased, correspondingly lowering the overall surplus of the relevant companies. Two companies—that were never close to insolvency—accepted relatively small amounts of Troubled Asset Relief Program (TARP) funding to cushion their surplus in 2009 and repaid those amounts in full with interest (and profits to the government from warrants) within a year, and insurance regulators closely and effectively monitored the exposure of the industry to these and other risks throughout the crisis.[38]

Ability of the Life and Health Insurance Guaranty System to Protect Consumers in Challenging Economic Circumstances

The experience of the recent financial crisis understandably has led people to inquire whether the insurance guaranty system has the financial ability to protect consumers if, for example, several major insurers were to fail simultaneously. Those who have reviewed the available evidence have been able to conclude both that the system has in fact met that challenge in the past, and that it could do so if necessary in the future.

Historical Performance While the recent financial crisis and recession caused the liquidation of relatively few operating insurers, that was not true of the preceding significant U.S. recession. As a consequence of the recession in the early 1990s, nearly 40 life and health carriers were liquidated, and their resolutions were addressed simultaneously by NOLHGA and its member guaranty associations. Three insurers ranking among the top 25 writers in the U.S. market were among those cases. Yet even in the worst years of that period, the costs to the guaranty system of protecting consumers (sometimes referred to as assessments "called," i.e., collected from member insurers) did not remotely approach the theoretical maximum annual assessment capacity of the life and health insurance guaranty system, as illustrated in Figure 11.2.[39]

Current and Projected Financial Ability As depicted in the chart, the maximum annual assessment capacity of the life and health guaranty system now

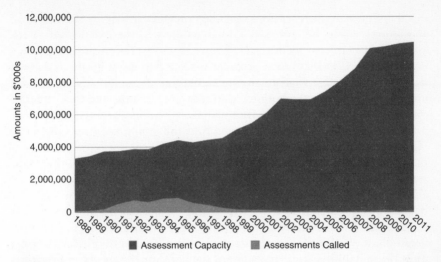

FIGURE 11.2   Assessment Capacity versus Assessments Called, 1988–2011

slightly exceeds $10.4 billion. That amount refreshes each year, meaning that for a two-year period (at the same maximum capacity) the total available to protect policyholders would be in excess of $20.8 billion, and so on. By comparison, the system's total net assessments (inception to date) required to provide all life and health guaranty protection—guaranteeing obligations on about $28.3 billion of policyholder obligations for over 2.8 million policyholders—has been roughly $6.4 billion. In other words, the current year's assessment capacity, by itself, is about 169 percent of the total net costs that have been required to protect consumers since the beginning of the life and health insurance guaranty system decades ago.

The financial ability of the guaranty system to respond in challenging times is not, however, limited to its annual assessment capacity. This is true for several reasons.

First, the liabilities of a troubled insurance company do not all come due on the date that an insurer enters liquidation. For a typical insurer, many or most of its liabilities will not come due until years, decades, or even generations after the company fails. For that reason, much less liquidity is required to meet the covered liabilities of a failing insurer than in the case of, for example, an FDIC-insured bank, whose consumer liabilities primarily consist of deposits contractually available to the consumer on demand.

Second, most life insurer insolvencies involve only small shortfalls of assets versus liabilities. The shortfalls are seldom more than 15 percent in larger cases and are more typically in the range of 5 percent to 10 percent.

As a consequence, the need that must be funded currently by the guaranty associations when the company fails is reduced to the extent that estate assets are available to the receiver in devising a resolution plan to protect policyholders. If the solvency problem is identified early by the regulator and prompt and effective regulatory intervention takes place, the cost of the insolvency is minimized—both for guaranty associations (and their funding sources) and for policyholders with claims exceeding guaranty association protection levels. (For further discussion of this point, see Appendix 11A, "The Critical Role of Prompt Corrective Action.")

Third, even a financial crisis of unprecedented proportions, involving insurers with unusually large shortfalls of assets to liabilities, could be addressed by utilizing the assessment capacity of guaranty associations that would develop in the years following the initiation of receivership proceedings. Because a significant proportion of the insurers' liabilities would mature in future years, a resolution plan could provide for the run-off of those liabilities (i.e., payment of the liabilities from the receivership estate, topped up or enhanced as necessary by guaranty associations, over the years in which the liabilities would by their terms mature). Such a run-off would be paid from the assessment capacity of the guaranty associations only in the years in which the payments would be made—not all in the year in which the receiverships commenced. In addition, associations have the ability to borrow today against future assessment capacity in the event a liquidity need might arise. Accordingly, an appropriate yardstick for the financial ability of the guaranty system to perform its mission is not the maximum assessment capacity of the system in the year a crisis arises, but rather the aggregate capacity of the system over the projected runoff period.

The point is illustrated in Figure 11.3, which assumes, for illustrative purposes, that capacity would remain level for the next 10 years, producing an aggregate maximum financial capacity of about $104 billion.[40]

Average Recoveries by Policyholders   One final point should be noted regarding the protection that has been achieved for policyholders in prior life insurer insolvencies. Because of factors noted previously—particularly the protections afforded through the guaranty system, the generally conservative nature of insurance company investments and reserving, effective solvency regulation, and general willingness of regulators to intervene promptly when life insurers face financial difficulties—actual losses typically suffered by consumers with life policy and annuity claims against insolvent carriers have on average been modest. The point is illustrated by the chart in Figure 11.4, which shows that, for the period 1991 through 2009, after application of estate assets to both the claims covered

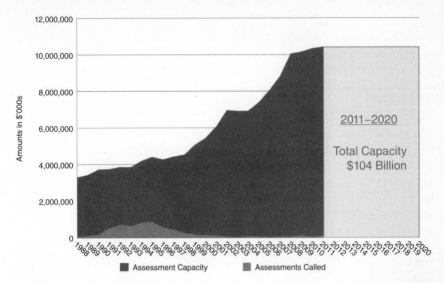

FIGURE 11.3 Assessment Capacity versus Assessments Called, Next 10 Years at 100 Percent of 2011 Capacity

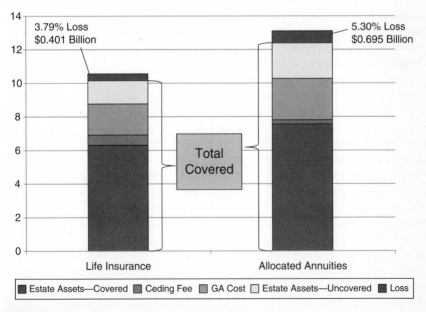

FIGURE 11.4 Multistate Insolvencies, 1991–2009

by guaranty associations and those policy claims exceeding coverage limits (or otherwise not covered), average recoveries have exceeded 96 percent on life claims and 94 percent on annuity claims.[41]

CONCLUSION

The recent financial crisis, like other adverse financial periods before it, has challenged both individuals and institutions. Fortunately, the insurance industry has weathered the storm rather well and continues to meet its commitments to consumers. In the few instances when life or health insurers have failed, the life and health insurance guaranty system has ably discharged its mission to protect consumers. It stands ready to do so in the future.

APPENDIX 11A: THE CRITICAL ROLE OF PROMPT CORRECTIVE ACTION

It is a common misunderstanding that policyholder recoveries in insurance liquidations are limited to the statutorily specified amounts of guaranty association (GA) protection provided under each GA's enabling legislation; these coverage amounts are sometimes described as *caps*, but that label is inaccurate and misleading. In reality, GA protection levels might more accurately be perceived as guaranteed *floor* levels of recovery, usually augmented substantially for claims exceeding those levels by recoveries from the estate of the failed insurer. Whether a policyholder recovers all or most of his or her claim *above* GA protection levels depends significantly on whether regulatory intervention occurs before the failed company's assets have been substantially dissipated, and whether assets are effectively protected and marshaled in the company's receivership.

That consumer recoveries are limited to GA "caps" is a subtle but critical misunderstanding suffered even by financially sophisticated people who do not often work with insurer insolvencies and the guaranty system.

Policyholders with claims against their insolvent insurer in excess of guaranty association protection levels have a priority claim against the insurer's assets for the excess amount. That excess claim ranks pari passu with all other claims at the policyholder level. For that reason, a policyholder can—and often does—recover most or all of his or her claim in the insolvency, *even above* the level covered by guaranty associations. The point can be seen in the following illustrations.

Imagine an insolvency in which a policyholder has a claim of $1 million, and suppose further that there was no guaranty association to provide a financial safety net. What would the policyholder recover? The answer: It would depend on the level of assets available in the insolvency estate, compared to the amount of the policy-level liabilities. This relationship is sometimes expressed as a *liquidation ratio*, or the number of cents on the dollar available for distribution to policy-level claimants.

Consider the outcomes illustrated in the chart in Figure 11A.1. If the estate has 95 cents on the dollar available—a 95 percent liquidation ratio—the policyholder will recover $950,000 on that $1 million claim, even with no guaranty association protection. However, if the estate has zero cents on the dollar available at the policyholder level, the policyholder will recover nothing.

Now imagine that the policyholder has the same claim for $1 million and resides in a state where guaranty association coverage is $100,000. Consider the outcomes illustrated in the chart in Figure 11A.2. In this case the policyholder will recover (from the guaranty association) 100 percent of the claim up to $100,000, and will recover on the rest of the claim an amount determined by multiplying the excess claim (here, $900,000) by the liquidation ratio for the insolvency. If the insolvency estate marshals 95 cents on the dollar for policyholder claims that policyholder will end up with a total of $955,000 on the $1 million claim: $100,000 from the guaranty association and $855,000 (95 percent of $900,000) in respect of the excess policyholder claim. However, if the estate marshals zero cents on the dollar, the policyholder's total recovery is limited to the $100,000 that will be paid by the guaranty association.

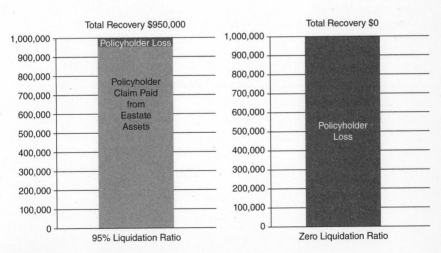

FIGURE 11A.1   Policyholder Claim with No GA Protection

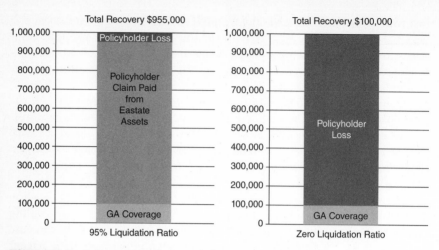

FIGURE 11A.2   Policyholder Claim with $100,000 GA Protection

Imagine next a slightly different set of facts, illustrated in the next chart in Figure 11A.3. Suppose the policyholder resides in a state with a $250,000 guaranty association protection level. In the first hypothetical outcome in this series of examples—a liquidation ratio of 95 percent—the policyholder's total recovery then would be $962,500 ($250,000 from the guaranty association and $712,500 from the excess claim): a modest increase of only $7,500 over what the policyholder would have received with guaranty

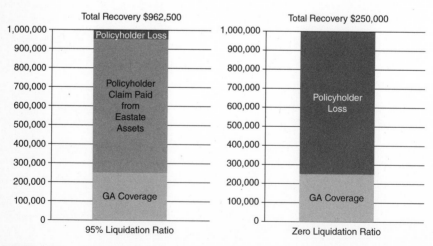

FIGURE 11A.3   Policyholder Claim with $250,000 GA Protection

association coverage to $100,000, even though the guaranty association "cap," in this new example, is two and one-half times larger. But in the second hypothetical outcome—with a liquidation percentage of zero—the total policyholder recovery is still only $250,000. That is to say that a very large loss—$750,000—is borne by the policyholder, even with much more guaranty association coverage than in the prior case.

A GA's protection level does set a floor for policyholder recoveries, no matter what else happens in the receivership case. But as the foregoing illustrations demonstrate, the much more important factor—at least for policyholder claims significantly in excess of GA protection levels—is the liquidation ratio achieved in the insolvency. How many cents on the dollar is the receiver able to pay on policy-level claims?

On that score, the historical averages are significant. In the insolvencies in the years 1991–2009 (the most recent insolvency outcome figures currently available), claims on life policies have been paid, on average, at a level of 96.21 cents on the dollar (see Figure 11A.4). Claims on annuity contracts have been paid, on average, at 94.70 cents on the dollar.[42]

In other words, in most (though unfortunately not all) life and annuity insolvency cases, the vast majority of policyholders have been made nearly whole, *regardless* of the statutory GA protection levels in their states. The

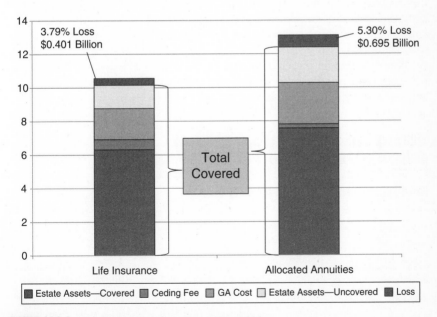

FIGURE 11A.4 Multistate Insolvencies, 1991–2009

obvious conclusion is that regulators, working with receivers and guaranty associations, have done an effective job of delivering real policyholder protection over the past two decades.

Prospectively, the key is to make sure that such outcomes (or better) are achieved in the future.

Experts in handling insolvencies of regulated entities—not just insurers, but other types of financial firms as well—have long recognized that the keys to doing so are, first, identifying financial problems early, and then acting promptly, decisively, and effectively to keep a bad situation from getting worse.

Spotting problems promptly is a function of financial supervision, and much of the success in delivering good insurance receivership outcomes to policyholders over the past 20 years is a direct result of better financial supervision. In this sense, "financial supervision" is intended broadly to include assessments by companies of their own risks, risk spotting by markets and insurance rating agencies, and better risk standards and evaluations by insurance regulators.

Beyond that, the recent financial crisis and attendant policy debates about regulatory reform have cast a bright light on the significance of effective resolutions of failing financial companies. Even if regulatory financial supervision is good, the regulated firm's stakeholders can still be harmed significantly by ineffective resolution of the failed company.

The two elements critical to a successful resolution are early intervention—invoking the liquidation process at a time when the assets of the failed company have not yet been substantially dissipated—and professional execution of a resolution strategy that marshals the assets of the failed firm as effectively as possible and maximizes their prompt application to proven creditors' claims as directed by law. In the world of banking resolutions, these concepts are sometimes referred to, respectively, as "prompt corrective action" and "least-cost resolution."

APPENDIX 11B: TABLE OF RELEVANT GUARANTY ASSOCIATION COVERAGE LEVELS BY STATE OR JURISDICTION

As of September 19, 2013 (Subject to Change)

Coverage Type	Life		Health	Long-Term Care	Annuity
	Death Benefit	Cash Value			
Alabama	300,000	100,000	500,000*	300,000	250,000
Alaska	300,000	100,000	500,000*	300,000	250,000[43]
Arizona	300,000	100,000	500,000*	300,000	250,000

Coverage Type	Life		Health	Long-Term Care	Annuity
	Death Benefit	Cash Value			
Arkansas	300,000	300,000	500,000[44]	300,000	300,000
California[45]	300,000	100,000	200,000†	200,000†	250,000
Colorado	300,000	100,000	500,000*	300,000	250,000
Connecticut	500,000	500,000	500,000	500,000	500,000
Delaware	300,000	100,000	500,000*	300,000	250,000
D.C.	300,000	100,000	100,000	***	300,000
Florida	300,000	100,000	300,000	300,000	300,000**
Georgia	300,000	100,000	500,000*	300,000	300,000**
Hawaii	300,000	100,000	500,000*	300,000	250,000
Idaho	300,000	100,000	500,000*	300,000	250,000
Illinois	300,000	100,000	500,000*	300,000	250,000
Indiana	300,000	100,000	500,000*	300,000	250,000
Iowa	300,000	100,000	500,000*	300,000	250,000
Kansas	300,000	100,000	500,000*	300,000	250,000
Kentucky	300,000	100,000	500,000*	300,000	250,000
Louisiana	300,000	100,000	500,000	500,000	250,000**
Maine	300,000	100,000	500,000*	300,000	250,000
Maryland	300,000	100,000	500,000*	300,000	250,000
Massachusetts	300,000	100,000	100,000	100,000	100,000
Michigan	300,000	100,000	500,000*	300,000	250,000
Minnesota	500,000	130,000	500,000	500,000	250,000[46]
Mississippi	300,000	100,000	500,000*	100,000	100,000
Missouri	300,000	100,000	500,000*	300,000	250,000
Montana	300,000	100,000	500,000*	300,000	250,000
Nebraska	300,000	100,000	500,000*	300,000	250,000
Nevada[47]	300,000	100,000	500,000*	300,000	250,000
New Hampshire	300,000	100,000	100,000	300,000	100,000
New Jersey	500,000	100,000	No limit††	No limit††	500,000**
New Mexico	300,000	100,000	500,000*	300,000	250,000
New York	500,000	500,000	500,000[48]	500,000	500,000
North Carolina	300,000	300,000	500,000*	300,000	300,000[49]
North Dakota	300,000	100,000	500,000*	300,000	250,000
Ohio	300,000	100,000	100,000	100,000	250,000

(continued)

| | Life | | | | |
| | Death Benefit | Cash Value | | Long-Term | |
Coverage Type	Death Benefit	Cash Value	Health	Long-Term Care	Annuity
Oklahoma	300,000	100,000	500,000*	300,000	300,000
Oregon	300,000	100,000	500,000*	300,000	250,000
Pennsylvania	300,000	100,000	300,000	300,000	300,000**
Puerto Rico	300,000	100,000	100,000	100,000	100,000
Rhode Island	300,000	100,000	500,000*	300,000	250,000
South Carolina	300,000	300,000	300,000	300,000	300,000
South Dakota	300,000	100,000	500,000*	300,000	250,000
Tennessee	300,000	100,000	500,000*	300,000	250,000
Texas	300,000	100,000	500,000*	300,000	250,000
Utah	500,000[50]	200,000	500,000	500,000	250,000
Vermont	300,000	100,000	500,000*	300,000	250,000
Virginia	300,000	100,000	500,000*	300,000	250,000
Washington	500,000	500,000	500,000	500,000	500,000
West Virginia	300,000	100,000	500,000*	300,000	250,000
Wisconsin	300,000	300,000	500,000*	300,000	300,000
Wyoming	300,000	100,000	300,000[51]	300,000	250,000

* Guaranty association provides $100,000 for health coverage not defined as disability insurance, long-term care, or basic hospital, medical, and surgical insurance or major medical insurance; $300,000 for disability insurance; $300,000 for long-term care insurance (with the exception of Mississippi, which provides $100,000 for long-term care insurance); and $500,000 for basic hospital, medical, and surgical insurance or major medical insurance (with the exception of Georgia, Idaho, Maine, North Carolina, and Wisconsin, which provide $300,000 instead of $100,000 for supplemental health coverage, and Texas, which provides $200,000 instead of $100,000 for supplemental health coverage).

** Guaranty association provides $300,000 (or $500,000 in New Jersey and $250,000 in Louisiana) coverage if annuity is in payout status; if not in payout status, the cash value limit is $100,000 (in Florida and Georgia the cash value limit is $250,000).

*** The District of Columbia GA does not provide coverage for long-term care insurance policies; however, legislation that would change this is being pursued.

† Increased by the change in the health care cost component of the consumer price index from January 1, 1991, to the date the member insurer becomes an insolvent insurer (approximately $450,000 in 2010).

†† New Jersey sets no cap on its medical coverage, covering claims up to the limits of the policy, but limiting the benefit to 80 percent coverage if the provider seeks coverage (as opposed to the insured).

NOTES

1. See, for example, Aaron Lucchetti and Julie Steinberg, "Life on Wall Street Grows Less Risky," *Wall Street Journal*, September 9, 2013, http://online.wsj.com/article/SB10001424127887324324404579044 503704364242.html; Andrew Ross Sorkin, "What Might Have Been, and the Fall of Lehman," *New York Times Dealbook*, September 9, 2013, http://dealbook.nytimes.com/2013/09/09/what-might-have-been-and-the-fall-of-lehman/. The fifth anniversary retrospectives relate back to the fateful week in mid-September 2008 when Lehman Brothers filed for bankruptcy. Most commentators now consider the financial crisis to have commenced early in 2008 or in late 2007.
2. Federal Deposit Insurance Corporation, Failed Bank List, www.fdic.gov/bank/individual/failed/banklist.html (last visited September 12, 2013).
3. Bear Stearns was acquired on the brink of bankruptcy by JPMorgan Chase. Merrill Lynch was sold to Bank of America. Lehman Brothers entered bankruptcy, and Goldman Sachs and Morgan Stanley were converted to commercial banks. Stephen Labaton, "Agency's '04 Rule Lets Banks Pile Up New Debt," *New York Times*, October 3, 2008, A1.
4. According to the Pension Benefit Guaranty Corporation annual reports for its five fiscal years ending September 30, 2008, through September 30, 2012, 665 underfunded, single-employer pension plans were terminated by the PBGC in involuntary terminations or by the sponsoring employers in distress terminations. The aggregate underfunding for those terminated plans was nearly $10 billion. Pension Benefit Guaranty Corporation, annual reports, http://pbgc.gov/res/annual-reports.html.
5. See Figure 11.1.
6. See Government Accountability Office, *Insurance Markets: Impacts of and Regulatory Response to the 2007–2009 Financial Crisis* (June 2013) (hereinafter referred to as GAO Insurance Study), 17.
7. The crisis did involve serious problems for several monoline financial and mortgage guaranty insurers, and it obviously included the near failure and government rescue of AIG, a near failure that was driven not by any problems that developed within the insurance subsidiaries but rather by credit derivative and corporate-wide securities lending programs originating from noninsurance segments of the overall enterprise. See discussion later in this chapter.
8. Dodd-Frank Wall Street Reform and Consumer Protection Act, Pub. L. No. 111-203, 124 Stat. 1376 (2010) (to be codified in scattered sections of 12 U.S.C.).
9. Direct writers are insurance companies that sell policies and contracts to individuals and businesses seeking protection against various

insurable risks covered by different types of policies; direct writers are often distinguished from reinsurers, which are insurance companies that contractually agree through the sale of reinsurance protection to assume from direct writers some part of the risks the direct writers have assumed by extending insurance protection to individual or business purchasers of that protection. In that sense, direct writers constitute the primary market for insurance, and reinsurance writers play an important role in the secondary market.

10. See discussion introduced at GAO Insurance Study, pp. 6–7.
11. In addition, a contract surrendered or lapsed as a result of economic worries may need to be replaced later to meet the insurance need that originally prompted its purchase. Many considerations (payment of a new commission, an insured's age or health, or changed market conditions) may make the replacement of the original contract significantly more expensive (if not impossible).
12. See generally, Therese M. Vaughan, "Insurance: Providing Long-Term Stability in a Volatile World," prepared for the Geneva Association Annual General Meeting, June 7, 2012 (hereinafter referred to as Vaughan, Geneva Paper).
13. "[T]he national state-based system of insurance regulation was specifically designed to address the unique nature of insurance products. The system's fundamental tenet is to protect policyholders by ensuring the solvency of the insurer and its ability to pay insurance claims." Examining the Impact of the Proposed Rules to Implement Basel III Capital Standards: Before the H. Subcomms. on Financial Institutions and Consumer Credit and Insurance, Housing and Community Opportunity, Comm. on Financial Services, 112th Cong. 2 (2012) (submitted testimony of Kevin McCarty, commissioner, Florida Office of Insurance Regulation, and president of the National Association of Insurance Commissioners).
14. "[T]he states have done a good job in solvency regulation of insurers in recent years." How Should the Federal Government Oversee Insurance?: Before the H. Subcomm. on Capital Markets, Insurance and Government Sponsored Enterprises, Comm. on Financial Services, 111th Cong. 91 (2009) (statement of Bob Hunter, Director of Insurance, Consumer Federation of America).
15. See generally GAO Insurance Study.
16. See Vaughan, Geneva Paper.
17. Since the U.S. Supreme Court's decision in *United States v. South-Eastern Underwriters Ass'n*, 322 U.S. 533 (1944), it has been clear that Congress has authority to regulate insurance under the Constitution's commerce power, but in the McCarran-Ferguson Act, 15 U.S.C. §1011-15 (2012),

Congress chose generally to defer to state regulation except when it conflicts with federal law. *U.S. Dept. of Treasury v. Fabe*, 508 U.S. 491 (1993). Effectively, the McCarran-Ferguson Act delegates insurance regulation to the states except to the extent that federal law overrides that delegation.

18. Domestic insurance companies are expressly excluded from the definition of *debtor* under the federal bankruptcy code and thus may not be subjects of federal bankruptcy proceedings. *See* Bankruptcy Code, 11 U.S.C §§ 109(b) and (d), preventing domestic insurance companies from qualifying as "debtors" under Chapter 7 and Chapter 11 bankruptcy. Rather, as discussed herein, an insurer resolution takes place in a bankruptcy-like judicial proceeding in the courts of the state where the subject insurer was chartered or domiciled, and is governed by the insurer receivership statute of that state. See, e.g., 215 Ill. Comp. Stat. 5/ Art. XIII.

19. GAO Insurance Study, pp. 7–8.

20. See, e.g., GAO Insurance Study, p. 8.

21. See generally GAO Insurance Study, pp.7ff.

22. See generally, NAIC, Statutory Accounting Principles Working Group, www.naic.org/committees_e_app_sapwg.htm (last visited September 17, 2013).

23. Largely because of the legal and operational distinctions between life and health insurance on the one hand and property-casualty insurance on the other, separate (but similar) regulatory laws, systems, and processes apply to these two main categories of insurance sold to consumers. For the same reasons, the safety net protections afforded U.S. owners of property-casualty contracts are provided through a system of property-casualty insurance guaranty funds that exists and operates separately from the system of life and health insurance guaranty associations. The resolution responses of property-casualty guaranty funds are coordinated through the National Conference of Insurance Guaranty Funds (NCIGF). See generally, www.ncigf.org/home. In general, the laws and procedures for the receivership of a troubled insurer are substantially similar for life and health insurers and for property-casualty insurers.

24. Also included in the larger number are some cases where failed property and casualty insurers wrote a small amount of health insurance, and where the insolvency case triggered obligations of both property-casualty guaranty funds and some life and health guaranty associations.

25. See generally GAO Insurance Study.

26. Compare, for example, the initial bank and bond debt of Lehman Brothers alone, which was reported on the first day of Lehman's bankruptcy as totaling approximately $613 *billion*. See "Lehman's Big Bankruptcy

Filing," *New York Times Dealbook*, September 15, 2008 (retrieved September 17, 2013), http://dealbook.nytimes.com/2008/09/15/lehmans-big-bankruptcy-filing/?_r=0.

27. See NAIC Life and Health Insurance Guaranty Association Model Act (hereinafter Model Act).

28. The development of the consensus favoring the guaranty system, the related model legislation, and enactment of the model legislation in the states are summarized in "The U.S. Guaranty Association Concept at 25: A Quarter Century Assessment," Christopher J. Wilcox, *Journal of Insurance Regulation* 14, no. 3 (Spring 1996): 370–372.

29. Certain conditions must exist in order for a guaranty association to have statutory responsibility to consumers. For example, in general the insured must be a "covered person" (see Model Act Section 3A); the contract under which the insured seeks coverage from the guaranty association must be a "covered contract" (see Model Act Section 3B(1)); the failed insurer must have been a "member insurer" of the guaranty association (see Model Act Sections 3B(1) and 5(L)); and no coverage "exclusions" must apply to the insured's claim for coverage (see Model Act Section 3B(2)). These conditions are routinely satisfied in cases involving typical insolvent insurers that wrote traditional consumer lines of life or health insurance.

30. See Bankruptcy Code, 11 U.S.C §§ 109(b) and (d), preventing domestic insurance companies from qualifying as "debtors" under Chapter 7 and Chapter 11 bankruptcy proceedings.

31. See, e.g., 215 ILCS 5/187 et seq.

32. See Model Act Section 8K.

33. See generally, "Communication and Coordination Among Regulators, Receivers, and Guaranty Associations: An Approach to a National State Based System," NAIC (2005).

34. In addition to a percentage-of-premium cap, the Life Insurance Guaranty Corporation of New York (that state's guaranty association) has a unique, cumulative, "inception-to-date" limit on assessments that may be imposed on its member insurers; N.Y. Ins. Law § 7709(e) (2012). A recent insurer liquidation triggered the New York guaranty association (for only the second time since the formation of its statutory predecessor entity in 1941). Unique circumstances of that case involved both an unusually high shortfall of assets to liabilities and an unusually large allocation of guaranty association costs to New York. As a consequence, the fulfillment of the New York guaranty association's obligations in that case caused the statutory cumulative limit to be approached. Legislation is currently being considered in New York to increase the cumulative funding limit and to update the New York enabling statute to align it more closely with the Model Act.

35. "Bernanke Says Insurer AIG Operated Like a Hedge Fund," Bloomberg .com, March 3, 2009 (retrieved September 17, 2013), www.bloomberg .com/apps/news?pid=newsarchive&sid=a0n7q0AGB_m4.
36. Id.
37. Copious details of the evolution of both the AIG Financial Products CDS program and the securities lending program are set forth in Roddy Boyd, *Fatal Risk: A Cautionary Tale of AIG's Corporate Suicide* (Hoboken, NJ: John Wiley & Sons, 2011).
38. See GAO Insurance Study, pp. 28, 34–37, 46–47.
39. The chart depicts the actual assessments collected from association member companies by year, charted against the aggregate theoretical maximum assessment capacity for all lines of insurance for all of NOLHGA's 51 member guaranty associations and the Puerto Rico life and health insurance guaranty association (which is not a member of NOLHGA but provides protections to Puerto Rico residents much like NOLHGA's 51 member associations). The entire theoretical maximum capacity may not be available for a particular insolvency, since each individual guaranty association generally covers only residents of its jurisdiction, so that—in theory—an individual association could meet its annual capacity limit before satisfying all of its obligations. In practice, even individual association "caps" are seldom approached in an insolvency, and in the rare cases when they are, associations have the ability to borrow against the security of pledged future assessments to meet current needs. Furthermore, insolvencies of life and annuity carriers generally tend to produce a relatively normal distribution of policyholders by state, with the result that association funding needs generally line up relatively well with association capacity, further minimizing the impact of what otherwise might be viewed as a silo issue. The chart also does not reflect any potential application of the unique, cumulative, "inception-to-date" assessment limit under the enabling legislation for the New York guaranty association, discussed in note 34.
40. See explanations in notes 34 and 41.
41. The figures in the chart reflect only multistate life insurer liquidations in which NOLHGA was involved and for which final outcome information is currently available. A small number of health insurance insolvencies in which the companies wrote de minimis amounts of residual life and annuity business have been excluded, as has one life insurer liquidation for which we do not possess reliable financial data. The figures are based on guaranty association records, financial information provided by receivers, and estimates on recoveries on "above coverage limits" amounts derived from guaranty association recoveries of their subrogation claims. The figures do not reflect the time value of

money, nor do they yet reflect recovery outcomes in a recent insolvency from New York, referenced in note 34, which will reduce the average recovery on annuity claims by a relatively modest amount.

42. See explanatory note 41.

43. Structured settlement annuities and individuals in governmental retirement plans are covered at the $100,000 benefit level.

44. Guaranty association provides $500,000 in coverage for health benefits except for disability insurance and long-term care insurance, which are covered at $300,000.

45. Benefits for life insurance and annuity policies in California are covered at 80 percent of the contractual obligation, subject to the statutory limits.

46. The $250,000 limit is for annuity net cash surrender and net cash withdrawal values; if annuitized, the benefit limit is $410,000.

47. Changes effective 10/1/13.

48. The $500,000 limit is for individual health policies issued by life companies; there is no coverage for policies issued by nonlife companies, and unlimited coverage for group or blanket health insurance issued by a life company.

49. North Carolina applies a $300,000 annuity limit except in the case of structured settlement annuities where the limit is $1,000,000.

50. The $500,000 limit applies if death occurs before the guaranty association is triggered. If death occurs after triggering, the benefit is limited to the covered portion of the policy as defined by statutory reference to covered cash value.

51. Guaranty association provides $100,000 for health coverage not defined as disability insurance, long-term care, or basic hospital, medical, and surgical insurance or major medical insurance; $300,000 for disability insurance; $300,000 for long-term care insurance and for basic hospital, medical, and surgical insurance or major medical insurance.

CHAPTER 12

Comparative Regulation of Market Intermediaries: Insights from the Indian Life Insurance Market

Santosh Anagol

The Wharton School, University of Pennsylvania

Shawn Cole

Harvard Business School

Shayak Sarkar

Harvard University

Global economic growth and financial liberalization are rapidly increasing the size and depth of insurance markets in emerging markets, and millions of consumers are purchasing life insurance for the first time. Insurance can be a complicated product, and many households in emerging markets have low levels of financial literacy. Many life insurance products are complex, and insurance companies, agents, and/or brokers may stand to profit by steering customers toward policies that offer relatively less value to consumers but relatively higher commissions to agents.

In this chapter, we consider regulation of the sales of insurance as a means for reducing the amount of misselling that occurs. This chapter was inspired by a field experiment we conducted in India, in which we sent mystery shoppers (experimental auditors) to visit life insurance agents and solicit financial advice. The experiment and results are reported in Anagol, Cole, and Sarkar (2013).[1] A key finding of the experiment was that life insurance agents often gave unsuitable advice: For some types of clients, agents recommended the wrong product more than 80 percent of the time.[2]

Because Indian insurance law is a work in progress, we ground our analysis in a consideration of the regulatory regimes used to govern insurance sales in the United States.

After providing background information on the life insurance markets in India and the United States, we focus on the regulation of commissions disclosure in the two countries, before proceeding to a discussion of the results of our field experiment in India, exploiting a recent disclosure mandate for a particular class of life insurance products. In the next section, we discuss the more general issue of regulation of advice, focusing on the three tiers of legal duty (caveat emptor, suitability, and fiduciary) present in U.S. law. These place differing duties upon different types of agents in their product recommendations to, and interactions with, consumers. We use this as a springboard to discuss the recent Indian "suitability" rhetoric appearing in both Indian insurance regulation and broader financial reform efforts. Next, we present our experimental evidence on how quality of advice responded to consumer sophistication, preferences, and needs, in addition to market competition. That evidence gives rise to our recommendations regarding the emerging Indian standards. The chapter ends with a brief conclusion section.

COMPARING LIFE INSURANCE MARKETS IN THE UNITED STATES AND INDIA

In both the United States and India, the life insurance markets involve significant amounts of money and people. In the United States, life insurance premium payments to insurers exceed $100 billion annually,[3] with the majority of people in the United States covered by some type of life insurance.[4] In India, life insurance premium payments to insurers were close to $60 billion,[5] but recent estimates suggest that less than 20 percent of Indians have life insurance.[6]

In contrast to the American system of private providers and state-level regulation, federal regulation and a dominant public provider define the Indian life insurance market.

In 1956, the Indian government nationalized the life insurance industry, and for over 40 years only one company, the government-owned Life Insurance Corporation of India (LIC), was permitted to offer insurance. In 1999, financial liberalization permitted the entry of private insurers; they introduced new products and distribution channels.[7] While competition from dozens of private-sector competitors has decreased LIC's market share since 2000, LIC continues to be the dominant player in the life insurance market in terms of both total premiums and new premiums. Due to greater competition, the largest market shares are much lower in the United States: The two market leaders, MetLife and Prudential, hold a combined market share of only 30 percent of the total life insurance premiums collected in 2012.[8]

In terms of regulation, state regulation defines U.S. insurance whereas India's regulation is largely national. One might point to the Dodd-Frank Act's creation of the Federal Insurance Office (FIO) as evidence of a federalizing trend in American insurance. Yet the FIO is neither a regulator nor a supervisor but rather only a data collection and monitoring entity.[9] In contrast, India's Insurance Regulatory and Development Authority (IRDA) regulates the national licensing requirements for insurers, including business conduct guidelines. One example of those guidelines, the IRDA's 2010 mandate on commissions disclosure for particular life insurance products, constitutes the basis of our analysis on the effect of such regulatory requirements on agent recommendations.

The qualifications and characteristics of agents selling life insurance differ between the United States and India. American insurance agents generally are licensed in the states where they work, most often work on commission, and possess at least a high school diploma.[10] The Bureau of Labor Statistics (BLS) predicts the number of jobs for insurance agents to grow more quickly over the next decade than most occupations, the growing role of the Internet in insurance marketing and sales notwithstanding.[11] Indian agents also work on commission, but they possess national licenses, for which a 12th-grade education is also the educational prerequisite, though for applicants from rural areas a 10th-grade education will suffice.[12]

India may technically have more insurance agents, even adjusted for its population, but they tend to work part-time and the profession may be losing its appeal. Around 2010, when the number of life insurance agents in the United States was just shy of 200,000,[13] India had already hit its peak of 3 million agents, many of whom were working in an ad hoc fashion.[14] However, decreased financial prospects, due to both regulatory reform and declining consumer demand, have led to annual attrition rates of over 50 percent, inspiring recent efforts to professionalize and stabilize the agent base.[15] Despite a recent contraction in new premiums,[16] analysts remain optimistic about growth in the Indian life insurance market given that the ratio of life insurance premium to gross domestic product (GDP) remains less than half of some developed countries.[17] In contrast, despite the BLS's prediction of growth in insurance agents generally (including life insurance, property insurance, and other types), the number of households with life insurance is decreasing in the United States.[18] In sum, the pervasiveness of life insurance agents and the nature of their employment differ between the two countries, though both employment sectors are experiencing uncertainty.

Last, life insurance customer behaviors and preferences regarding agents differ between the United States and India. These differences are highlighted in a recent 2012 global life insurance customer survey by Ernst & Young.[19] While the survey's online platform overrepresents the urban and affluent, the survey provides preliminary insights.[20] First, Indian consumers do more research than consumers in any other country—nearly three-quarters of respondents said they did a fair amount or a great deal of research before buying a product, as compared to less than a third of American respondents, who typically take a more passive approach.[21] This may be a partial response to Indian consumers' expressed concerns about misselling, where agents focus on commissions over consumer needs.[22] Second, despite the emergence of online platforms, both Americans (82 percent)[23] and Indians (94 percent)[24] cite personal interactions with intermediaries (agents) as important to the purchase process. Yet while surveyed Indians steadfastly believed that insurers make an effort to retain them as customers (77 percent), a faith surpassing every other country,[25] American consumers feel the exact opposite (12 percent).[26] Third and finally, an important commonality underlies the desire for personal product advice: A majority of consumers cite product complexity as a reason for seeking out advice, noting that experts are needed to decode the technicalities.[27] Thus, while Indian customers tend to conduct more independent research and to perceive more agent effort, the very existence of agents comports with customers' preferences and needs for advice in both countries. Our research uses a unique field experiment to test the quality of this advice, particularly whether agents' advice accords with customers' stated product preferences and needs.

COMPARING DISCLOSURE MANDATES

Before discussing quality of advice, we first turn to the issue of commissions disclosure, discussing commissions disclosure in the United States before turning to India.

The United States

As noted before, insurance is regulated at the state rather than federal level, leading to differing disclosure mandates across the United States. Recently enacted New York state law, for example, mandates insurance agents to disclose affirmatively, either orally or in writing, the general compensation incentives of the agent.[28] The law does not, however, require general disclosures of compensation quantities.[29] The agent must only disclose, in written form, quantities and sources of compensation in response to a consumer inquiry.[30]

The New York law was particularly significant as a catalyst for national reform. Prior to the law's passage in January 2011, the National Association of Insurance and Financial Advisors, a prominent trade group that includes licensed life insurance agents, had no policies regarding commission disclosure.[31] In response to the New York law, the group changed its agnostic stance and now encourages the more than 45,000 agents that belong to its local associations to disclose fully all commission amounts on securities and insurance products, *if* a consumer asks.[32] This change accorded with other nongovernmental groups advocating for commissions disclosure in the life insurance industry.[33] New York is a significant example, but its disclosure standards are not universal. Colorado requires disclosure of a standard compensation schedule to the purchaser, while California requires disclosure only after the sale is completed, and only to certain classes of consumers.[34]

These contemporary commissions disclosure debates are taking place around the world, motivating our research in India. As of April 2013, Hong Kong required disclosure of fees on insurance sales by insurance brokers, but only when those fees exceed the "usual market rate."[35] These regulations emerge from a highly publicized court case in which the plaintiff sued his financial adviser for losses on insurance instruments, alleging a conflict of interest.[36] Similarly, the Netherlands imposed a ban on commissions on life insurance products, while the United Kingdom imposed a ban on life insurance investment and savings products but carved out an exception for term (protection only) products.[37]

Experimental Evidence from an Indian Disclosure Mandate

A particularly salient example of such a disclosure policy from an emerging market is India's commissions disclosure mandate for equity-linked insurance products. On July 1, 2010, the Indian insurance regulator mandated that insurance agents must disclose the commissions they would earn when selling a specific type of whole life insurance product called a unit-linked insurance product (ULIP). ULIPs are very similar to whole life insurance policies, except that the savings component is invested in equity instruments with uncertain returns. This regulation was enacted as the Indian insurance regulator faced criticism from the Indian stock market regulator that ULIPs should be regulated in the same way as other equity-based investment products. The insurance regulator responded to these criticisms by requiring agents to disclose commissions when selling ULIPs.

There are two specific features of this policy. First, it is important to note that the disclosure of commissions required as of July 1, 2010, is in addition to a disclosure requirement on total charges that came into effect earlier in 2010. Prior to July 1, agents were required to disclose the total charges (i.e., the total costs, including commissions) of the policies they sold, but they were not required to disclose how much of those charges went to agent commissions. Thus, the new legislation requiring the specific disclosure of commissions gives the potential life insurance customer more information on the agency problem between himself or herself and the agent, but does not change the amount of information on total costs. This allows us to interpret our results as the effect of better information about agency, rather than better information about costs more generally.

Our empirical research documents two important effects of the regulation: First, the percentage of ULIP recommendations made to our experimental auditors dropped precipitously after the regulation came into effect.[38] Yet agent recommendations shifted from high-commission ULIPs to high-commission whole life insurance products, and this effect was not contingent on whether auditors affirmatively inquired about commissions. Mandating commissions disclosure of particularly high-commission products may therefore affect product recommendations, but if the disclosure mandate is not universal, agents may simply recommend other high-commission products.

QUALITY OF ADVICE

In contrast to the relative simplicity of disclosure, regulating the quality of advice is a much more difficult task and often hinges on the legal duties of intermediaries to the insurance consumer (prospectively, the insured). As with the earlier discussion of commissions disclosure mandates, we begin by discussing quality of advice in the United States and then turn to India.

Agent Duties in the United States

In the United States, these intermediary legal duties can roughly be grouped into three categories: caveat emptor (the buyer must beware as the intermediary possesses little or no duty), suitability, and fiduciary (the highest duty). In discussing these categories, we discuss two examples of intermediaries, agents and brokers, which typically refer to slightly different relationships in the American context. While both serve as market intermediaries, agents are tied to insurers and act as their company representatives or legal agents. Brokers are independent intermediaries who often represent the insured.[39] New Jersey law, for example, explicitly incorporates this distinction, though the legal distinctions hinge on functional rather than nominal labels.[40]

Retail life insurance agents usually fall into the caveat emptor category of duty. These agents explicitly serve as salespeople in arm's-length transactions with individual consumers, and therefore have minimal legal duties, if any, to those consumers. As a Pennsylvania federal court articulated the legal standard, such an agent does not act "out of a special duty to act for the consumer's exclusive benefit, but rather out of a duty to his employer—and to his own self-interest—to sell its products as successfully as possible."[41] The only legal proscriptions on agent advice arise from liability for negligent or fraudulent misrepresentation; material falsities or omissions can potentially give rise to common law tort liability where such acts are the proximate cause for insurance-related damages. Yet agents' opinions about the quality, suitability, or desirability of a policy will not give rise to such claims.[42] State administrative agencies follow similar legal standards in addressing consumer complaints.[43] State law thus provides few bounds to the quality of advice by insurance agents.

Brokers, on the other hand, may be held to a higher standard that we call professional negligence or suitability. Generally, when a broker agrees to obtain insurance for a client for the purposes of a commission, the broker is held to a duty of care that reflects reasonable skill and diligence.[44] This duty is often called professional negligence because states tend to impose liability when brokers "fail to exercise the care that a reasonably prudent businessman in the brokerage field would exercise under similar circumstances."[45] In instances where an insurance agent consensually undertakes to act on behalf of the insured, a higher (broker) duty might arise even for an individual otherwise labeled as an agent for the insurer.[46] The requirement that a broker "use reasonable care, diligence, and judgment"[47] reflects a higher standard for quality of advice than caveat emptor, though the interpretation of those terms across jurisdictions can vary.

Generally, insurance brokers are not held to the highest duty, that of a fiduciary. As opposed to reasonableness or general suitability, the term *fiduciary* can be defined as a strict duty to a high standard of care based on good faith, trust, and confidence.[48] It is a duty of loyalty that precludes conflicts of interest, burdening insurance brokers who may be dual agents, purportedly serving the insured while responding to incentives by the insurer. However, in 2011, New York's highest court held that an insurance broker does not have a common law fiduciary duty to disclose to its customers incentive arrangements that the broker has entered into with insurance companies.[49] The case relied on existing jurisprudence holding that, absent special circumstances, the relationship between brokers and clients is not fiduciary in nature.[50] Yet in some states, such as California, there is no clear answer as to whether the highest fiduciary duties apply to insurance agents and brokers.[51] When courts hesitate to create common law fiduciary duties, legislative or regulatory responses may nonetheless create heightened standards.[52]

One complicating aspect of insurance regulation is where products marketed as life insurance fall under the purview of stricter, federal securities regulation. Annuities are a classic example. Yet even securities regulation faces its own internal tensions, disparate duties, and evolving, politically responsive regulation. When Congress raised the standard of conduct of securities brokers from caveat emptor to one of professional duty in 1934 with the creation of the Securities and Exchange Commission (SEC), it was responding to the Great Depression. Nonetheless, the legislation was a compromise, establishing a duty but measuring that duty in terms of internal industry standards rather than well-defined extrinsic metrics.[53] Similarly, in the wake of the financial crisis, the Dodd-Frank Act has tasked the SEC with investigating the merits of establishing a fiduciary standard for securities broker-dealers, who are currently subject to a suitability standard.[54] Licensed investment advisers (who are fee rather than commission based and regulated by a different statute)[55] are subject to the highest fiduciary standard, whereas broker-dealers may provide, for example, a higher-priced (and higher-commission) product even if a lower-cost one with better returns exists. The latter product might theoretically meet the suitability, but not fiduciary, standard. Higher duties therefore limit the recommendations made, and commissions received, by agents in their interactions with consumers.

In summary, American retail life insurance agents who act as representatives of the insurer are legally held to minimal standards of conduct in the quality of advice they offer to consumers. Brokers, where they act as representatives of the insured, are held to a higher professional standard, though not necessarily a fiduciary one. However, where particular life insurance products implicate securities such as annuities or mutual fund–linked term insurance, the fiduciary standard more likely applies.

Emerging Standards in India

The term *suitability* became a significant factor in the Indian life insurance regulation in 2013. The IRDA issued regulations requiring a standardized suitability analysis to form the basis for recommendations by a spectrum of intermediaries: "agents, bancassurance [sale of insurance through a bank], brokers and its [the insurer's] employees."[56] The mandated suitability analysis involves three main stages: data collection, analysis, and verification. First, the IRDA's standardized form asks the intermediary to collect consumer information including demographics, current assets, expected family liabilities (education, health, etc.), and expected future income.[57] After this data collection phase, a mandatory section requires the insurer to answer two queries: why the "policy is most suited for the proposer" and whether the product proposed is based on need, demand, or agent recommendation.[58] The regulations provide little insight on how these questions should be answered—they do not demand that the preceding quantitative information be referenced, nor do they specify the level of detail required in substantiating the recommendation. Nonetheless, in the third stage, both the intermediary and the customer must sign an acknowledgment that the "product recommended is suitable for the proposer."[59] In the alternative, where the customer rejects the agent's recommendation and chooses a different product, the intermediary and consumer must document this divergence with a signed acknowledgment.[60]

Despite requiring detailed data upon which to make product recommendations and requiring both intermediaries and consumers to verify "suitability," suitability is not defined. The regulatory language lends itself to the logical inference that suitability is something more than a caveat emptor regime and something less rigid than a fiduciary duty. In that sense, retail sales agents in India under the Draft Code would be held to a higher standard than retail sales agents in the United States, who are governed by the caveat emptor regime.

In terms of implementing these suitability regulations, insurers are instructed (1) to train their agents on the new documentation requirements as well as the suitability analysis, (2) to monitor agent documentation to assure that suitable recommendations are in fact being made, and (3) to maintain the records for five years for inspection by the IRDA.[61] Yet the lack of regulatory clarity on which vectors of underlying data are "suitable" for which life insurance products means that the regulations leave a definitional hole in consumer protection despite this extensive record keeping.

The suitability rhetoric is not limited to the life insurance context; it pervades India's broader financial reform. In 2013, India also released the Report of the Financial Sector Legislative Reforms Commission based on a perceived need to modernize its financial regulation.[62] At the agency level, this modernization incorporated regulatory consolidation, with the report recommending the merger of the IRDA with the Securities and Exchange Board of India (SEBI), Forward Markets Commission (FMC), and Pension Fund Regulatory and Development Authority (PFRDA) to create a new, unified regulatory agency.[63] The report, which included a Draft Code, also offered language regarding "fair disclosure," "suitability of advice," and their intersection to be implemented by the regulator.

In addressing "fair disclosure," the Draft Code incorporates both substantive and procedural mandates. Procedurally, the Draft Code mandates that the disclosure be made "sufficiently before entering into a contract," in writing, and in a manner "that enables the customer to make reasonable comparison of the financial product."[64] Substantively, the Draft Code only provides suggested topics, noting that the regulator (proposed as the newly unified agency described earlier) may require disclosures regarding product benefits and risks, effects of contractual terms, and consumer rights under any law or regulation.[65]

The Draft Code's ambitious "suitability" requirement, only partially exposed through statutory language, parallels the IRDA regulations' similarly promising but ambiguous language. The Draft Code demands that the "retail advisor must ensure that the advice given is suitable for the retail consumer after due consideration of the relevant personal circumstances of the retail consumer."[66] In the Draft Code, as in the IRDA regulations, if the consumer forgoes the adviser's recommendation and purchases a different product, a signed acknowledgment of the divergence is required.[67] While the Draft Code language defines (or, more accurately, fails to define) suitability as broadly as the IRDA regulations, the Draft Code, as a model statute, explicitly leaves the task of administration and clarification to the regulator, who can implement clarifying regulations. In contrast, with the current life insurance suitability mandate, the IRDA, as a regulatory agency, is the final implementer, leaving only the courts and subsequent regulation as a source of specificity.

The Draft Code also explicitly addresses the interaction between disclosure and suitability. While the Regulator must ultimately decide which financial products fall under the purview of the suitability regulations, the Draft Code mandates that, in exercising this judgment, the regulator must take into account the "sufficiency of the disclosures made . . . to allow retail consumers to assess the suitability of the financial product or financial service for their purposes."[68] A retail adviser must also disclose to consumers "any conflict of interests, including any conflicted remuneration that the retail advisor has received or expects to receive for making the advice to the retail consumer."[69]

Before discussing the results of our experiment, we summarize our discussion of quality of advice in the United States and India with three basic observations. First, suitability of advice pervades modern insurance regulation, whether in American common law professional negligence claims or in emerging Indian financial regulation architecture. Nonetheless, the Indian standard is at least ostensibly higher, given that agents fall under a suitability purview as opposed to the caveat emptor standard in the United States. Second, suitable advice in the Indian context takes on the stature of an affirmative right, yet the lack of clarity on how suitability is defined and evaluated jeopardizes that right's practical implications. Finally, the acknowledgment that consumer preferences may often conflict with consumer needs and therefore the agent's suitability analysis gives rise to the question of how those conflicts shape the quality of advice. That question constitutes the basis of a second component of our research, discussed in the next section.

QUALITY OF ADVICE IN INDIA: AN EXPERIMENT WITH ASSOCIATED RECOMMENDATIONS

In addition to measuring the effects of disclosure regimes on product recommendation (discussed earlier in the chapter), our field experiment in urban India also pursued a second goal: documenting the responsiveness of quality of advice in a setting in which one product is unambiguously more appropriate than other products. Whole life insurance, a popular product in the Indian market, is economically inferior to a combination of investing in savings accounts and purchasing term insurance, and yet we find that life insurance agents overwhelmingly encourage the purchase of whole life insurance and rarely recommend term insurance.

The generally poor quality of advice is confirmed by our findings. For individuals for whom term insurance is the most suitable product, only 5 percent of agents recommend purchasing only term insurance, while 74 percent recommend purchasing only whole life insurance.[70] We also documented a range of wildly incorrect statements made by agents, such as: "You want term—are you planning on killing yourself?," "Term insurance is not for women," and "Term insurance is for government employees only."[71]

Experimental Evidence from Auditor Cues

Beyond documenting the generally poor quality of advice, by randomizing the content of our scripts for our experimental auditors we also specifically explore how four different attributes affect the quality of advice: customer needs, customer bias (stated preference for a product), competition, and customer sophistication.

First, with regard to bias and need, we varied the auditors' stated preferences for term insurance as well as their need for it. In the latter case, need for term insurance was signaled by the auditor mentioning concerns about the effects on his family's position of dying early, as well as wanting to cover risk affordably. The need for whole life insurance was signaled by mentioning the desire to save and invest money for the future through a product that would provide financial discipline. We found that neither an initial customer bias nor customer need for term insurance increases the probability of a recommendation of buying *only* term life insurance. However, both the bias and need increase the probability of a product recommendation that *includes* term insurance. Such a bias or need also increases the amount of risk coverage recommended by the agent, but does not increase the corresponding premium, largely because term insurance provides more risk coverage per rupee of premium. Agents thus cater to customers (either their beliefs or their needs) primarily by recommending term insurance products as an addition to high-commission whole life insurance products, rather than recommending only the purchase of term insurance.

Second, with regard to competition, we experimentally reduced the agent's perceived amount of market power by varying whether the customer mentioned that he had talked to other providers and wanted to compare offers. The auditors lacking the competition treatment only mentioned having discussed life insurance with a friend. We were particularly interested in competition's effect where the customer is biased toward whole life insurance but demonstrates a need for term insurance. In this setting the agent has the potential to debias customers (auditors) as their beliefs are inconsistent with their insurance needs. When the threat of competition looms, we find that the agent is substantially more likely to debias customers by recommending a product that includes term insurance. However, when the dependent variable is a binary indicator for a product recommendation of term insurance only, there is no longer a competition effect. Moreover, we do not find that competition leads agents to debias customers who have a belief that term insurance is a good product but express a need for whole life insurance. In summary, in the limited circumstances where competition has an effect, we find that agents mainly compete by recommending term policies on top of whole life insurance policies, as opposed to completely debiasing the customer and recommending only term insurance.

Finally, we varied auditor cues of sophistication. In this experiment, sophisticated auditors mentioned that they had spent time shopping for policies and were familiar with the different types of policies. The unsophisticated auditors affirmatively conveyed their lack of knowledge and their confusion. We found that sophistication does in fact lead to higher-quality advice. Yet, similar to the results in the bias versus needs experiment, it appears that agents attempt to cater to more sophisticated types by including term insurance as a part of a recommendation, as opposed to exclusively recommending term insurance.

Recommendations

Our findings lend themselves to three particular critiques of both the IRDA regulations and the Draft Code. First, insofar as commissions-motivated agents improve their quality of advice by creating composite recommendations that mix suitable products with unsuitable products as opposed to recommending only the suitable products, the IRDA regulations should clarify how the suitability analysis judges such composite recommendations. If the practice is a professional norm across licensed agents, extrinsic suitability standards (rather than professional negligence standards alone) would be needed to truly protect consumers. While suitability standards provide a middle ground between caveat emptor and fiduciary standards, adding a suitable product to an unsuitable product does not clearly make the composite recommendation more suitable.

Second, since our research suggests that agents may in fact cater to consumer preferences even when they conflict with consumer need, the relationship between preferences and suitability analysis needs elaboration.

In addition to our research, a recent American audit study examining the quality of portfolio allocation guidance found that agents recommend higher-risk portfolios for wealthier individuals, are biased toward active management, and do not do a good job of undoing customer biases; the phenomenon of catering is thus not limited to the financial products market in India.[72] On the one hand, the IRDA regulations may address this conflict by requiring consumers to acknowledge when their product purchases diverge from the agent's "suitable" recommendation. Yet, in the absence of a clearer suitability standard, it's possible that such customer preferences will be incorporated into the agent recommendation, particularly when those preferences are in line with the agent's compensation interests. Our research also suggests that competition among agents will not necessarily remedy this catering. Thus, the role (if any) of consumer preferences in suitability analysis needs to be clarified by the IRDA.

Third, we caution against the Draft Code's suggestion that disclosures may sufficiently promote suitable financial product recommendations, exempting certain product classes from suitability requirements. For example, we find evidence that commissions disclosure causes agents to shift recommendations toward other high-commission products where disclosure is not required, not necessarily to more suitable products. Our research exploits a disclosure mandate that applies to a single class of products, so commissions disclosure across *all* products might produce a different equilibrium. Yet given the practical limits on how much disclosure can be mandated, how well individual consumers can incorporate multiple disclosures, and the efficacy of such disclosures, the IRDA should move cautiously before relying on disclosure as a substitute for suitability regulation.[73]

In sum, India's recent reforms in the insurance industry and prospective reforms in the financial industry endeavor to create substantive rights to suitable advice, exceeding American standards in certain regards. Experimental evidence, such as the research we summarize here, can play an important role in testing the theoretical limits of these frameworks and ensure that the regulations effectuate the consumer protection they are meant to accomplish.

CONCLUSION

As consumers, particularly in emerging markets, begin to engage in complicated financial products markets, the role of intermediaries as sources of advice will come under further scrutiny. Our comparative regulation analysis has, we hope, crystallized two overarching themes. First, even seemingly disparate markets such as the life insurance markets in India and the United States often overlap in their market characteristics and their regulatory regimes. Second, financial regulatory efforts do not always create the intended impacts in human behavior, but creative field experiments can shed light on regulatory limitations and identify promising interventions.

NOTES

1. Santosh Anagol, Shawn Cole, and Shayak Sarkar, *Understanding the Advice of Commissions-Motivated Agents: Evidence from the Indian Life Insurance Market* (2013), 20 (manuscript on file with the author).

2. See the section "Quality of Advice in India: An Experiment with Associated Recommendations," this chapter, for relevant statistics.

3. American Council of Life Insurers, *2011 Life Insurers Fact Book*, xiii; Insurance Information Institute (India), "Life Insurance—Life/Health Insurance Industry Statement, 2008–2012" (2013), www.iii.org/facts_statistics/life-insurance.html.

4. Insurance Information Institute (India), "Life Insurance" (2013), www.iii.org/facts_statistics/life-insurance.html ("Sixty-two percent of all people in the United States were covered by some type of life insurance in 2013, according to LIMRA's 2013 *Insurance Barometer*.").

5. Insurance Regulatory and Development Authority (IRDA), *Annual Report* 2011–2012 ("Life insurance industry recorded a premium income of 2,87,072R crore during 2011–12 as against 2,91,639R crore in the previous financial year, registering a negative growth of 1.57 percent.").

6. Bharati Pathak, *The Indian Financial System: Markets, Institutions and Services*, 3rd ed. (Upper Saddle River, NJ: Pearson Education, 2011), 697 ("The outreach of insurance is equally modest at 20 percent of the insurable population in case of life."); Kartik Goyal, "Hidden Cash Lures Subbarao to Rural India Worth $24 Billion," *Bloomberg*, March 20, 2013, www.bloomberg.com/news/2013-03-19/hidden-cash-lures-subbarao-to-indian-villages-worth-24-billion.html ("Sixty percent of the 1.2 billion population remains outside the formal banking system. Only 10 percent has life insurance and 0.6 percent uses non-life insurance.").

7. Insurance Regulatory and Development Authority (IRDA), "History of Insurance in India" (2007), www.irda.gov.in/ADMINCMS/cms/NormalData_Layout.aspx?page=PageNo4&mid=2.

8. Federal Insurance Office, U.S. Department of the Treasury, *Annual Report on the Insurance Industry* (2013), 10.

9. U.S. Department of the Treasury, Federal Insurance Office, www.treasury.gov/initiatives/fio/about-fio/Pages/default.aspx.

10. Bureau of Labor Statistics, *Occupational Outlook Handbook: Insurance Sales Agents—Summary* (2010), www.bls.gov/ooh/sales/insurance-sales-agents.htm#tab-4 ("A high school diploma is the typical requirement for insurance sales agents, although more than one-third of insurance sales agents have a bachelor's degree. Public speaking classes can be useful in improving sales techniques, and often agents will have taken courses in business, finance, or economics. Business knowledge is also helpful for sales agents hoping to advance to a managerial position.").

11. Bureau of Labor Statistics, *Occupational Outlook Handbook: Insurance Sales Agents—Job Outlook* (2010), www.bls.gov/ooh/sales/insurance-sales-agents.htm#tab-6.

12. IRDA, Reg./7/2000, Insurance Regulatory and Development Authority (Licensing of Insurance Agents) Regulations 3(4) (2000) ("Qualifications of the applicant. The applicant shall possess the minimum qualification of a pass in 12th Standard or equivalent examination conducted by any recognised Board/Institution, where the applicant resides in a place with a population of five thousand or more as per the last census, and a pass in 10th Standard or equivalent examination from a recognised Board/Institution if the applicant resides in any other place.").

13. Leslie Scism, "A Hot Job for Hard Times: The Life-Insurance Agent," *Wall Street Journal*, March 19, 2010 ("In all, the number of U.S. life-insurance agents affiliated with a specific company today is down nearly a third since the 1970s, to 174,000, according to Limra. Their average age is up to 56.").

14. "Indian Insurance: Rogue Agents," *The Economist*, October 29, 2011 ("At the peak of India's strange insurance hysteria a few years ago there were almost 3m people flogging life-insurance policies.").

15. Devina Sengupta and Sreeradha D. Basu, "Life Insurance Companies Struggling to Retain Employees, Pursue Change," *Economic Times of India*, April 26, 2013.

16. Megha Mandavia, "Bajaj Finserv Sees Life Insurance Industry Contracting This Year," DNA *India*, May 16, 2013, www.dnaindia.com/money/1835342/interview-bajaj-finserv-sees-life-insurance-industry-contracting-this-year ("As far as life insurance is concerned we have seen total premiums drop by 8%, though new business premium are up 10%. However, because of all these new regulatory changes that have again recently happened in February, we think the industry can contract in 2013–14 before growth comes back in 2014–15."); Towers Watson, *India Market Life Insurance Update* 50 (April 16, 2013), www.towerswatson.com/en-IN/Insights/Newsletters/Asia-Pacific/india-market-life-insurance/2013/India-Market-Life-Insurance-Update-April-2013

("Pulled down by the 22 per cent fall in weighted new premium collections of the Life Insurance Corporation of India (LIC), the life insurance
industry recorded a decline of approximately 15 per cent year-on-year
in weighted new business premium collections in the first 11 months of
FY2012–13 (April 2012 to February 2013). Private players were relatively more stable and recorded a decline of approximately 3 per cent in
weighted new premiums in this period.").

17. See, for example, McKinsey and Co., "India Life Insurance 2012,"
available at www.mckinsey.com/locations/india/mckinseyonindia/pdf/
insurance_a_summary.pdf ("But the market is still at a nascent stage
in its evolution. The ratio of life insurance premium to GDP in India is
currently about 4 per cent, much lower than developed market levels
of 6 to 9 per cent. In several segments of the population, penetration is
lower than potential. For example, in urban areas, penetration of life
insurance in the mass market is about 65 per cent, and it is considerably
less in the low-income unbanked segment. In rural areas, life insurance
penetration in the banked segment is estimated to be about 40 per cent,
while it is marginal at best in the unbanked segment.").

18. Life Insurance and Market Research Association (LIMRA), "Ownership
of Individual Life Insurance Falls to 50-Year Low," August 30, 2010,
www.limra.com/Posts/PR/News_Releases/Ownership_of_Individual_
Life_Insurance_Falls_to_50-Year_Low,_LIMRA_Reports.aspx?
LangType=1033.

19. Ernst & Young, *Americas: Global Consumer Insurance Survey 2012*;
Ernst & Young, *India: Global Consumer Insurance Survey 2012*.

20. Ernst & Young, *Americas*, 35.

21. Ernst & Young, *India*, 11 ("Our survey indicates that customers around
the world are increasing their use of research before buying a policy.
This is particularly true in India, where 74% of consumers surveyed say
they perform a fair or great deal of research before buying a product—
a higher proportion than any other location that we surveyed. While
some of this can potentially be attributed to differing understanding of
what constitutes research, the difference is still quite marked. In China,
another fast-growth market with a rapidly growing middle class, the
equivalent percentage is 44% and in more mature economies like the UK
and US the percentages are even lower—37% and 31% respectively.").

22. Ernst & Young, *Americas*, 13 ("In the Americas, the two most common reasons consumers cite for seeking assistance are that they need
expert assistance to make important financial decisions (52% of consumers) and that they do not know which products best meet their
needs (41%)"); Ernst & Young, *India*, 8 ("Mis-selling is also a concern
in India, where a belief persists that distributors are sometimes more

focused on selling products to trigger commission payments than on meeting customers' needs. There is a further idea that agents do not always share the correct information on returns or the timeframe in which payments will be made. This implies that many consumers feel confident at the time of purchase, but at a later date realize that some features of the policy are not in line with what was promised by the agent. The Insurance Regulatory and Development Authority (IRDA) has intervened and reviewed the commissions on unit-linked products in an attempt to increase transparency and has indicated that it might do the same for traditional products.").

23. Ernst & Young, *Americas*, 14.
24. Ibid., 13.
25. Ernst & Young, *India*, 18.
26. Ernst & Young, *Americas*, 19.
27. Ernst & Young, *India*, 13 ("The main barriers that prevent customers from transacting for themselves are product complexity and a lack of transparent information about how products will meet their needs. The most common reasons cited for the continuing use of agents in India are that the products on offer are 'too technical and complicated' (53%) and that consumers feel they need expert assistance to make more important financial decisions (42%). Forty-two percent also state that they are unclear which products best suit their needs and just over a quarter (26%) use an agent because they are unsure how to measure product performance.").
28. 11 NYCRR (Reg. 194) § 30.3(a).
29. Ibid.
30. 11 NYCRR (Reg. 194) § 30.3(b).
31. Leslie Scism, "Insurance Fees, Revealed," *Wall Street Journal*, March 30, 2012, http://online.wsj.com/article/SB10001424052702304177104577305930202770336.html.
32. Ibid.
33. Meg Fletcher, "NAIC Moves Forward on Disclosure Rule for Producers," *Business Insurance*, December 12, 2004, www.businessinsurance.com/apps/pbcs.dll/article?AID=9999100015882 (discussing how the National Association of Insurance Commissioners embraced the beginnings of a commissions disclosure standard nearly a decade ago).
34. Ameritas, *Commission Disclosure Requirements for Producers* (2010), newyork.ameritasgroup.com/producer/737_4747.asp.
35. Rick Adkinson, "New Insurance Rule Far from Transparent on Fee Disclosure," *South China Post*, March 25, 2013, www.scmp.com/business/money/markets-investing/article/1198780/new-insurance-rule-far-transparent-fee-disclosure.

36. Ibid.
37. Lachlan Colquhoun, "Australia Proposes Ban on Commission," *Financial Times*, September 4, 2011, www.ft.com/intl/cms/s/0/c8bf2050-d536-11e0-bd7e-00144feab49a.html#axzz2Wc1kafgC. See also Jeremy Forty and Keith Walter, "Commissions—The Beginning of the End?," Towers Watson *Emphasis* 3 (September 2011).
38. Santosh Anagol, Shawn Cole, and Shayak Sarkar, *Understanding the Advice of Commissions-Motivated Agents: Evidence from the Indian Life Insurance Market* (2013), 20 (manuscript on file with the author).
39. Francis J. Deasey, "The Liability of Insurance Agents and Brokers," *The Brief* 29, no. 4 (Summer 2000), 44.
40. *Polar Int'l Brokerage Corp. v. Investors Ins. Co. of Am.*, 967 F. Supp. 135, 139 (D.N.J. 1997) ("New Jersey law distinguishes between insurance agents and insurance brokers. An insurance broker is a 'person who, for a commission, brokerage fee, or other consideration, acts or aids in any manner concerning negotiation, solicitation or effectuation of insurance contracts as the representative of the insured . . .' An insurance agent is a 'person authorized, in writing, by any insurance company to act as its agent to solicit, negotiate or effect insurance contracts on its behalf or to collect insurance premiums and who may be authorized to countersign insurance policies on its behalf.'") (internal citations omitted).
41. *Weisblatt v. Minnesota Mutual Life Insurance Co.*, 4 F. Supp. 2d 371 (E.D. Pa. 1998).
42. Douglas R. Richmond, "Insurance Agent and Broker Liability," *Tort Trial & Insurance Practice Law Journal* 40, no. 1 (2004): 13.
43. California Department of Insurance: General Inquiries and Complaints, available at www.insurance.ca.gov/contact-us/0200-file-complaint/ (stating that the agency will address complaints based on "misconduct or theft of premiums"); Maryland Insurance Administration: File a Complaint, available at www.mdinsurance.state.md.us/sa/consumer/file-a-complaint.html (noting that the primary role of the Maryland Insurance Administration is to protect consumers from illegal insurance practices by ensuring that insurance companies and producers that operate in Maryland act in accordance with state insurance laws).
44. Richmond, "Insurance Agent and Broker Liability," 10.
45. David Paige, "Potential Sources of Legal Liability for Life Insurance Agents and Brokers," § 7:2 in *The Law of Commercial Insurance Agents and Brokers*, ed. Britton Weimer, Clarence Hagglund, and Andrew Whitman (New York: Thomson West, 2007).
46. Richmond, "Insurance Agent and Broker Liability," 10.

47. Mher Asatryan, "What Are the Fiduciary Duties of Insurance Agents and Brokers?," *Los Angeles Lawyer* 35 (September 2012), 16 (quoting *Kotlar*, 83 Cal. App. 4th at 1123).

48. *Black's Law Dictionary*, 9th ed. (2009) ("[O]ne who owes to another the duties of good faith, trust, confidence.").

49. "The Fiduciary Duty of Insurance Brokers in NY," *Law360*, March 2, 2011, www.willkie.com/files/tbl_s29Publications%5CFileUpload5686 %5C3695%5CThe-Fiduciary-Duty-Of-Insurance-Brokers-In-NY.PDF (discussing *People ex rel. Cuomo v. Wells Fargo Insurance Services Inc.*).

50. Ibid.

51. Mher Asatryan, "What Are the Fiduciary Duties of Insurance Agents and Brokers?," 16, www.lacba.org/Files/LAL/Vol35No6/2953.pdf ("While there is no appellate precedent in California permitting an insured to sue an insurance broker or agent on a common law cause of action for breach of fiduciary duty, California courts have been hesitant to confirm outright that this cause of action is inapplicable to insurance brokers and agents. For example, in *Workmen's Auto Insurance Company v. Guy Carpenter & Company, Inc.*, the Second District Court of Appeal initially definitively answered the question of whether insurance brokers owe any fiduciary duties to insureds in the negative. However, any relief this decision brought to insurance agents and brokers was short-lived, as the opinion was vacated and depublished by a subsequent rehearing, which affirmed the initial opinion but remained unpublished.").

52. The Employee Retirement Income Security Act (ERISA), for example, requires the naming of fiduciaries and outlines their functions ("For purposes of this subchapter, the term 'named fiduciary' means a fiduciary who is named in the plan instrument, or who, pursuant to a procedure specified in the plan, is identified as a fiduciary (A) by a person who is an employer or employee organization with respect to the plan or (B) by such an employer and such an employee organization acting jointly."), 29 U.S.C.A. § 1102 (West).

53. Matthew P. Allen, "A Lesson from History, Roosevelt to Obama—The Evolution of Broker-Dealer Regulation," *Ohio State Entrepreneurial Business Law Journal* 5, no. 1, 20 ("Broker dealers were and are regulated under the '34 Exchange Act. Before the Great Depression, there were no standards governing the conduct of those selling securities to the public. Roosevelt and Congress used the 1934 Exchange Act to raise the standard of professional conduct in the securities industry from the standardless principle of caveat emptor to a 'clearer understanding of the ancient truth' that brokers managing 'other people's money' should be subject to professional trustee duties. But neither Roosevelt nor Congress wanted the federal government to regulate the brokerage industry

on a wide scale. This was because industry participants were seen as better able to more quickly respond to regulatory problems given their expertise and intimate knowledge of the securities industry.").

54. Dodd-Frank Wall Street Reform and Consumer Protection Act § 913; see Elizabeth MacBride, "Fiduciary Standard Soon May Regulate Brokers-Dealers Deals," CNBC, April 29, 2013, www.cnbc.com/id/100662116.

55. Investment advisers are governed by the Investment Advisers Act of 1940 whereas brokers are governed by the Securities Exchange Act of 1934.

56. IRDA, Reg./10/68, Standard Proposal Form for Life Insurance Regulations § 8(a) (2013).

57. IRDA, Standard Proposal Form for Life Insurance Regulations, 22–30.

58. Ibid., 30.

59. Ibid., 30.

60. Ibid., 31.

61. Ibid., §§ 8–10.

62. Government of India, *Report of the Financial Sector Legislative Reforms Commission* (2013), ix ("Dozens of legislations enacted from the 1870s were the foundations of this important catalytic sector. Many of them were enacted when financial economics was not born and the financial sector was at its infancy. In the last 100 years financial policies and practices have undergone many paradigm shifts. But its legal foundations, though amended in piecemeal fashion at times, remained more or less static with serious fractures visibly harming the system. These 'fault lines,' once more or less hidden, are now evident openly in the form of lack of legal clarity on responsibility and powers of regulators, inter-regulatory disputes, regulator-regulated court battles, adventurism of market participants and the growing shadow banking and shadow financial sector. How do we address the new world of finance with the institutions and the equipment from a non-financial era?").

63. Ibid., xxv.

64. Government of India, *Report of the Financial Sector Legislative Reforms Commission*, Draft Code Ch. 20, § 95(2) (2013).

65. Ibid., Ch. 20, § 95(3).

66. Ibid., Ch. 22, § 100(1)(b).

67. Ibid., Ch. 22, § 100(3)(a).

68. Ibid., Ch. 22, § 101(3).

69. Ibid., Ch. 22, § 102(1)(a).

70. Anagol, Cole, and Sarkar, *Understanding the Advice of Commissions-Motivated Agents.*

71. Ibid.

72. Sendhil Mullainathan, Markus Noth, and Antoinette Schoar, *The Market for Financial Advice: An Audit Study*, mimeo, Harvard University, 2012.
73. See generally Omri Ben-Shahar and Carl E. Schneider, "The Failure of Mandated Disclosure," *University of Pennsylvania Law Review* 159 (2011): 647. "Not only does the empirical evidence show that mandated disclosure regularly fails in practice, but its failure is inevitable. First, mandated disclosure rests on false assumptions about how people live, think, and make decisions. Second, it rests on false assumptions about the decisions it intends to improve. Third, its success requires an impossibly long series of unlikely achievements by lawmakers, disclosers, and disclosees." Ibid., 651. "But even for food labeling—the simplest and most understandable case of daily disclosures—evidence is mixed." Ibid., 675.

About the Authors

Viral V. Acharya is the C. V. Starr Professor of Economics in the Department of Finance at the New York University Stern School of Business (NYU Stern). He completed a bachelor of technology in computer science and engineering from the Indian Institute of Technology, Mumbai, in 1995 and PhD in finance from NYU Stern in 2001. Prior to joining Stern, he was a professor of finance at the London Business School (2001–2008). His primary research interest is in theoretical and empirical analysis of systemic risk of the financial sector, its regulation, and its genesis in government-induced distortions, an inquiry that cuts across several other strands of research—credit risk and liquidity risk, their interactions and agency-theoretical foundations, as well as their general equilibrium consequences. He is the recipient of the inaugural Banque de France—Toulouse School of Economics Junior Prize in Monetary Economics and Finance, 2011. He is the current PhD coordinator in the finance department at Stern.

Santosh Anagol is an assistant professor in the Business Economics and Public Policy Department at the Wharton School of the University of Pennsylvania. His research focuses on financial market issues in emerging markets. One recent project studies how the regulation of fees has shaped the Indian mutual fund industry. Another project studies the behavior of life insurance agents and how they respond to changes in regulatory policy. His dissertation studied inefficiencies in the Indian market for dairy cows and buffaloes, which are commonly purchased by microfinance borrowers. His teaching focuses on the effects of economic regulation on business. He received his PhD from Yale University in 2009 and his undergraduate degree from Stanford University in 2002, and was a Fulbright Scholar to India in 2002 and 2003.

John H. Biggs is an executive-in-residence and adjunct professor of finance at the Stern School of Business, New York University. He served as President and then Chairman and CEO of TIAA-CREF, a multiline pension and insurance company, for 14 years. Prior to his retirement, he has served as a director of many public companies, including recently five years at JPMorgan Chase and 22 years at the Boeing Company. He continues to serve as a trustee or director of a number of nonprofit companies, including Washington University in St. Louis, where he chaired its Investment Management Company, and the National Bureau of Economic Research, which he once chaired. He served as a pension actuary and then the chief financial officer of a Midwestern life insurance company before becoming Vice-Chancellor of Washington University in 1977. He also served as a trustee of the foundations overseeing the Financial Accounting Standards Board (FASB) and the International Accounting Standards Committee. Dr. Biggs earned a BA in classics from Harvard University and a PhD in economics from Washington University. He is a Fellow in the Society of Actuaries, and a member of the American Academy of Arts and Sciences and the Council on Foreign Relations.

Shawn Cole is an associate professor in the Finance Unit at Harvard Business School. His research examines corporate and household finance in emerging markets, with a focus on banking, microfinance, insurance, and the relationship between financial development and economic growth. He is an affiliate of the National Bureau of Economic Research, MIT's Jameel Poverty Action Lab, and the Bureau for Research and Economic Analysis of Development. Before joining the Harvard Business School, Professor Cole worked at the Federal Reserve Bank of New York in the economic research department. He currently serves on the Boston Federal Reserve's Community Development Research Advisory Council, and has served as an external adviser to the Gates Foundation and as the chair of the endowment management committee of the Telluride Association, a non-profit educational organization. He received a PhD in economics from the Massachusetts Institute of Technology in 2005, where he was a National Science Foundation and Javits Fellow, and an AB in economics and German literature from Cornell University.

J. David Cummins is the Joseph E. Boettner Professor of Risk Management and Insurance at Temple University and Harry J. Loman Professor Emeritus at the Wharton School of the University of Pennsylvania. Dr. Cummins's research interests include economics of insurance markets, productivity and efficiency of financial institutions, financing of catastrophic risk (including reinsurance and securitization), systemic risk in the insurance industry, financial pricing of insurance, and estimation of the cost of capital. Dr. Cummins has published more than 100 refereed journal articles and 39 book chapters, and has written or edited 16 books. His publications have appeared in many refereed journals, including the *Journal of Risk and Insurance*, the *Journal of Banking and Finance*, *Insurance: Mathematics and Economics*, the *Journal of Financial Economics*, and *Management Science*. He has received more than 20 prizes for his research. Among his recent books are *Catastrophe Risk Financing in Developing Countries* (The World Bank, 2008), *Handbook of International Insurance: Between Global Dynamics and Local Contingencies* (Springer, 2007), and *The Bermuda Insurance Market: An Economic Analysis* (Bermuda Insurance Market, 2008). Dr. Cummins also has served as consultant to numerous business and governmental organizations, including the Association of Bermuda Insurers and Reinsurers, Allstate Insurance Group, and the Federal Reserve Bank of New York. He is a past president of the American Risk and Insurance Association and past editor of the *Journal of Risk and Insurance*, and is currently an associate editor of eight refereed journals. He recently headed a team of researchers who were awarded a Centers of Actuarial Excellence research grant from the Society of Actuaries to study systemic risk in the insurance industry.

Eric R. Dinallo is a partner in the New York office of Debevoise & Plimpton LLP and member of the Financial Institutions Group. Prior to joining Debevoise in 2010, Mr. Dinallo served as the New York State Superintendent of Insurance (2007–2009) and was a Democratic candidate for the Office of New York State Attorney General. Mr. Dinallo has also served as the General Counsel of Willis Group Holdings (2006–2007), as Managing Director, Global Head of Regulatory Affairs of Morgan Stanley (2003–2006), as Chief of the Investment Protection Bureau in the Office of Attorney General Eliot Spitzer (1999–2003), and as an Assistant District Attorney in the New York County District Attorney's office (1995–1999). Mr. Dinallo received his BA in philosophy in 1985 from Vassar College, and his MA in 1987 from Duke University School of Public Policy. He earned his JD from New York University in 1990, where he was Review and Essay Editor of the *New York University Law Review*. He clerked with the Honorable David M. Ebel of the United States Court of Appeals, Tenth Circuit, in Denver (1990–1991). Mr. Dinallo serves on the board of directors of the American Institute for Stuttering.

Roger W. Ferguson Jr. is President and CEO of TIAA-CREF and a former Vice Chairman of the Board of Governors of the Federal Reserve System. Prior to joining TIAA-CREF in April 2008, he was head of financial services for Swiss Re and Chairman of Swiss Re America Holding Corporation. Earlier in his career, he was an associate and partner at McKinsey & Company and an attorney at Davis Polk & Wardwell. Dr. Ferguson is a fellow of the American Academy of Arts and Sciences and co-chair of the Committee on Economic Development. He serves on the boards of International Flavors & Fragrances Inc. and Audax Health and on the advisory board of Brevan Howard Asset Management LLP. He is a board member of the American Council of Life Insurers, the Institute for Advanced Study, and Memorial Sloan-Kettering Cancer Center. He serves as vice chair of the Business–Higher Education Forum and was co-chair of the National Academy of Sciences' Committee on the Long-Run Macroeconomic Effects of the Aging U.S. Population. He served on President Obama's Council on Jobs and Competitiveness and Economic Recovery Advisory Board. He holds a BA and JD, and a PhD in economics, all from Harvard University.

Peter G. Gallanis has served as President of the National Organization of Life & Health Insurance Guaranty Associations (NOLHGA) in Herndon, Virginia, since 1999. Before that, he served as CEO of the Illinois insurance receiver's office, chaired the National Association of Insurance Commissioners' (NAIC) Receivership and Insolvency Task Force, and was an adjunct professor of insurance law at the DePaul University College of Law in Chicago. Prior to joining the Illinois insurance receiver's office, he was a partner at a large law firm in Chicago, where he engaged in the private practice of law from 1978 through 1991. He received an AB from the University of Chicago in 1975 and a JD from the University of Illinois College of Law in 1978.

Scott E. Harrington is the Alan B. Miller Professor in the Health Care Management and Business Economic and Public Policy departments at the Wharton School, University of Pennsylvania. He is also Academic Director of the Wharton/Penn Risk and Insurance Program, a Senior Fellow with the Leonard Davis Institute for Health Economics, an adjunct scholar at the American Enterprise Institute, and a member of the U.S. Treasury's Federal Advisory Committee on Insurance. A former president of both the American Risk and Insurance Association and the Risk Theory Society, he is a co-editor of the *Journal of Risk and Insurance* and has published widely on the economics and regulation of insurance. He has conducted research, consulted, or served as an expert for many organizations and has testified before the U.S. House and Senate on insurance regulation, including testimony on the identification of systemically significant insurance organizations. His recent policy research has focused on the causes and implications of the financial crisis for insurance regulation, on the potential identification and regulation of systemically important insurance entities, and on the regulation of health insurers under healthcare reform. He earned an AB in 1975 and a PhD in 1979, both from the University of Illinois.

Dirk Kempthorne, as president and CEO of the American Council of Life Insurers (ACLI), is the chief representative and spokesman for the life insurance industry before Congress, before the administration, in all state capitals, and in the international arena. His focus is on the important role life insurers play in providing financial and retirement security to many millions of American families. His efforts shape public policies that make it easier for families to manage risk and ensure they have protection, long-term savings, and guaranteed income-for-life options in retirement. In 1985, he was elected Mayor of the City of Boise, Idaho. After serving seven years as Mayor, he was elected to the United States Senate in 1993. With Idaho issues close to his heart, he left the Senate after one term and was elected Governor of Idaho in 1998, and reelected for a second term in 2002. In 2006, Governor Kempthorne returned to Washington, D.C., to serve President George W. Bush as the 49th Secretary of the Interior, charged with resurrecting the Department of the Interior's tradition of responsible stewardship of public lands. In this role, Governor Kempthorne managed 20 percent of U.S. lands with an annual budget of $18 billion.

Robert McMenamin is the Team Leader of the Chicago Federal Reserve Bank's Insurance Initiative. He conducts analysis on academic and policy issues relating to the insurance industry and its role in the broader financial system. He received a BA in economics from Northwestern University and an MBA from the Booth School of Business at the University of Chicago.

Zain Mohey-Deen is a business economist in the economic research department at the Federal Reserve Bank of Chicago. He is also a member of the Chicago Fed's Insurance Initiative. He has worked in risk management in banks and insurance companies, where he has developed and implemented asset liability management models. He is a Fellow of the Society of Actuaries. He holds an MS in financial mathematics from the University of Chicago and a BSc from the London School of Economics.

Anna Paulson is a vice president and director of financial research in the economic research department at the Federal Reserve Bank of Chicago. She also leads the Chicago Fed's Insurance Initiative, which aims to understand the role of the insurance industry in the overall economy, with an emphasis on the industry's role in the financial sector. Her research, which focuses on financial stability issues and insurance and on how households cope with risk and incomplete financial markets, has been published in scholarly journals, including the *Journal of Political Economy*, the *Review of Economics and Statistics*, and the *Journal of Corporate Finance*. Before joining the Fed in November 2001, she was an assistant professor in the finance department at the Kellogg School of Management. She received a BA from Carleton College and a PhD in economics from the University of Chicago.

Thanases Plestis is an associate economist in the economic research department at the Federal Reserve Bank of Chicago. He is also a member of the

Chicago Fed's Insurance Initiative. Prior to joining the Chicago Fed, he received a BA in economics from Brown University.

Matthew Richardson is the Charles E. Simon Professor of Applied Financial Economics at the Leonard N. Stern School of Business at New York University. He currently holds the position of the Sidney Homer Director of the Salomon Center for the Study of Financial Institutions, which is a leading financial research center. In addition, he is a research associate of the National Bureau of Economic Research. Professor Richardson has done research in many areas of finance, including both theoretical and empirical work, publishing in the major journals. He has been associate editor of the *Journal of Finance, Review of Financial Studies,* and *Journal of Financial and Quantitative Analysis.* He recently co-edited two books on the financial crisis titled *Restoring Financial Stability: How to Repair a Failed System* (John Wiley & Sons, 2009) and *Regulating Wall Street: The Dodd-Frank Act and the New Architecture of Global Finance* (John Wiley & Sons, 2010), and is a co-author of *Guaranteed to Fail: Fannie Mae, Freddie Mac and the Debacle of Mortgage Finance* (Princeton University Press, 2011). Professor Richardson completed both his bachelor's and master's degrees in economics concurrently at the University of California at Los Angeles. He received his doctor of philosophy in finance from the Graduate School of Business at Stanford University.

Richard Rosen is a senior financial economist and research adviser in the economic research department at the Federal Reserve Bank of Chicago, and is part of the Chicago Fed's Insurance Initiative leadership. He also conducts research on issues relating to financial intermediation, bank regulation, mergers, and housing. Prior to coming to the Chicago Fed, he taught in the finance departments at the Kelley School of Business at Indiana University, the Wharton School at the University of Pennsylvania, and the School of Business at Georgetown University. He has also worked at the Board of Governors of the Federal Reserve System. Dr. Rosen received a BA in mathematics from Swarthmore College and a PhD in economics from Princeton University.

Shayak Sarkar is finishing his PhD in Harvard University's Department of Economics with primary fields of development and econometrics. He uses legal and economic analysis to research educational quality and financial access for the poor. He received his JD from Yale University Law School, where he was active in the Worker and Immigrant Rights Advocacy Clinic and received the Paul and Daisy Soros Fellowship for New Americans. Before coming to Harvard, he earned master's degrees, with distinction, in social work and development economics from Oxford University as a Rhodes Scholar and Knox Fellow. Sarkar graduated magna cum laude and Phi Beta Kappa from Harvard College with an AB in applied mathematics and an AM in statistics.

Therese M. Vaughan has spent the bulk of her career in academia and insurance regulation. From February 2009 to November 2012, she served as the Chief Executive Officer of the National Association of Insurance Commissioners (NAIC). As CEO, she oversaw the operations of the NAIC and served as its primary representative and chief spokesperson in Washington, D.C. Dr. Vaughan was actively involved in developing and promoting NAIC international policies, in the NAIC's response to the Dodd-Frank Act, and in the development and implementation of the NAIC's Solvency Modernization Initiative. In 2012, she chaired the Joint Forum, a Basel, Switzerland–based group of banking, insurance, and securities supervisors focused on cross-sectoral issues. In 2013, she was named a distinguished fellow of the International Association of Insurance Supervisors in recognition of her contribution to its work. Prior to joining the NAIC, Dr. Vaughan was the Robb B. Kelley Distinguished Professor of Insurance and Actuarial Science at Drake University. From 1994 to 2004, she was the Iowa Insurance Commissioner. While Commissioner, she led activities related to the implementation of the Gramm-Leach-Bliley Act, coordinating with federal regulators, modernizing producer licensing, working toward passage and implementation of the Terrorism Risk Insurance Act of 2002, reengineering the NAIC financial database, and creating the NAIC's Interstate Insurance Product Regulation Compact. She was NAIC President in 2002. Dr. Vaughan earned a PhD in risk and insurance at the University of Pennsylvania and a BBA in insurance and economics at the University of Iowa. She is a CPCU, an associate of the Society of Actuaries, an associate of the Casualty Actuarial Society, and a member of the American Academy of Actuaries. She is the coauthor of two college textbooks on insurance, *Essentials of Insurance* and *Fundamentals of Risk and Insurance* (11th edition forthcoming).

Mary A. Weiss is the Deaver Professor of Risk, Insurance, and Healthcare Management at the Fox School of Business and Management of Temple University. She is a past president of the American Risk and Insurance Association (ARIA) and the Risk Theory Society. She is Editor of *Risk Management and Insurance Review* and a Co-Editor for the *Journal of Risk and Insurance*. She has published more than 30 refereed journal articles, focusing on financial services conglomeration, efficiency measurement of insurers, no-fault automobile insurance, reinsurance, regulation, and underwriting cycles. Her research has appeared in the *Journal of Law and Economics*,

Journal of Business, Management Science, Journal of Financial Intermediation, Journal of Risk and Insurance, Journal of Banking and Finance, Geneva Papers on Risk and Insurance Theory, and *Contingencies*. Her articles have received awards from the *Journal of Risk and Insurance*, the Casualty Actuarial Society (CAS), and the *Journal of Financial Intermediation*. Professor Weiss has made numerous research presentations at academic and professional associations worldwide. Her research also has been presented at the National Bureau of Economic Research, the Brookings Institution, the Casualty Actuarial Society, the Risk Theory Society, the Financial Management Association, the Western Economic Association, the Competitive Enterprise Institute, and the Allied Social Sciences Association, as well as at conferences sponsored by the Federal Reserve Banks of Atlanta and New York. She obtained her PhD degree at the Wharton School of the University of Pennsylvania and has been on the faculty of Temple University since 1986. She served as the Distinguished Scholar at the NAIC's Center for Insurance Policy and Research (a think tank) in 2009 and 2010.

Index

ABX.HE index, 63, 80
Accident and health (A&H)
    reserves, 67
Accounting, global standards for, 23
ACE Group, 112
Advice. *See* Quality of advice
Aegon, 193
Agents:
duties of, 246–248, 258
  licensing of, 16
  use of, 257
AIG. *See* American International
    Group (AIG)
AIG CI, 158
AIG CM, 156, 157, 158
AIG Financial Products:
  complexity and, 93
  credit default swaps and, 43, 45,
    47, 50, 54, 58, 91, 93–94, 111,
    213, 239
  losses reported by, 195
  OTS and, 131
  regulation and, 121
  systemic risk and, 55
Ambac, 112
American Council of Life Insurers
    (ACLI), 4, 21, 23, 24, 154
American International Group (AIG):
  Capital Markets (*see* AIG CM)
  Commercial Insurance
    (AIG CI), 158
  commercial insurance services, 148
  corporate bonds and, 158
  credit rating and, 54, 58
  creditors of, 99

deregulation and, 43–44
failure of, 2, 153
federal bailout of, 44, 138,
  146, 195
federal intervention and, 11
Federal Reserve and, 147
financial crisis and, 63
Financial Products (*see* AIG
  Financial Products)
FSOC and, 8, 138,
  142–143
government rescue of, 54
history and, 53
holding company, 5
interconnectedness and, 157
Life Insurance and Retirement
  Services, 156
liquidity problem at, 58–59
losses reported by, 196
OTS and, 44
parent level of, 157, 158
precrisis history of, 44
product offerings of, 160
prudential requirements for, 147
ratings downgrade, 52
securities lending and, 35,
  54–58, 161, 177
SIFI designation, 146,
  146–147, 156
SIFI determination and, 3,
  8, 152
state insurance regulation
  and, 60
subprime mortgages and, 161
systemwide runs and, 158–159